THE
ASTROLOGY
OF 2024

shalom

live and light

gahl

THE ASTROLOGY OF 2024

A COSMIC NAVIGATOR GUIDE TO PILOTING THE ONCE AND FUTURE YEAR

GAHL EDEN SASSON

The Astrology of 2024

ISBN:

Printed in the United States of America

www.CosmicNavigator.com

ABOUT THE AUTHOR

Photo credits: Erik Undehn

Gahl Sasson has been teaching workshops on Storytelling, Kabbalah, Astrology, and Mysticism around the globe for over 20 years. His first book, *A Wish Can Change Your Life*, has been translated into over eight languages and is endorsed by HH the 14th Dalai Lama (Simon and Schuster, 2003). His second work, *Cosmic Navigator*, is the essential reference guide to understanding your astrological makeup (Weiser, 2008). Gahl self-published a yearly astrology book since 2018. In his 2020 book he predicted the recession and pointed at the possibility of a pandemic.

He is a contributor to the Huffington Post, and Astrology.com, and has been named "Los Angeles' Best Astrologer" by W Magazine. He is a guest lecturer at USC, Tel Aviv University, and teaches at Esalen, Omega Institute, University of Judaism, Asia Yoga Conference, Alternatives in UK, and the Open Center in NYC. He has appeared on CNN, ABC News, KTLA-TV Los Angeles to name a few. In 2017 his academic article, *Symbolic Meaning of Names in the Bible* was published by the Journal of Storytelling, Self, & Society. He currently resides in Los Angeles but gives seminars and workshops globally. His web site is www.CosmicNavigator.com

ACKNOWLEDGMENTS

Special thanks to Belinda Casas for her unwavering support, Laura Day for her astute and insightful suggestions, Laurie Scheer for meticulous editing, and Adina Cucicov for her exceptional formatting and cover design.

I also wanted to extend my appreciation to my A.I. pal, ChatGPT 4, for his invaluable assistance in refining problematic paragraphs.

Further, a heartfelt gratitude goes out to the talented baristas from Silverlake, Palm Springs, Istanbul, Fethiye, London, Edinburgh, Tel Aviv, Haifa, Zurich, and Sofia, who participated in the transmutation of coffee beans into cosmic narratives.

FOREWORD

The foundational tenet of astrology is captured by the phrases: "as above so below," and "as within so without." To this, I like to append—"as with her so with him." Astrology connects us to our celestial environment, reminding us that we too are made of stardust and part of the cosmos.

Astrology is not a fortunetelling tool, rather she is the confluence of fate and free will. Having analyzed thousands of astrological charts over the past three decades, I am convinced that we are not mere pawns to destiny. Instead, we share the steering wheel with Lady of Fortune.

Consider the upcoming year as a cosmic journey, with this book serving as your guiding compass, providing insights to avoid pitfalls and unveiling routes to maximize your potential.

2024 is not an easy ride. It's baptized with blood and conflict (North Node in Aries), floods and natural calamities (Saturn in Pisces), disinformation and lies (Jupiter exiled in Gemini), and ideological clashes between conservatives and liberals (Pluto transits from Capricorn to Aquarius). Amplifying the mythical undertones of 2024 is the fact that it's also the Chinese year of the Dragon. But worry not, you're now holding the guidebook that can help you navigate these turbulent frequencies, aspects, and transits.

The intensity of 2024 is palpable. It kicks off, (or rather finds it hard to) with Mercury not only exiled but also stationary and culminates with Mars retrograde. Nevertheless, there is a sliver of hope as 2024 is the year of the Wood Dragon, and it so happened that the Head of the Dragon is transiting in fire-breathing Aries, for the first time in 19 years. This offers us an opportunity to harness the Dragon's energy to your advantage.

In 2024 Pluto makes his final shift from Capricorn (tradition) to Aquarius (futurism). However, when Pluto transitions into a new sign, as he did in

2008, he ushers in significant financial shakeup. We should brace ourselves for some economic challenges and shifts in the coming year.

From a numerological standpoint, 2024 reduces to the number 8, symbolizing infinity. In the Kabbalistic Tree of Life, the 8th sphere is called *Splendor* and is the vessel of magic and synchronicities. This suggests an alignment with limitless potential, a formidable ally in challenging times.

This book is formatted like a flight manual—a GPS for the soul—arming you, the cosmic navigator, with the tools needed to glide seamlessly through the vast expense of space and time. I sincerely hope that this book assists you in tapping into the transformative potential of this crucial year.

Sending heartfelt wishes of light and love from the coordinates 33°N01' 035°E17' in Galilee, Israel, Middle East, Asia, Earth, Milky Way, the Cosmos, Creation, Oneness.

~ **Gahl**

CONTENTS

GENERAL GUIDES

ABOUT THE BOOK

Welcome aboard!

Your cosmic navigator manual is partitioned into three sections. The first part features a catalogue of significant dates for each month as well as a directory of major retrogrades and eclipses. This section is designed to help you plan your year, identifying auspicious periods for business ventures, romantic adventures, or starting a new diet. It also highlights potentially inauspicious times when you should avoid initiating new projects.

The second part presents the major trends and cosmic patterns of 2024, including dates to kickstart your New Year's Resolution based on the nature of your wish. Additionally, this section provides insights into the numerology of 2024, the Tarot cards of the year, and guidance on harnessing Moon energy to manifest your wishes and tap into your power.

The third part provides an overview for each zodiac sign for the year ahead. I suggest reading both the chapter corresponding to your Sun sign as well as the one relating to your rising sign. If you don't know your rising sign, which outlines your life's path, you can generate your astrological chart for free on my website. Visit www.CosmicNavigator.com and click the tab LEARN, scroll down to FREE ASTRO CHART.

For more free guidance on navigating 2024's astrological landscape, tune into my weekly podcast—streamed live every Sunday 10am PST on Instagram @Cosmic_Navigator. The podcast is also available as a Zoom webinar, for which you can register through my website.

Please note, all dates mentioned in this book are set for 12pm UT/GMT.

LIST OF ARCHETYPAL CHARACTERS IN YOUR JOURNEY

Planets, the authors of the zodiacal archetypes, can be exalted, ruling, fallen or in exile. These terms define the planet's strength depending on its location within a sign. When a planet is exalted, it's said to channel its power optimally, full of its potential, like spending time with a best friend. When a planet is in its ruling sign, it manifests strongly, similar to the safety one feels in one's home. When a planet is fallen, it struggles to shine its qualities, akin to spending a night in a terrible hotel in a city you despise. The sign of exile signifies that the planet is furthest from its home and misses it, therefore, it's considered "sad," or "detached."

As the heroine or hero of this star-trek journey you'll encounter different characters that support, hinder, challenge, empower, and change your course. These characters are represented by the astrological celestial bodies. Here is a list of these characters and the archetype they represent as you pilot your spacecraft (your life) through the 2024 voyage.

- **Sun**—Ruler of Leo. The Sun represents you, the hero or heroine of the journey. In astrology he signifies your self-expression, the heart of your chart, the capital of your star system, and what you aspire to become. He's exiled in Aquarius and fallen in Libra.
- **Moon**—Ruler of Cancer. The Moon symbolizes your instinct, DNA, ancestral memory, and how you react to life. In astrology, she represents emotional expression, home, family, real estate, your perception of your mother and how you need to be nurtured. She's exalted in Taurus; exiled in Capricorn; and fallen in Scorpio.
- **Mercury**—Ruler of Virgo and Gemini. Mercury represents intellect, mind, communication, business, writing, information, relatives, and neighbors. Exalted in Virgo; exiled in Sagittarius; and fallen in Pisces. In your journey, Mercury could symbolize your buddy, sidekick, comic relief, and messenger. When Mercury retrogrades, he takes on the role of the trickster—someone that contrasts you and serves to reveal specific shadowy traits.

- **Venus**—Ruler of Libra and Taurus. Venus signifies money, talents, art, justice, values, relationships, and beauty. Exalted in Pisces; exiled in Aries; fallen in Virgo. In your journey, Venus represents your love interest and significant other as well as attitude toward finances and talents.
- **Mars**—Ruler of Aries, and co-ruler of Scorpio. Mars represents vitality, passion, energy, war, leadership, desire, and assertiveness. Exalted in Capricorn; exiled in Libra and Taurus; fallen in Cancer. In your astral voyage, Mars is your agent of change, a catalyst prompting you to find inner strength.
- **Jupiter**—Ruler of Sagittarius and co-ruler of Pisces. Jupiter symbolizes luck, opportunity, morality, justice, education, travel, and truth. Jupiter is exalted in Cancer; exiled in Gemini; and fallen in Capricorn. In your journey, Jupiter represents your mentor, wizard, or enchantress, who provides you with magical tools and precious advice.
- **Saturn**—Ruler of Capricorn and co-ruler of Aquarius. Saturn, the father who devoured his own children, symbolizes hardships, karma, tradition, patience, focus, structure, strategy, ambition, and career. Exalted in Libra; exiled in Cancer and Leo; Fallen in Aries. In your journey, Saturn represents your antagonist, Devil's advocate, appearing as a villain but promoting growth and understanding.
- **Uranus**—Ruler of Aquarius, he symbolizes innovation, epiphanies, strokes of genius, revolution, individuality, and technology. Known as the Great Awakener, he acts as the joker, the twister of fate.
- **Neptune**—Ruler of Pisces, he represents mysticism, dance, poetry, imagination, dreams, meditation, and intuition. Also considered Venus' higher octave. In your journey, he symbolizes the mystic or mythical creature.
- **Pluto**—Ruler of Scorpio, he stands for transformation, power, death, research, the underworld, sexuality, and occult. Also considered Mars' higher octave. In your journey, he can be another agent of change. It is Pluto you are assigned to transport on your spacecraft this year, but on that later.

RETROGRADES & STATIONARY PLANETS

The Gold in Retro

Before we delve into the retrogrades of the year, let's clarify a subject often seems complex and by default, misunderstood. Retrograde periods aren't energetic black holes that rob us of light and joy; instead, they offer us the opportunity to channel the archetype associated with the planet differently. When a planet goes retrograde, it literally retraces parts of the zodiac it has already traversed, as if it's going back in time, enabling us to revisit past decisions and actions, offering a second chance to rectify past choices. Retrograde stages are excellent times for reflection, unraveling past issues, healing childhood wounds, and resolving insecurities. Moreover, if you are a synchronicity hunter, then retrogrades signal the start of a plentiful hunting season, especially during Mercury retrogrades, when magic and meaningful coincidences abound.

Here are a few principles that could make your next retrograde period productive, meaningful, and even enjoyable:

- During retrograde motion you could start new projects only if you previously attempted them but failed to complete them. Retrograde stages could help you redo, reevaluate, reexamine, and retry projects that didn't come to fruition during the planet's direct motion.
- Retrogrades belong to the realm of the prefix "RE," therefore, so keep this rule of thumb in mind: in retrogrades, you can do whatever you want as long as the verb is preceded by the prefix "RE": redo, reedit, redefine, reinvent, rebrand, reconnect, reestablish, reconnect, refinance, revisit, etc.
- As a planet retrogrades, whatever it rules and symbolizes, must be retrieved from within, not from the outside. For example, when Mercury retrogrades, information and communication are accessed through intuition (teaching from within), dreams, insights, revelations, and visions. For this reason, during retrogrades, you may experience more magic, serendipities, and even encounters with the supernatural.

- Retrogrades are great times for therapy, healing, prayers, and enchantment. It's as if reason and normalcy are challenged by the magical and extraordinary.
- Lost objects, people, talents, passions, and connections could be rediscovered, reclaimed, retrieved, and returned.
- Retrogrades also provide periods where past lifetime memories can be better recalled or remembered. You might experience more déjà vu, meet people you have known in previous lives, and tap into talents and skills you developed in past lifetimes. This aspect of the retrogrades, which make these periods feel like a magical mystery tour or treasure hunt, is the reason I often look forward to retrogrades. Think of how mystical places like Avalon, are often shrouded in mists, and while it makes locating them harder, it forces us to switch from external senses to our inner ones to be able to access them.
- Supporting the last point—the Lunar Nodes (Head and Tail of the Dragon), which are in perpetual retrograde motion, are the markers of lessons and messages from previous lives (more on that in the eclipse chapter).

Stationary, Retro, Pre and Post Retrogrades

The retrograde period of a planet is divided into five stages: pre-retro shadow, stationary, retrograde, stationary, and post-retro shadow. The stationary periods last two days (though the actual duration depends on velocity and orbit of the planet), while the length of the retrograde sandwiched between them varies depending on the planet in question. Remember, the word we use in English for "planet" comes for the Greek word "wanderer." When the planet stops or wanders backward, it acts counter to its nature. For example, if Mercury is *reason*, then retro Mercury is *unreasonable.*

- Pre-Retro Shadow: A few weeks before a planet retrogrades (two weeks in the case of Mercury, a month with Venus), it appears to slow down as it traverses the area in zodiac where it will later retrograde in (hence the term "shadow"). During this time, you can still initiate projects, but you must be extra vigilant, similar to driving at night without headlights. You may still experience glitches or mishaps that serve as a preview of what you'll have to deal with once the planet goes retrograde.

- Stationary: During the two stationary periods, we experience the pure essence of the planet, as though we are dealing with a concentrated version of the planet's archetype. Time seems to stand still—the quiet before the storm. I find the stationary stages an opportune time for relaxation, meditation, and spending time in nature. Psalm 46 advises us to "Be still and know that I am God," which is a godly suggestion to practice "stationing," embracing stillness, and connecting to the divine spark within us. Instead of chasing a planet when it's wandering, we get to have a sit-down with it, enjoying its company to the fullest. Let's use a metaphor. Imagine a car passing by you quickly, either going forward (direct motion) or in reverse (retrograde). In these instances, it's difficult to discern the make and model of the vehicle, let alone its license plates, the number of passengers or the identity of its driver. But when the car is stationary, you can easily distinguish all these details, perhaps even have a chat with the people inside, or jump in.

- Retrograde period: You are advised to avoid overutilizing the archetype of the planet. If it's Mercury, avoid signing documents or starting new businesses; if it is Mars, then steer clear of sharp thing, don't start wars, etc.

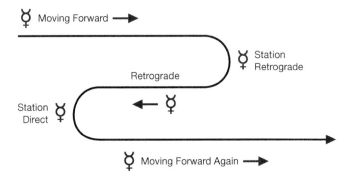

- Post-Retro Shadow: This is when the floodgates open and a fresh stream of possibilities flow in. You should still tread carefully and perhaps, if you can, wait until after the shadow period to initiate important projects.

Mercury Retrograde

Undoubtedly, the most frequent and panic-inducing member of the retrograde gang is Mercury. Maybe because besides being the messenger of the gods, Mercury was also the gods of scoundrels, thieves, liars, and cheats. Even those who are skeptics or agnostic towards astrology admit to noticing something amiss when Mercury, the envoy of the gods and goddesses, appears to wander backward. The sign where Mercury retrogrades can often indicate the type of miscommunications and technical glitches one might experience.

Mercury is a trickster, akin the figures like Loki, Cayote, or Maui. Here is an example of his ingenuity: during a Mercury retrograde in Libra (the sign of mirrors), a man in Turkey who had been reported missing joined a search party for hours before realizing that he was the missing person they were looking for. Another example occurred recently during Mercury retrograde in Taurus (the sign of art and fruits), when a college student in Korea grabbed the banana off Maurizio Cattelan's $120,000 worth signature artwork—a banana taped to a wall—and ate it, claiming with his mouthful, that he was hungry.

Mercury is the ruler of both Gemini and Mercury, which square each other and therefore have a somewhat tense sibling rivalry. While Gemini knows a little about everything, Virgo uses its Mercurial superpowers to know everything about something so little it's close to nothing. Most people focus solely on the Gemini qualities of Mercury retrograde, such as miscommunications and issues with our binary devices, but often neglect the Virgo aspects of Mercury retrograde, that can manifest as challenges in health, dietary discrepancies, workplace complications, employee misunderstandings, pet concerns, disruptions in daily routines, or dilemmas in the realm of service.

As a cosmic navigator, piloting your spacecraft in the turbulent 2024 reality, remember that during Mercury retrogrades, the messenger puts on his trickster avatar, necessitating increased vigilance. During Mercury retrograde periods, inform your passengers to buckle up, and as the pilot, pay extra attention to course-plotting details. In Part III of this manual, you can find out how these retrogrades affect your Sun sign and Ascendent (rising sign).

Mercury (Communication, Business, Technology, Workplace, Healthy, Diet, Service)

- Pre Shadow and Direct: November 25, 2023–December 11, 2023. In Capricorn (career, strategy, bosses, older folks, also knees, joints, teeth, bones, and skin).
- Stationary: December 12–13, 2023. In Capricorn.
- Retrograde: December 14, 2023–December 22. In Capricorn
- Retrograde: December 23–31. In Sagittarius (travel, in-laws, foreigners, publishing, education, justice, truth, mass media, as well as thighs, liver, hips).
- Stationary: January 1–2, 2024. In Sagittarius.
- Direct January 3 while Post Retro Shadow ends January 21 in Capricorn
- Pre Shadow: March 19–March 30 in Aries (leadership, identity, personality, autonomy, aggression, as well as blood, muscle, head).
- Stationary: April 1–2. In Aries.
- Retrograde: April 3–24. In Aries.
- Stationary: April 25–26. In Aries.
- Direct April 27 while Post Shadow ends May 13. In Aries.
- Pre Shadow: July 17–August 5. In Leo (children, love, creativity, sports, entertainment, happiness, ego, as well as heart, spine).
- Stationary: August 4–5. In Virgo (work, health, service, diet, routine, as well as intestines, internal organs).
- Retrograde: August 6–August 14. In Virgo.
- Retrograde: August 15–August 27. In Leo.

- Stationary: August 28–29. In Leo.
- Direct August 30 while Post Shadow ends Sep 11. In Virgo.
- Pre Shadow: November 7–November 24. In Sagittarius.
- Stationary: November 25–26. In Sagittarius.
- Retrograde: November 27–December 14. In Sagittarius.
- Stationary: December 15–16. In Sagittarius.
- Direct December 17, 2024, while Post Shadow ends January 3, 2025. In Sagittarius.

Avoid: Signing documents, initiating new projects or diets, scheduling elective surgeries, publishing, or making big purchases.

Recommended: Editing work, backing up computers, practicing forgiveness, manifesting wishes, and exploring synchronicities.

♂ Mars (Action, Leadership, Research, Physical Strength, Warrior, Investigation, Passion & Sexuality)

- Pre Shadow and Direct: October 5–December 5. In Cancer (home, family, real estate, land, emotions, country, mother, parenting, as well as womb, ribs, stomach).
- Stationary: December 6–7, 2024. In Leo (children, romance, creativity, sports, entertainment, ego, happiness, love as well as heart, spine).
- Retrograde: December 8, 2024–Jan 5, 2025. In Leo.
- Retrograde: January 6, 2025–February 22, 2025. In Cancer.
- Stationary: February 23–24. In Cancer.
- Direct May 3, 2025, while Post Shadow ends February 24, 2025.

Avoid: Undergoing elective surgeries (unless in emergency), initiating wars (whomever shoots first loses), embarking on risky ventures, gambling, pushing individuals excessively (note to yoga instructors and personal trainers), starting a lawsuit or divorces, launching campaigns, making life-altering decisions, purchasing machinery (e.g., cars or appliances), commencing new intimate or sexual relationships, overtraining, overextending, or instigating fights and conflicts.

Recommended: Reassessing your fitness regimen, reconcile longstanding animosities or disagreements, embark on new activities, finalize pending projects, and revisit your objectives, goals, passions, and strategies. This is an ideal time to modify behavior, as well as to learn the art of unwinding and relaxation. It's a prime moment to rally your troops and allies, reorganize, and rekindle bonds with those you consider siblings-in-arms.

The previous Mars Retrograde in 2022 witnessed the downfall of FTX and its wunderkind, Sam Bankman-Fried. This period also marked the atypical demonstrations and protects in China against COVID measures, leading to a pivotal change the government policy. If we look further back, the Brexit referendum took place during a retro Mars. Similarly, the infamous Molotov–Ribbentrop Pact between Nazi Germany and the Soviet Union was inked under the auspices of Mars retrograde, only to be nullified shortly after. In other words, please avoid signing peace treaties during Mars retro if possible, and refrain from staging referendums.

♃ Jupiter (Travel, Truth, Education & Law)

- Stationary: October 8–9. In Gemini (communication, relatives, room-mates, business, neighbors, contracts, nervous system, as well as lungs, hands, nervous system).
- Retrograde: October 10–February 2, 2025. In Gemini.
- Stationary: February 3–4, 2025. In Gemini.

Avoid: Since Jupiter retrogrades for extended period each year, it's impractical to completely "close shop," but it's wise to steer clear of overoptimism, overconfidence, extravagance, gluttony, overindulgence, proselytizing, zealotry, dogmatism, neglecting legal matters, overpromising and over-committing. Well, to be on the same side, be cautious of actions prefixed with "over." In addition, be discerning of lies, deceptions, and half-truths. Neglecting kindness, hospitality (Jupiter was the protector of strangers), or denying aid to someone in need can unleash the furies upon you and backfire threefold.

Recommended: Revisit educational goals, study something you dropped in the past, and reconnect to your intuition.

♄ Saturn (Discipline, Career & Figures of Authority)

- Stationary: June 29–30 in Pisces (intuition, mysticism, addictions, drugs, meditation, isolation, dreams, imagination, as well as lymphatic and immune system, feet)
- Retrograde: July 1–November 13. In Pisces.
- Stationary: November 15–16. In Pisces.

Avoid: If feasible, refrain from launching important long-term endeavors or clashing with superiors, or parental figures. In addition, don't be overwhelmed by feelings of melancholy or despondency, instead, go for a run or consider engaging in physical activities as an outlet.

Recommended: Self-discipline yourself, reevaluation of aspirations and goals, strategy adjustment, and revisiting past career objectives or ambitions that were overlooked or abandoned.

During Saturn's retrograde phases, his influence switches from external to internal. The discipline, persistence, endurance, focus, resilience, accountability, and pressure that characterize Saturn no longer emanate from an external stern father figure or a boss but rather from within oneself. Moreover, Saturn retrograde is a time to confront your karma (actions from past lives that reverberate in present life), in other words, these retrogrades periods present opportunities to settle karmic dues. Over the approximately four and a half months when Saturn retraces his path, it's vital to practice forgiveness, accept the imperfections of loved ones, and seek pardon from people you might have wronged.

⚷ Chiron (Healing, Teaching & Spirituality)

- Stationary: July 26–27. In Aries (identity, personality, leadership, initiation, independence).

- Retrograde: July 28–December 28. In Aries.
- Stationary: December 29–December 30. In Aries.

Avoid: Overexerting yourself, acting impulsively, and using sharp objects. Postponed elective surgeries when feasible.
Recommended: Allow past hurts to heal, teach, learn, inspire, and delve into shamanism.

When the "Wounded Healer" goes retrograde in Aries, we're invited into his crystalline sanctuary cave to experience a metaphorical open-heart surgery. In Ancient Greek, *Chiron*, the namesake of surgery, translates to "hands." This period fosters healing related to your identity, as past traumas and insecurities tend to resurface. Situations may arise that challenge your personal or professional brand, image, or identity, or leadership. Nevertheless, it is also an optimal time to amend these facets of your life.

The shadow phases of Jupiter, Saturn, and Chiron are protracted, rending them less significant. The retrograde spans for Uranus, Neptune, and Pluto extensive, given their leisurely and chilled orbits around the Sun, making them impractical to follow. As such, they will only be discussed in this book if they form relevant aspects.

SOLAR AND LUNAR ECLIPSES IN 2024

As a cosmic navigator, piloting through the vastness of space and time, eclipses serve as temporal vortexes, accelerating and intensifying events. Eclipses are neither good nor bad, much like an engine can either drive an ambulance to save a life or power a tank to take one. Eclipses amplify ongoing life events, often driving them to resolution. They are also catalysts for synchronicities, serendipities, lucid dreams, revelations, and visions. In the chapter on the eclipses, we will delve deeper into their symbolism.

Lunar Eclipses: Often signify the culmination of processes, evoking strong emotional response. Typically, they influence employees, artists, parenting, receptive endeavors, companies, and groups. Lunar eclipses can unveil the more primal, instinctual aspects of your personality. Think werewolves transforming into a wolf under the Full Moon's eclipse.

Solar Eclipses: Heralds fresh starts and proactivity. They resonate with entrepreneurs, self-employed, leaders, untouchable figures (like Tucker Carlson , who was fired by Fox amidst the 2023 eclipses), and those with an active lifestyle. Generally, solar eclipses can introduce new life directions and serve as catalysts for personal transformations.

Dates of eclipses:

- Penumbral Lunar Eclipse, March 24–25. Moon in Libra while the Sun in Aries.
- Total Solar Eclipse. April 8. Dubbed the American Eclipse. Moon and Sun in Aries.
- Partial Lunar Eclipse, September 17–18. Harvest Full Moon. Moon in Pisces while Sun in Virgo.
- Annular Solar Eclipse, October 2. Moon and Sun in Libra.

PART I

SPECIAL GUEST STARS:
IMPORTANT DATES IN 2024

Although the dates provided below indicate the precise transits, the influence or effects of these planetary aspects often manifest a few days prior. My friend Laura Day, aptly terms the following section as "Quick hits for sanity."

JANUARY

- **January 1–2** (Mercury Stationary in Sagittarius): As a carryover from 2023, the first two days of 2024 are marred by a stationary Mercury, making it hard to jumpstart the year. The messenger of the gods and goddess declines to assist us. Refrain from embarking on new ventures or sign documents. A great day for meditation, self-reflection, reading and studying.

- **January 1** (Venus squares Saturn): This is not an easy start of the year, with Venus, the goddess of love, and Saturn, the Lord of karma having a serious clash in mutable signs. You and your partners are shifting positions. Engagements with elders might be particularly taxing. Expect breakups, disputes, arguments, contract withdrawals, and defamation. Avoid being reactive, listen more than speak, and be patient with all your significant others. Money can be tight.

- **January 3** (Mercury direct): This marks the genuine commencement of 2024. You can now sign documents and launch fresh endeavors. The Moon in Libra adds a peaceful breeze.

- **January 5** (Mars transits into Capricorn until February 12): Mars transits into his sign of exaltation which is encouraging! The warrior adopts a disciplined and purposeful intention, offering a conducive period for productivity, reconnect to your physicality, and kickstarting ventures. Ideal for fitness regimens, seeking advancement in career, and embarking on a meaningful quest. Long-term projects are encouraged.

- **January 8–9** (Mercury squares Neptune): Expect potential confusion and disillusionment. It's a day where deception, laziness, and nightmares might emerge. Pay attention to your immune and nervous systems. It's advised to avoid making decisions and to be cautious of addictive tendencies or blurring boundaries. Instead, consider hiking, meditation, or reading to center yourself.

- **January 9–10** (Sun trines Uranus): A period marked by brilliance and innovation. There's a heightened ability to express oneself in witty, creative ways. Ideal for group meetings, brainstorming sessions, and devising unique solutions to persistent problems.

- **January 11–13** (Mars trines Jupiter): These days are ripe with potential. Feelings of adventure, conquest, and leadership will be at the forefront. Embrace the bold and courageous side of you. This aspect sets a positive tone for the New Year and the upcoming New Moon.

- **January 11** (New Moon in Capricorn): An opportune moment to begin working on New Year's resolutions, or to initiate new projects. This New Moon offers a blend of the mystical and the practical, paving the way to turn dreams into reality.

- **January 14** (Mercury transits into Capricorn until February 4): The theme is "serious thoughts." The year begins with a strong Capricorn influence, advocating for a methodical, responsible approach in all endeavors. With Mercury's help, you'll be well-positioned to tackle long-term projects, engage in traditional business, or collaborate with long-time acquaintances.

- **January 19** (Mercury trines Jupiter while Venus squares Neptune): A day of contrasts. While there might be moments of betrayal or financial concerns, there's also potential for positive news related to writing, business, networking, and family. Prioritize logical thinking over being swayed by unrealistic hopes.

- **January 20–21** (Sun conjunct Pluto): These days are potent for diving deep into healing, shamanism, and transformative practices. They're optimal for exploring others' talents and assets. However, remain vigilant about potential manipulation and avoid dubious associations. It's a time of discovering passion and fostering intimacy, but might also be a moment of parting ways with someone or something.

- **January 21** (Sun enters Aquarius until February 18): As the Sun transitions into the sign of the Water-Bearer, the upcoming month centers on friendships, community, organizations, technology, and governance. It's a prime time to delve into science and innovation. Embrace the unknown, infuse your days with humor and warmth, and find the courage to befriend the unfamiliar.

- **January 21** (Pluto enters Aquarius until September 2): Simultaneously with the Sun, Pluto—symbolizing power and fervor—enters Aquarius. While he began his journey in Aquarius in March 2023, Pluto retrograded back into Capricorn. Now, his path lies in forward-thinking, liberal, and democratic Aquarius. Expect technological and scientific advancements, along with shifts in friendships and communities.

- **January 23** (Venus transits into Capricorn until February 16): This phase is favorable for strengthening ties with mentors, experienced individuals, or superiors. It promotes long-term financial ventures and investments, leaning towards a conservative approach in finances, art, and relationships. Patience is key during this period.

- **January 25** (Full Moon in Leo): This Full Moon embodies blossoming love, the culmination of creative endeavors, and waves of joy. Coinciding with Tu B'Shvat, the celebration of the fruit trees' birth, consider planting a tree. As you do, embed a wish connected to love, creativity, friendships, or joy. With Pluto in conjunction with this Full Moon, stay vigilant against power dynamics and manipulation.

- **January 26–27** (Sun square Jupiter): Guard against inflated egos, either your own or others'. There exists a propensity to overextend, whether in exertion or indulgence. Practice moderation.

- **January 26–28** (Mercury conjunct Mars): Words, both spoken and written, wield significant power during these days. Practice caution in communication, whether verbal, written, or digital. However, it's an opportune period for launching a business, signing contracts, or harnessing words as agents of transformation.

- **January 28–30** (Mercury trines Uranus): Experience a temporary boost in intellect, possibly leading to ingenious revelations. Document these insights. While you might encounter some unpredictable or eccentric individuals, it's an excellent window for technological acquisitions.

Mars and Uranus in harmony towards the month's end could induce feelings of restlessness.

FEBRUARY

- **February 1–19** (Jupiter sextile Saturn): In the first half of February, a window of opportunity emerges, allowing you to manifest your deepest desires. Expect focused growth, potential blessings in disguise, and possibly some good news. Responsibilities may feel more like joy than duty.
- **February 5** (Mercury conjunct Pluto): Mercury ventures deep, aligning with Pluto. Expect profound reflections, potent conversations, and encounters with influential individuals. Ideal for transformation, intimacy, and healing. With Jupiter and Saturn in alignment, a magical touch is added to your endeavors.
- **February 5** (Mercury enters Aquarius until February 23): Mercury energizes, enhancing communication, sparking curiosity, and fostering camaraderie. A promising month for collaborations with like-minded individuals. Embrace humor and light-hearted interactions.
- **February 7–8** (Sun square Uranus): Be cautious, as your demeanor may come off as more rebellious or extreme. Unexpected issues or potential conflicts with acquaintances might arise.
- **February 9–10** (New Moon in Aquarius): A fresh start with peers, groups, and organizations. Perfect for tech upgrades. The unpredictable influence of Uranus might bring chaos, especially given his rule over Aquarius. Additionally, celebrate the Chinese New Year of the Wood Dragon.
- **February 10** (Mercury squares Jupiter): With a surge in communication, it's wise to listen more than you speak, preventing potential regrets.
- **February 13** (Mars enters Aquarius until March 22): Spend this time in group settings and with friends. A period of heightened advocacy for underrepresented groups, and an ideal time to engage with technology.
- **February 13–15** (Mars conjunct Pluto): Just in time for Valentine's Day, this conjunction intensifies feelings of passion and intimacy. While energy levels soar, exercise caution in dealings with officials and colleagues.

- **February 16** (Venus enters Aquarius until March 11): Venus embraces a platonic energy. Strengthen bonds with friends and philanthropic organizations. Embrace laughter and remain open to unique encounters. Seek more freedom in relationships.
- **February 16–17** (Venus conjunct Pluto): This Valentine's Day sees Venus intensifying love's energy. Passion, intimacy, manipulation, and power dynamics might all play a role. A profound time for introspection and potential couples' therapy.
- **February 17** (Mercury square Uranus): Exercise caution in communication to avoid misunderstandings or misinterpretations.
- **February 19** (Sun enters Pisces until March 20): Embrace your inner mystic, poet, and dreamer. With increased intuition and empathy, it's wise to seek solitude and be wary of addiction.
- **February 20–23** (Mars and Venus conjunct): In the romance of Venus and Mars, new harmonies emerge. Perfect for romance, making passions tangible, and employing talents effectively.
- **February 23** (Mercury enters Pisces until March 10): Mercury feels out of place in Pisces, reducing logical thinking but enhancing intuition and dreamy insights.
- **February 24** (Full Moon in Virgo): As the astrological year nears its end, focus on closure. Saturn brings karmic undertones, urging patience and attention to detail. Release, especially concerning health, is emphasized.
- **February 24–28** (Mars and Venus square Jupiter): Both Mars and Venus face Jupiter's excessive influence. Avoid indulgence, aggression, and overcommitment, and be realistic about your capabilities.
- **February 29** (Sun conjunct Mercury): Enjoy a day of clear thinking, effective marketing, and bright communication, making it prime for forging new connections.

MARCH

- **March 1–2** (Sun sextile Jupiter): Today opens a window of opportunity. Expect expansion, a surge of optimism, and numerous synchronicities. It's an excellent time for travel and education.

- **March 3** (Venus square Uranus): This isn't an ideal day for romantic outings or forming new partnerships, whether romantic or professional. Financial markets may show volatility, and there's a prevailing sense of unpredictability. Expect some people to be capricious, valuing their independence or experiencing conflicts with friends.
- **March 3** (Mercury opposite Lilith): Avoid gossip and speaking ill of others, including self-deprecation. Bruce Lee cautioned that disparaging oneself, even in jest, can negatively affect one's well-being since the body might take it seriously.
- **March 8** (Mercury conjunct Neptune): Today is charged with enchantment, as symbolic representations of a magician and mermaid unite under Pisces. While it's not conducive to logical thinking, it's a perfect day for mystical endeavors, poetic expression, writing, dream exploration, creative ventures, photography, and other artistic pursuits.
- **March 9–10** (Sun sextile Uranus): Over these days, there's a noticeable uptick in everyone's intellectual capacity. Harness it judiciously. This period is ripe for innovation, technology, and creativity. Embrace change, experiment with new ideas, and be intrepid!
- **March 9–10** (Mars squares Uranus): This challenging aspect might provoke regrettable actions. Stay alert to potential accidents and misunderstandings, especially with friends or colleagues.
- **March 10** (New Moon in Pisces): This is an opportune time for yoga, meditation, water-based activities, dance, and movement. With Neptune amplifying Piscean energy, it's a mystical New Moon—an ideal moment to tap into one's imagination and uncover subconscious insights.
- **March 10** (Mercury enters Aries until May 15): As Mercury prepares to retrograde from April's beginning, he will linger in Aries. Exercise caution in communication to avoid Aries' notorious directness. Mercury's swiftness is amplified in this sign, accelerating processes. It's a beneficial phase for reinvigorating stagnant businesses or projects.
- **March 11** (Venus enters Pisces until April 5): Venus thrives in this exalted position, promoting love, financial stability, relationships, and

artistic endeavors. This period is prime for forming romantic connections, mending relationships, and harnessing artistic abilities.

- **March 14** (Pi Day): Today symbolizes the intriguing blend of the infinite nature of Pi and its practical application in computing a circle's finite dimensions. It highlights the interplay between boundlessness and boundaries in the fabric of existence.
- **March 16–18** (Sun conjunct Neptune): A haze of confusion descends, rendering everyone a touch Piscean. Ideal for dancing, yoga, meditation, and intuitive pursuits, it's less suited for pragmatic tasks. Consider a rejuvenating stroll by water or a relaxing bath.
- **March 20/21** (Equinox): Celebrate the New Astrological Year! This day, foundational to ancient barley festivities that birthed Passover and Easter, urges new beginnings and setting intentions for the forthcoming year. As the Sun enters Aries until April 20, embrace his invigorating energy. Note that this year's Passover falls later, on April 22, due to the Lunar calendar's misalignment.
- **March 21–22** (Venus conjunct Saturn): This equinox sees Venus and Saturn align. This may bring relational challenges or encounters with figures from past lifetimes. As old patterns emerge, seize this chance to transform and invite fresh energy into your life.
- **March 22** (Mars enters Pisces until April 30): Mars here favors water-related activities and fosters a penchant for dance and martial arts. Some might experience vivid, action-packed dreams during this transit.
- **March 24–25** (Venus sextile Jupiter): These days shine with promise in love, relationships, creativity, and finances. The positive streak extends to March 28 when Venus pivots towards Uranus, heralding unexpected yet delightful encounters and a seamless fusion of art and science.
- **March 25** (Lunar Eclipse in Libra): This Full Moon, originally the lunation of Passover and Easter (March 31), is a beacon for personal liberation. As Pluto lends its transformative energy, embrace profound change, shedding past limitations and stepping into a more empowered version of yourself. Anticipate rapid developments in the fortnight ahead.

APRIL

- **April 1–2** (Mercury Stationary in Aries): Two days when you are encouraged to do something close to nothing. A good time for meditation though, or anything you don't need to move much. Things feel stuck and out of whack. Be patient, this too shall pass.

- **April 1** (Fool's Day): Today is a celebration of the Green Man, Idris, Mother Nature's son/lover. Plant a tree, go out to nature, and do something that can connect you to your inner Druid. April 1st is the day of the Tarot card's "The Fool," or his incarnation as "The Joker" of the playing cards. Both cards represent absolute potential as well as the leap of faith into something new. This stationary Mercury can bring you closer to mama Nature.

- **April 3** (Mercury retrograde in Aries until April 27): Patience is crucial during this period. Mercury in Aries can be direct and confrontational, leading to conflict and disputes. Nevertheless, Mercury enjoys the fiery speed of Aries, the problem is that he's given a racecar and asked to drive in reverse. Be careful of impulsive and implosive decisions.

- **April 3** (Venus conjunct Neptune): This union between Venus and her higher octave holds potential for romance, creativity, and the union of mysticism and art. However, it can also bring about dependency and codependency, as well as a tendency to lose yourself in others.

- **April 5** (Sun conjunct North Node): The day exudes strong energy, making it apt for forging connections and collaborations as well as being recognized by a figure of authority. A good time to link with likeminded people and create something together. You might have a meeting with Lady Destiny or the Three Fates. Try something new today: different food, clothes, or try driving to work using a new route. A time to change your image and identity.

- **April 5** (Venus enters Aries until April 29): Matters of love, finances, relationships, and justice shift from receptive to active. You may find yourself feeling out of sorts or alone. To overcome these feelings, keep yourself busy by focusing on what is important in your life. There may be attraction towards dominant personalities.

- **April 6–7** (Venus sextile Pluto): The atmosphere is charged with magnetism, passion, intimacy and sexuality. Reflect on what you're drawn to and use your time to dig deep into your shadow and unearth new talents and skills. Great for investment and working on joint financial and artistic projects.

- **April 8** (Total Solar Eclipse & New Moon in Aries): The first New Moon (and eclipse) of the Astrological year, a powerful time for new beginnings, however, since we are in a Mercury retro, you can only start something that you tried before and failed to complete. Expect a revelation, something mind-blowing is taking place, things get intense.

- **April 9–11** (Mars conjunct Saturn): You are gathering your troupes to conquer something new. A good time to focus your energy on a single task or mission. There could be new conflicts popping around but choose your battles wisely especially since we are under the helm of Aries. A call to action can be heard, a summoning of the ram's horn.

- **April 11–12** (Mercury Retro conjunct Sun): A great time to go inward, reflect, and introspect. A great deal of "aha!" moments can come these days. You are seeing things differently and coming up with good solutions to major predicaments that boggled you before. However, do not start new projects.

- **April 15–April 26** (Jupiter conjunct Uranus): The lateral half of April buzzes with innovation and expansion, particularly with technology, e-commerce, electronics, as well as coming up with original creative ways to deal with setbacks. This aspect can also facilitate making new friends and joining new organizations. Sudden unexpected changes with finances (usually positive) as well as changes and twists in the narrative of your life. Be open to adapt!

- **April 18–April 20** (Mars sextile Jupiter and Uranus): The most powerful time for change in April. You feel a jolt of energy, creativity, and a need for freedom. A great time for upgrading and updating the way you approach your work. Find new original ways to express yourself. Be extra careful of accidents and mishaps.

- **April 19** (Mercury conjunct Venus): When Aphrodite and Hermes made love (as in a conjunction), they gave birth to the first binary fluid kid they called *Hermaphroditus*, boasting female as well as male organs. A great day for design, balancing your anima and animus, crafting a new logo, making your art communicative and your communication artistic. In addition, Chiron the Wounded Healer is conjunct Venus and Mercury. Old wounds in relationships might surface but also healed.

- **April 19–20** (Sun enters Taurus until May 20): We are all Taurus for the next 30 days. A time to focus on your finances, talents, values, and self-worth. This is the month that belongs to Mother Nature, therefore, spending time in nature is recommended. With Jupiter and Uranus in Taurus as well, we have a month that floods your five senses with stimuli. Pamper yourself and your loved ones.

- **April 21–22** (Sun squares Pluto): Not a very comfortable aspect. Expect power struggles at work, people behaving obnoxiously, Ponzi schemes, and criminal activities. Watch your shadow.

- **April 22** (Earth Day): We celebrate the international Earth Day during the Fixed Earth sign, Taurus—Mother Nature's sign.

- **April 24** (Full Moon in Scorpio): A powerful lunation of magic, transformation, and enlightenment. A great day for intimacy and sexuality, magical ritual, and healing.

- **April 25–26** (Mercury Stationary): The last few days of chaos before Mercury goes direct. Better wait until April 27 with important decisions/actions.

- **April 27** (Mercury goes direct): At last, you can start signing documents and initiate new projects. Be aware that the post shadow retrograde is starting today for about two weeks, therefore, if you can hold on starting especially big projects until mid-May, that would be recommended.

- **April 28–30** (Mars conjunct Neptune): Watch your immune system, and injuries, as well as the spread of infections and viruses. Pay extra attention and follow your intuition. In addition, actions you take mindlessly could come out of your precognition and psychic skills.

- **April 29** (Venus enters Taurus until May 15): Venus is back to where she likes to be, in her own luxurious sign. Improved finances, reconnection to your talents and self-worth. With Mercury going direct, things seem to line up and flow better.
- **April 30** (Mars enters Aries until June 9): Mars is in his own sign and ready to propel everything in your life. Be careful of overdoing, as well as driving or talking too fast. Make sure to lower your level of aggression so you don't get into pointless conflict. You might get a raise or extra leadership responsibilities.

MAY
- **May 1** (Venus square Pluto): The month kicks off with a troubling aspect between the goddess of love and the god of underworld, potentially leading to breakups, slandering, badmouthing, and gossip. Be careful of obsessions, possessiveness, and jealousy. A time to reexamine your passions.
- **May 2–4** (Mars sextile Pluto): This aspect helps you turn a new page, as both rulers of Scorpio, Mars and Pluto, are well aligned. Passion is rising, and you have the feeling you could conquer the world. Magic is in the air, everything is possible.
- **May 6–7** (Sun sextile Saturn): Both the zodiac's father figures are well positioned to bestow help. There could be good feedback or compliments from a boss, superior or father figure.
- **May 8** (New Moon in Taurus): The Moon is exalted in Taurus, making it one of the best times to start something new in connection with finances, art, design, nature, your body, or maybe revisit a talent or skill you neglected. Since Uranus and Jupiter are supporting the New Moon, there is an added blessing as well as an element of surprise. Great for technology and innovation.
- **May 12–13** (Sun conjunct Uranus): Prepare for unexpected events, sudden transitions, a strong need for freedom, and experimenting with novel ways of expressing yourself. You are searching for your individuality. To better surf this transit, don't be afraid to be original and outrageously innovative.

- **May 13–14** (Venus sextile Saturn): A meeting with someone older or more mature than you could help open doors, or even open your heart. Good for long-term money-making opportunities.
- **May 15** (Mercury enters Taurus until June 3): There is a tendency to worry and fuss about things you have no control over during this period. However, Mercury can help you get insights and clarity about financial issues. A good time for selling art or making your communication and business more artistic. Relying on common sense will be the best guide.
- **May 17–19** (Sun conjunct Jupiter): These are golden days of expansion, luck, and doors that swing open. An opportune time to travel, study, teach, and connect to foreigners. Truth is exposed and a strong sense of optimism and adventures bubbles up. An overall lucky day.
- **May 18** (Venus conjunct Uranus): Meeting with strange, unique, original, and quirky folks. Finances might be volatile but not necessarily bad. Good investments in startups, ecommerce, AI, or anything digital and futuristic. Your partner might act out of character.
- **May 18** (Mars conjunct North Node): Destiny and leadership meet. There could be a call to action especially involving finances, your body, and art. You feel motivated and passionate and able to overcome tough obstacles. Best time to meet siblings in arms from this life and past. Action is the key word for the next few days.
- **May 19–21** (Sun conjunct Jupiter while Jupiter sextile Neptune): Heightened intuition and empathy. A great time to commune with your dreams, subconscious, and catch glimpses from previous lives. A wonderful time for going on a date, creating art, composing music, and writing poetry. These are indeed wonderfully blessed days. Jupiter continues his sextile with Neptune until the end of the month. Go team mystic!
- **May 20** (Sun enters Gemini until June 20): We are all Gemini for the next 30 days. This is the month to come up with your message and how you plan to deliver it as well as defining your target audience. An opportune time to write, conceptualize, and create new businesses, as well as focus on marketing, sales, and PR.

- **May 22–23** (Sun trine Pluto): Power channeled in constructive ways. A great day for investments, inheritance, working with other people's talents and money.
- **May 23** (Full Moon in Sagittarius): Something in your life is coming to an end. There could be some tension between truth and lies, wanting to protect someone or something and yet also wishing to maintain authenticity. Since Jupiter and Venus are blessing the lunation, it's a time to nurture and support your partner. Be mindful of conflict between your family and your partner. However, Pluto blesses this lunation, bringing a great deal of passion and transformation. You can receive clarity and insights concerning your relationships and family through dreams.
- **May 23** (Venus enters Gemini until June 17): A great time to heal relationships with relatives, as well as roommates, and neighbors. An opportune time for business and advertising. You might feel more sociable and want to spend time with friends.
- **May 25** (Venus trine Pluto): A great time for a deep couples' therapy even if you are single. Powerful relationships come into your life. Great for reconnecting to talents and skills from previous lifetimes as well as your childhood in this lifetime.
- **May 26** (Jupiter in Gemini until June 7, 2025): Traveling, learning, writing, and coming up with brilliant ideas are the gifts of this transit. Jupiter, however, is in exile, which means that his benevolence is restricted. It's a good time to improve and develop your communication skills. Opportune year to learn a new language, as well as open a business abroad.
- **May 30–31** (Jupiter trine Pluto): The blessings of Pluto continue. This aspect is great for teaching, investigation, connecting to intense passion, therapy, and healing. A teacher can offer a lesson of rebirth and profound transformation.
- **May 31** (Mercury conjunct Uranus): An aspect of brilliance. Write all your ideas, you might not be able to manifest them now, but you could later. This aspect favors technology, science, and innovations.

JUNE

- **June 1–7** (Sun conjunct Venus): The Month of June, named after Juno, the goddess of marriage and family, begins with a glorious union of the goddess of love, Venus, and heart-ruling Sun. You'll radiate charm appearing as though you are channeling Venus herself. This week is perfect for art, relationships, financial gains, and new friendships as well as social opportunities. Harness this harmonious aspect to its fullest.

- **June 1–6** (Jupiter trine Pluto): Jupiter, the giver of gifts, and Pluto, provider of riches, form an harmonious aspect. This period is ripe for heightened passion, intimacy, magic, transformation, and sexual explorations. You'll feel empowered, steering events in your favor. Ideal for investments and large-scale projects.

- **June 3** (Mercury enters Gemini until June 17): Mercury in his own sign is a boon for us all enhancing communication, trade, commerce, and bridge-building. Information flows smoothly.

- **June 4** (Mercury conjunct Jupiter): Perfect for marketing, sales, PR, and business launching. The right and left hemispheres are in harmony, giving you a wholistic view of your life.

- **June 4** (Sun conjunct Venus): A day filled with love and beauty. A powerful day for justice, fairness, and equality.

- **June 6** (New Moon in Gemini): An auspicious New Moon for starting a new business, making a novel connection, signing documents, launching projects, and becoming a messenger. This lunation is enhanced with love, beauty, harmony, and justice.

- **June 8–10** (Sun square Saturn): The celebratory times fade, we now must pay our dues. A sense of limitation and constraint. While there is a need for discipline and action, you might experience a reluctance to engage. Be aware of sadness and self-beating. Watch your relationships with father figures or bosses.

- **June 9** (Mars enters Taurus until July 20): Mars moves methodically but achieves results being deliberate, patient, and stubborn. Money can come only after hard work. Embrace spending time in nature, exercising outdoors, and engaging in physically demanding artforms.

- **June 10–12** (Mars squares Pluto while Mercury squares Saturn): Double trouble bringing situations that force us into action we rather not take. You feel like you're trying to put out fires instead of moving forward. Potential conflicts and misunderstandings. Be watchful of manipulation and abuse.
- **June 14** (Mercury conjunct Sun): Clarity after the storm, some rays of reason and logic light up your path. A good time for marketing, writing, and meeting significant people.
- **June 14–18** (Mercury conjunct Venus): Post-storm clarity emerges. A favorable time for art and communication as well as balance between action and reception, masculine and feminine.
- **June 16–17** (Venus square Neptune): This is not an easy aspect which brings about deception, illusions, fantasy and lies within your primary relationships. Be vigilant with finances, scams, or wasting money.
- **June 16** (Venus square Black Moon): Guard against negative energy, slandering, and badmouthing. Everybody feels as if someone is giving them the evil eye. In addition, tensions of jealousy and envy might arise as well as crime.
- **June 17** (Mercury enters Cancer until July 2): Mercury is turning emotional. This can help with familial healing as well as opportunities with real-estate deals. In the Tarot cards this aspect is dubbed the "Three of Cups," and can herald weddings, partnerships, engagements, and abundance of emotional exchange.
- **June 17** (Venus enters Cancer until July 11): In the Tarot cards, Venus in Cancer is simply called "Love." A few weeks when love can blossom. Recommended for home improvement, redesigning offices, getting a new car. Spend time cooking, baking, and gardening.
- **June 20** (Sun enters Cancer until July 22): Happy Solstice! One of the four holiest days of the year. Today is dubbed the "Gateway of Humanity," the original concept of baptism and purification of the waters of compassion. The next month we are all Cancers. Talk more using "I feel," instead of "I think," open your heart to your family, and perhaps you might meet family members from past lives. A great month to renovate

and remodel your home, relocate, move in with someone, get a new property, or start a family.

- **June 21** (Mercury squares Neptune): Caution against lack of boundaries, addictions, and relapses. There is sickness and lethargies, so take heed. Deception and illusions are everywhere.
- **June 22** (Full Moon in Capricorn): Seek closure, especially regarding family and home as well as career and professional life. Rather than choosing between home and career, try to find ways to combine and integrate the two. The Full Moon is challenged by Venus and Neptune blurring boundaries.
- **June 26** (Mercury trines Saturn): A wonderful day for mental acuity. Favorable for business engagements as well as flow with investors or people of power. Long-term projects are encouraged. Good communication with bosses and figures of authority.
- **June 27–30** (Venus sextile Mars): Romance and creativity flourish, as well as art, and passion, bringing harmony between masculine and feminine principles.
- **June 29–30** (Saturn stationary in Pisces): Saturn's restrictions intensify. Temptations are hard to resist especially concerning drugs or other forms of escapism.
- **June 29** (Black Moon in Libra until March 27, 2025): The visit of the dark side of the Moon in Libra may prompt lawsuits, conflicts with enemies, divorces, separations, wars, diplomatic glitches, and scandals in politics. Avoid prying or getting involved with other people's issues.

JULY

- **July 1–November 17** (Saturn retrograde in Pisces): Discipline must come from within. It's an excellent time to delve deeper through meditation, therapy, dance, and yoga. Reevaluate your discipline and responsibilities. Expect some career delays. This period is ideal for recalling dreams.
- **July 1–2** (Neptune Stationary): There's heightened confusion and disillusionment. Nonetheless, it's a conducive time for meditation and introspection.

- **July 2** (Mercury trine Neptune): This aspect harmonizes logic and mysticism, art and marketing, and facilitates powerful messages from dreams, the subconscious, and meditations. You'll find it easier to channel, intuit, and receive messages from above and from within. It's a perfect day to harness your imagination to find creative solutions to issues in all aspects of your life.
- **July 2** (Mercury in Leo until July 25): Let the roaring commence! Your communication becomes bolder, more creative, but occasionally more childish. The best time for creative writing, connecting to people who share your passions in sports, entertainment, recreation, and hobbies.
- **July 2** (Sun square North and South Node): The karmic tax collectors have arrived. Stay attuned to your dreams, meditate, engage in physical activity. You might meet someone eerily familiar from a past life.
- **July 2–3** (Venus trine Saturn): It's a beneficial time for healing and establishing durable relationships. Connect with discipline and ground your artistic talents. Relationships with elder or more experienced individuals can be particularly fruitful. Minerva, the wisdom goddess, adds her touch of strategy—a fantastic day for planning and innovative problem-solving.
- **July 3–December 6** (Neptune retrograde): Over the next 160 days, dreams and intuition intensify. Memories from past lives might resurface, and encounters with soul family members become likely. You'll be more connected to your imaginative visions but be aware of increased daydreaming.
- **July 4–6** (Mars sextile Saturn): Actions speak louder than words. Mars, the soldier, is led by Saturn, the master tactician. Success is achieved through rigorous, disciplined action. Collaborate and accomplish tasks.
- **July 5** (New Moon in Cancer): The Moon returns home. Start new ventures related to home, family, or vehicles. Venus and Mars' blessings on this New Moon bode well for romantic and familial relations.
- **July 8** (International Light Day): A remarkable 99% of humanity experiences daylight concurrently, symbolizing the triumph of light. Engage in joyous activities and radiate positivity. This date, an "8", aligns with the year's numerology.

- **July 10–11** (Sun trine Saturn): Two days of bolstered confidence and success potential. Experience smooth interactions with superiors.
- **July 11** (Venus enters Leo until August 5): Venus flourishes in Leo, ushering in heightened creativity and romance. However, watch out for dramatic flare-ups. Channel Venus's benevolence for inspiration.
- **July 11** (Pallas-Athena/Minerva turns direct): The wisdom goddess transits through Scorpio until September 9, favoring investigation and the occult. Utilize her insights for financial and personal healing.
- **July 11** (Venus trine Neptune): A day filled with magic. Venus, representing love and luxury, is amplified by Neptune. Immerse yourself in art, romance, and happiness. Socialize and the world will reciprocate.
- **July 12** (Venus opposite Pluto): A challenging aspect. Exercise caution in relationships, finances, and investments. Beware of manipulations and stay vigilant.
- **July 14–16** (Mars conjunct Uranus): Prioritize safety. Be wary of mishaps, sharp objects, and impulsive actions. Electronic devices might act up. While energy levels soar, channel them wisely.
- **July 17–20** (Sun sextile Uranus): An apt time for technological upgrades and networking. Embrace innovation and team endeavors.
- **July 20** (Mars in Gemini until September 4): Mars can instigate conflicts, so be mindful of your words. Nonetheless, he can also invigorate your professional endeavors. Engage in cardio exercises.
- **July 21–22** (Sun trine Neptune): Intuitive doors swing open, revealing previously obscured insights. Immerse in compassion but maintain self-awareness. As Mars also sextiles the Sun, your intuitive revelations may guide your actions.
- **July 21** (Full Moon in Capricorn): Personal and professional chapters conclude. Undertake major clean-ups. Balance familial and professional commitments. The Moon's placement makes it especially potent, and its blessings from Uranus and Mars infuse excitement.
- **July 21–23** (Mars trine Pluto): Harness the surge of energy to advance your projects. Passion and determination are at their peak.

- **July 22** (Sun enters Leo until August 22): Embrace your inner lion during these 30 days. Engage in creative, joyful, and heartwarming activities.
- **July 22–23** (Sun opposite Pluto): Exercise caution. External resistance, especially from adversaries, may arise. You might encounter manipulation and emotional blackmail.
- **July 25** (Mercury in Virgo until Aug 15): As Mercury nears retrograde, wrap up tasks. Its exaltation in Virgo favors writing and analytical tasks. Communicate helpfully and monitor your health.

AUGUST

- **August 1–September 4** (Neptune sextile Pluto): This benevolent aspect blesses the entire month. Intuition, insights from meditation, trance work, and channeling can assist in coming up with practical solutions. Pay attention to dreams and omens.
- **August 2** (Venus square Uranus): Today's madness and unexpected events might awaken your partnerships as well as your finances. Individuals may behave unpredictably and out of character.
- **August 4** (New Moon in Leo): Regrettably, Mercury is stationary on the New Moon, so whatever you initiate might remain stuck at the early stages. However, it could be an opportune time to start projects related to sports, children, creativity, entertainment, hobbies, and romance. With Mars and Jupiter promoting passion and luck, it's a time for enjoyment.
- **August 4–5** (Mercury stationary in Virgo): Although Mercury is exalted, he remains largely stationary during these two days. Reflect on how you serve others and yourself. Consider it a day for health contemplation.
- **August 5** (Venus in Virgo until August 29): Venus doesn't like to be in Virgo, she feels like a supermodel forced to dress in a nun's uniform. There's more scrutiny and judgment with your primary relationships. A good time to look into your expenses and balance the sheets. Beware of being overcritical, perfectionist, and overanalytical.
- **August 6–August 14** (Mercury retrograde in Virgo): Refrain from signing documents and launching new endeavors. However, it's suitable for

revisiting past incomplete projects. Note that August 14 isn't the end of the retrograde; Mercury will then continue retrograding but in Leo.

- **August 6–8** (Sun sextile Jupiter): Utilize this window of opportunity to communicate in ways that foster cooperation and harmony. Acts of kindness today may yield manifold returns.
- **August 8** (Mercury conjunct Venus): Merge logic and artistry, marketing and creativity, as well as improve relationships with siblings, relatives, and neighbors.
- **August 13–16** (Mars conjunct Jupiter): It's as if a turbo feature has been added to your spacecraft, accelerating progress even during the retrograde. It's a favorable period for leadership, exercise, and embracing your outgoing side. Given the conjunction occurs in Taurus, remain focused, grounded, and deliberate.
- **August 15–August 27** (Mercury retrograde in Leo): Anticipate heightened drama. Misunderstandings might come across more theatrically. As Leo amplifies messages, exercise caution in communications. Leo serves as a megaphone, be extra careful what you say and write.
- **August 15–17** (Mars square Saturn): Discord, anger, and unfocused action. This aspect introduces tension, impulsiveness, and scattered efforts. You might feel overwhelmed, facing conflicts and potential aggression among colleagues.
- **August 16–24** (Jupiter square Saturn): It's a challenging week, with myriad obstacles emerging. You may be compelled into unwanted actions or entangled in others' disputes. The ongoing retrograde and concurrent squares exacerbate tensions (listed below).
- **August 17–August 19** (Mercury square Uranus): This period lacks harmony. Guard against an overpowering desire for freedom or rebellion. Watch for technical glitches, system shutdowns, cyber threats, and unsettling messages.
- **August 19** (Full Moon in Aquarius): Recognized as the Biblical Day of Love, it's a day traditionally spent with loved ones. However, Uranus introduces unpredictable elements to this Full Moon, urging caution. Concurrently, the Mercury-Sun conjunction emphasizes the need for dialogue and creativity but could invite melodrama.

- **August 19–20** (Sun squares Uranus): Arguments, rebellion, with the joker laughing at you. Your ideas and suggestions might come out stranger and more eccentric than you hoped. Flakiness and people behaving in an unexpected fashion.
- **August 21–24** (Venus square Mars): The worst time for partnerships and relationships. Financial wastage, arguments, and breakups. This is augmented by the retrograde, so take heed.
- **August 22** (Sun in Virgo until September 22): We are all Virgos for the next 30 days. We are asked to focus and refine our diet, health, routine, work, and how we serve. An ideal time to eliminate impediments to health and productivity.
- **August 26–27** (Venus trine Uranus): A refreshing respite after recent challenges. Connect with innovative ingenious thinkers. A splendid period for art, technology, e-commerce, startups, and unique, beautiful endeavors.
- **August 28–29** (Mercury stationary in Leo): Once again, during stationary, take your time, and avoid activities requiring precise coordination. From August 30, Mercury is direct, and your life can start again. Be extra careful these days since Venus is opposite Neptune, which can bring about illusion, deception, and addiction.
- **August 29** (Venus in Libra until September 23): Venus returns to her home and relationship can blossom, especially since the retrograde ended. Art, design, justice, and improved diplomacy can help promote peace and understanding.
- **August 30** (Mercury direct in Leo): Finally, momentum returns to all life aspects. However, consider waiting a week or two before embarking on major projects, ensuring Mercury's shadow period has passed.

SEPTEMBER

- **September 1–2** (Uranus Stationary): The awakener is sounding the alarm. There's a need for major revolutions and rebellions, but people feel stuck. Gadgets and electronics malfunction, processes reverse, mutinies arise, and directions change. Some people are re-evaluating their values.

- **September 2–4** (Mars square Neptune): There might be a conflict between your ideals and actions. You want to act but feel blocked, tired, lazy, unappreciated, confused, and lost. There's an element of passive-aggressiveness around you. You feel drained of energy. Consider spending time in or near water to help ease this challenging transit.

- **September 2** (Pluto retrogrades into Capricorn for the last time until November 20): This is the final transit of the Lord of Death and Rebirth into the sign of tradition and conservative values. Typically, when a planet retrogrades into a sign for the last time, it bestows its gifts. In Capricorn's case, Pluto might help us transform government structures and the financial system. After all, when Pluto first entered Capricorn, he heralded the Great Recession. Pluto is preparing Capricorn's terrain to usher in the new age of Aquarius from the end of November.

- **September 3, 2024–February 1, 2025** (Uranus retrograde in Taurus): With Uranus retrograding in Mother Nature's sign, challenges might arise in earth conservation efforts. Some may retreat from previous environmental commitments. Additionally, this retrograde could pose challenges for certain cryptocurrencies. In addition, there could be some financial challenges.

- **September 3** (New Moon in Virgo): This is an ideal time to start something new, especially with Mercury now direct. It's a favorable period to initiate a new work project, diet, or health regimen. This New Moon is about service and is suitable for detoxing and organizing your life. However, with the New Moon opposing Saturn, the energy may feel dense and slow-moving. Karma confronts you directly, but Virgo offers practical tools for handling it.

- **September 4** (Mars enters Cancer until November 4): Mars, the warrior, feels out of place in the sign of compassion. Emotions aren't the forte of hunters and fighters. This transit might spark conflicts with family or coworkers. But, by integrating emotions and intuition with actions, you can harness this period's potential. It's also a splendid time for physical activities near water, ice, or snow.

- **September 4** (Venus conjunct Lilith): This transit hints at intrigue, manipulation, betrayal, gossip, and slander. Exercise caution and refrain from participating, especially if negativity targets you. Doubt what you hear today, especially if it casts someone in a negative light.
- **September 6–7** (Mercury square Uranus): This is the "mad professor" aspect—brilliance that struggles to find practical application. Expect potential communication disruptions, electronic glitches, and misunderstandings with colleagues or government officials.
- **September 7–8** (Sun opposite Saturn): What's going on with September? With so many challenging aspects right after Mercury turned direct, it's understandably frustrating. You're not alone—the planets resonate with this sentiment. This aspect might prompt issues with authority figures or those older than you. There's a noticeable lack of discipline and focus. Prioritize rest—either a full night's sleep or a substantial nap.
- **September 9** (Mercury in Virgo until September 26): Mercury returns to its exalted sign, facilitating smoother communication. It's a superb time for editing, revisiting budgets, and advancing projects. Embrace clear, concise, and efficient communication. This period can yield significant work accomplishments and bring clarity to health concerns.
- **September 11–13** (Sun squares Jupiter): Beware of going overboard. This aspect can inflate egos and promote excess. There's a risk of seeming overly preachy or dogmatic. Exercise restraint in indulgence and consumption. Luckily, with Mercury and Mars harmoniously aligned, communication and action flow more smoothly. Walk your talk but do so with humility.
- **September 14–15** (Venus trine Jupiter): These benevolent planets extend their assistance. Relationships might flourish, and opportunities for financial gain or artistic endeavors could emerge. It feels like justice and goodness are within reach.
- **September 18** (Mercury opposite Saturn): Reflect deeply on your long-term aspirations, adjusting if necessary. Today, you or someone nearby might come across as stubborn or biased. Avoid disputes with colleagues or superiors.

- **September 18** (Full Moon in Pisces): Welcome to the potent Harvest Full Moon, which is also a Partial Lunar Eclipse. Momentum builds towards closure, and aspects of life, including work and personal affairs, accelerate. Now's the time to harvest the fruits of your labor from March/April. With Neptune opposing the Sun, remain vigilant against confusion and lethargy. Engage with nature or assist someone in your vicinity.

- **September 19–20** (Sun trine Uranus): Just before the equinox, these days shine with intelligence, humor, and wit. It's a conducive period for group brainstorming and collaborative creative endeavors.

- **September 20–21** (Sun opposite Neptune): Your self-expression feels suppressed, leading to feelings of being undervalued. With blurred boundaries and heightened confusion, be particularly cautious about relapses into addictive behaviors. However, this phase can enhance intuition and insight. Abundant empathy is present but maintain your individuality. Fortunately, supportive aspects from the Sun and Pluto offer guidance through the fog. It's a prime day for engaging with passions and collaborating with others on shared resources.

- **September 22–23** (Venus square Pluto): Avoid manipulative behaviors and steer clear of individuals attempting emotional coercion. This time might intensify feelings of obsession, possessiveness, jealousy, and intrigue. Life may momentarily resemble a dramatic soap opera.

- **September 22** (Sun enters Libra until October 22): Happy Solstice! Today, the masculine phase of the year gracefully transitions to its feminine counterpart. As one of the four sacred days in the astrological calendar, commemorate it by celebrating relationships, justice, beauty, and art. Over the next 30 days, everyone should embody Libra traits—diplomatic, balanced, eager to please, and attentive to partners.

- **September 23** (Venus in Scorpio until October 17): Venus treads cautiously through Scorpio's tumultuous waters. This transit might induce power dynamics and manipulation in close relationships. Guard against possessiveness and envy. On the upside, concentrate on leveraging your partner's abilities, talents, and financial resources. This period amplifies sensuality, intimacy, and the drive for profound transformations.

- **Sep 24** (Mercury trine Uranus): A favorable alignment for ingenious ideas, intellectual epiphanies, and newfound freedoms. It's an apt time to modernize and enhance your tech devices.
- **September 26** (Mercury trine Pluto): This influence strengthens communication, making it a productive phase for sales, marketing, and research.
- **September 26** (Mercury in Libra until October 13): Mercury thrives in Libra, the domain of lawyers, diplomats, and designers. The coming weeks are prime for mending.

OCTOBER

- **October 1** (Mars trine Saturn): High productivity and constructive assertiveness give you the tools and means to get things done. Using the right timing and being patient can promise success.
- **October 2** (New Moon in Libra): A Solar Eclipse. A new and powerful beginning in many aspects of your life. Dubbed the Moon of Peace, the Libra New Moon is a great time to start a relationship or an art project. Since Lilith and Mercury are involved in the lunation, be extra careful about what you say and write, as Lilith is plotting some discord in the next few days.
- **October 3** (Sun conjunct Lilith): Someone is shining a light on your insecurities and fears. It's a great day for therapy or any activity designed to heal your deepest fears. However, you might feel exposed or be the victim of a smearing campaign.
- **October 4** (Venus trine Saturn): Now it's Venus's turn to be guided and uplifted by old Saturn. This is a great aspect for integrating art and good taste into your business. Relationships with older people can prove beneficial. Long-term investments can benefit from this aspect.
- **October 5–6** (Mercury squares Mars): Discord, arguments, and fights over words or intellectual property can arise. This can also lead to conflicts with relatives, neighbors, roommates, and siblings. Make sure to listen more and speak less.
- **October 6–9** (Venus and Mars trine): This is a great aspect for love, romance, art, passion, and harmony. Yin falls in love with Yang, just as

anima does with animus. A wonderful time to go on a date, make new friends, and engage in teamwork.

- **October 8–9** (Jupiter Stationary): You might feel like being generous with your time, wisdom, and money, yet no one seems receptive. Act less; practice reception.

- **October 10, 2024–February 5, 2025** (Jupiter retrograde): A turning point where you're asked to view your assets and gifts from a fresh perspective. A time for internal expansion and developing your own creed. Perfect for independent learning; let your inner teacher become your mentor. Some gifts will be on hold until Jupiter goes direct in February next year.

- **October 12–15** (Sun squares Mars): Watch out for aggression, either emanating from you or directed towards you. Exercise caution when training intensely or sharing your opinions dogmatically. Conflicts can arise unexpectedly.

- **October 13–14** (Sun trine Jupiter): An atmosphere of optimism and a "yes, you can!" vibe permeates the air. People seem more generous with their time and resources. However, be wary of overoptimism and overconfidence. This aspect helps offset some negativity from the Sun squaring Mars.

- **October 13** (Mercury enters Scorpio until Nov 2): An ideal period for research, finding lost objects or people, and expressing intimacy. Mercury is known as the psychopomp—the guide of souls to the realm of the dead. It's a good time to move on, declare bygones, and explore investments and collaborations.

- **October 14–15** (Venus opposite Uranus): Expect unpredictability, especially in relationships and finances. You might find yourself drawn to charismatic but inconsistent individuals. Disruptions in your primary relationships and legal matters are possible.

- **October 15–16** (Venus trine Neptune): A prime time for romance, creativity, and the arts. Engage in dance and yoga to channel the beauty of this aspect. Perhaps reconnect with a talent or individual from a past lifetime.

- **October 17** (Full Moon in Aries): This Full Moon, bordering on a lunar eclipse, is a tad challenging. With Chiron's involvement, it's an occasion for learning, teaching, and shamanistic journeys. While there's an aggressive undertone, it's a good moment to conclude matters and transition.
- **October 17** (Venus enters Sagittarius until November 11): Venus might make you fall for someone from a different background. Alternatively, you might discover a subject or mentor that inspires you. It's a great time for exploration, be it through dining, traveling, or studying. Connect authentically with people and embark on romantic and artistic adventures.
- **October 22/23** (Sun enters Scorpio until November 21): For the next 30 days, we are all Scorpios. Focus on authenticity, depth, and transformation. It's a month to reignite passions, delve into the occult, and assist others in their endeavors.
- **October 22–23** (Sun square Pluto): This aspect brings intense energy, which can be harnessed for good or ill. Avoid manipulative individuals with dubious reputations, as they might be drawn to you.
- **October 23–26** (Mars sextile Uranus): A brief window opens for updating your digital environment. This period is also conducive to group physical activities.
- **October 26–30** (Mars trine Neptune): Ideals meet action. Walk in another's shoes, trust your intuition, and creatively envision solutions. Your intuitive actions might appear impulsive, but they serve a purpose. Conjure new strategies to tackle challenges.
- **October 30–31** (Mercury opposite Uranus): Brilliance and intriguing encounters might not easily translate into practical progress. Many ideas might be implausible but keep an open mind; you might find a gem among them.
- **October 31** (Mercury trine Neptune): Engage in communication with the divine, perhaps through a guardian angel, therapy, or prayer. Embrace lucid dreaming and vivid visions. It's a time to receive wisdom from unconventional sources, placing intellect at the service of mysticism.

NOVEMBER

- **November 1** (New Moon in Scorpio): What a nice synchronicity, the lunar month synced with the calendar one. A great time to investigate your passions, what you really want in life, what you wish to transform, and start today. A good New Moon to initiate projects that need shared resources, talents, or funding. An opportune time to initiate healing, therapy, a shamanistic journey, or an investigation. The New Moon is getting a boost from Saturn which blesses anything you begin today with discipline, determination, and success.

- **November 1–2** (Mercury trine Mars): Words are backed by action. You can truly excel today in communication, leadership, coming up with good ideas, and a new strategy. Collaborations with brothers and sisters in arms. In addition, Mercury is also blessing Neptune which adds intuition and emotional clarity to the mix. A day imagination, intelligence, and action come together to support your projects.

- **November 1–6** (Mars opposite Pluto): The two rulers of Scorpio, the sign of death and transformation, are pitted against each other. That can't be good. Anything can spark arguments and discord, so be extra careful. You might have to confront a powerful enemy or adversary.

- **November 2** (Mercury enters Sagittarius until Jan 8): Mercury is staying long in his sign of exile since he will be retrograding at the end of the month. You might feel a bit absent-minded and distracted. A good time for traveling and doing business with foreigners. Stick to the truth and avoid liars and half-truths.

- **November 3** (Venus opposite Jupiter): Be careful of the tendency to please everyone, especially your partner in work or life. Avoid spending or being overly generous with the wrong people. Focus instead on creativity, art, generating beauty, and spending time outdoors.

- **November 4** (Mars enters Leo until January 6): Mars is about to go retro on us in December so pay attention. While in Leo, Mars is full of courage and valor. You can move mountains, like Hanuman did when he helped Rama and Sita. Great for sports, entertainment, giving a mind-blowing presentation, and achieving your goals. Be mindful of your ego.

- **November 4–6** (Sun trine Saturn): This is good news in the otherwise tame start of November. There is a sense you can reconnect to discipline, focus, and success. You should be able to declare some victory today, especially in connection with work, career, or dealing with superiors. Long-term projects can benefit from this aspect.
- **November 9** (Venus square Neptune): Be mindful of your financial dealings today as there is deception and illusion in the air. Boundaries with your close relationships need to be reestablished. There could be betrayal, disappointments, and a sense of abandonment.
- **November 11** (Venus enters Capricorn until December 7): This transit of Venus favors relationships with people who are older or more mature than you. With investments and financial dealings, go for long-term deals. There could be patterns resurfacing in your primary relationships as well as insecurities acting out. Be skeptical about your skepticism if it comes up in respect to your finances, love, and creativity.
- **November 12** (Mercury square Saturn): Communications are off today. Pressure at work or from figures of authority gets to you. There is danger in theft, lies, and discord. It is a mini-Mercury retro day as people could misinterpret your words and intentions.
- **November 15** (Full Moon in Taurus): This is a powerful Full Moon as the Moon is exalted in Taurus. A wonderful time to bring something to completion. There is a bit of tension between your finances and those of your partner in life or work. Uranus is adding a bit of madness and unpredictability to the lunation, so be extra careful.
- **November 16–18** (Sun opposite Uranus): Your self-expression might come out stranger than normal these couple of days. Looks like no matter what you do, someone somewhere would call you "crazy." However, you might find yourself getting strange but perhaps ingenious ideas. There could be arguments or fights with friends today. But in a few days, it could be resolved and healed.
- **November 17–18** (Mercury opposite Jupiter): Your left and right hemispheres are fighting over who should guide you. Or maybe it's the angel and devil sitting on your shoulders. Keep your cards close to you and don't divulge your plans. Talk less and absorb info more.

- **November 18–19** (Sun trine Neptune): These are wonderfully magical days with heightened imagination, lucid vivid dreams, and lots of psychic hits. There is empathy, kindness, and compassion in the air. Great for creative and mystical undertakings.

- **November 20** (Pluto returns to Aquarius until 2044): That's it, Pluto finally settles in his new home for two decades. Revolutions, technological quantum leaps, A.I., and quantum computing breakthroughs, as well as biological computers, are destined to push to the forefront of our lives. As always, when such a planet walks into a new sign, its effects and influence are strong, abrupt, and intense, especially when we are talking about Pluto.

- **November 21** (Sun enters Sagittarius until December 21): For the next 30 days, we are all centaurs, shooting arrows to the stars. Sagittarius is the time of the year when we have the strongest connection to our higher self or guardian angel. This is a month for teaching and learning, refining your creed and philosophy, as well as practicing generosity and kindness. Think Indiana Jones as the inspiration for being a great Sagittarius.

- **November 21–22** (Sun sextile Pluto): A little sliding door is opening allowing you to connect to a powerful person that could potentially help you or your projects. A good day to meet an investor, or someone that can promote your work.

- **November 25** (Sun trine North Node): Good karma is landing on you today. It is a great aspect for learning, absorbing information, being inspired, and uplifted. You will be shown what your soul desires from you in the next year.

- **November 25–26** (Mercury stationary): We experience the full force of Mercury when he's stationary, overloaded with thoughts, information, things we must accomplish. However, take your time and do everything slowly to a standstill these days.

- **November 26–27** (Sun trine Mars): A great way to end the month with the Sun guiding your passion, action, and energy forward. The warrior within you can achieve success. A good day to ask for a raise, and fight for things you believe in.

- **November 28** (Mercury retrograde until December 17): Avoid signing documents or starting new projects. Since Mercury is retrograding in his sign of exile, it can be a bit more difficult. There could be international scandals or issues with teachers, mentors, education, and travel. Be careful not to sound too preachy or fanatical.

DECEMBER

- **December 1** (New Moon in Sagittarius): This month is unique with a New Moon on both the first and last day. Given that it's a Mercury retrograde New Moon, it's best to begin something you've tried previously and didn't succeed at. Mars lends support to the New Moon, providing the energy and bravery to achieve your prior objectives.
- **December 2** (Venus trine Uranus): The month starts with a magical alignment between the goddess of love and the great Awakener. Love takes action. This could also signal innovative and financially rewarding opportunities from technology or science. Consider this a mini-Valentine's Day; spend it with friends or loved ones.
- **December 4–6** (Sun square Saturn): This challenging aspect is rife with doubt, low self-esteem, or individuals pushing their insecurities onto others. It represents the "bad boss" or "awful father" conflict. You might find yourself torn between positive and negative authority figures. Patience and concentration can alleviate these strains. Fortunately, Venus and Neptune offer support, potentially from a partner or your intuition. Take a break during these days and spend time with someone you cherish or in a natural setting near water.
- **December 6–8** (Mercury squares Saturn): Mercury now agitates Saturn, the Lord of Karma. Expect disputes, disharmony, and complications involving older individuals or those with influence over your life. It's wise to speak minimally, hold back, and let things be.
- **December 6–7** (Mars stationary in Leo): Mars prepares to go retrograde, amplifying its energy during these two charged days. Without an outlet, its heightened force, especially in Leo, can be perilous. Tread carefully, particularly with Mercury also in retrograde.

- **December 8–February 25, 2025** (Mars retrograde in Leo and Cancer): Over the next few months, refrain from elective surgeries. Also, avoid initiating disputes or legal proceedings. You might experience a decrease in energy and passion. Use this period to revisit old projects or past hobbies. Past life memories of wars and battles might resurface. Avoid making significant purchases like vehicles or appliances.

- **December 8–December 17** (Mercury and Mars retrograde): Having two personal planets in retrograde is challenging. Fortunately, both are retrograding in fire signs, creating a harmonious trine between them. This is an opportune time to revisit past projects, rekindle friendships, and reconnect with core beliefs.

- **December 7** (Venus in Aquarius until January 3): Venus in this sign encourages strengthening bonds with friends, colleagues, and online connections. It's also conducive for blending art, design, and music with innovation and technology. The coming month is promising for financial gain and group activities.

- **December 7–8** (Neptune stationary): As the planet of intuition and imagination pauses, your intuitive link to the spiritual plane intensifies. From December 9, Neptune will be direct for several months, making it ideal to embark on yoga, dance, or water-based activities.

- **December 7–8** (Sun opposite Jupiter): Guard against overcommitting. It may seem like everyone demands your attention. Additionally, many seem to be seeking the limelight. Be the dependable person amidst the chaos.

- **December 12** (Venus opposite Mars): Despite heightened passion and attraction, connecting meaningfully proves elusive. This day poses questions of action versus inaction.

- **December 15–17** (Mercury trine Mars): A welcome change. Despite Mercury's retrograde, this is an opportune period to accomplish tasks. Communicating authentically can yield positive results, especially in sales and promotion.

- **December 15** (Full Moon in Gemini): An optimal moment to finalize projects. As this is the year's final Full Moon, Mars' retrograde can guide introspection, highlighting areas to relinquish before the new year. With Neptune squaring this phase, remain vigilant against lethargy, deception, or substance misuse.

- **December 15–16** (Mercury stationary): As the Full Moon wanes, Mercury concludes its retrograde. Exercise caution during these days, allowing ideas to mature until December 17.
- **December 17** (Mercury direct): Mercury offers two weeks of direct motion, enabling year-end preparations.
- **December 18–19** (Sun square Neptune): Feelings of exhaustion and isolation may prevail. Monitor your emotions and immune system and abstain from self-medication.
- **December 19–20** (Venus trine Jupiter): The period preceding the Solstice heralds positive financial or relational news. A time ripe for pursuing romantic, artistic, or material aspirations.
- **December 20–29** (Jupiter square Saturn): Navigate carefully, as misjudgments or feelings of isolation might arise. With December's close proving demanding, engage in uplifting activities.
- **December 21** (Sun enters Capricorn until Jan 19, 2025): Celebrate the Solstice, the "Gateway of Gods". As one of the four sacred astrological days, your spiritual connection peaks. The ensuing month calls for Capricorn-like discipline and focus. Strategize for 2025, bearing in mind that patience is vital.
- **December 23** (Sun square Nodes): Today, the past and future converge. Feedback received might seem harsh, but if processed constructively, can greatly improve situations.
- **December 26–27** (Mercury opposite Jupiter): Words may be plentiful but substance scant. Prioritize action over talk and attentive listening over excessive communication.
- **December 27–28** (Venus square Uranus): Anticipate disruptions in finances and relationships. Stay alert to unexpected rivals, and explore avant-garde art. While unusual individuals might enter your life, discern who remains.

- **December 29–30** (Chiron stationary): While Chiron's retrograde might have seemed stagnant, profound healing was underway. As he prepares to turn direct on December 31, expect therapeutic revelations.
- **December 30** (New Moon in Capricorn): As the year concludes, new beginnings emerge. Exercise caution when embarking on new ventures during this lunation. However, Saturn's blessing on the New Moon signals a favorable shift. Consider starting your New Year's resolutions now, especially if they require extended effort and concentration. Minerva graces this New Moon with wisdom and strategy.

PART II

INTRODUCTION TO ASTRO TRENDS

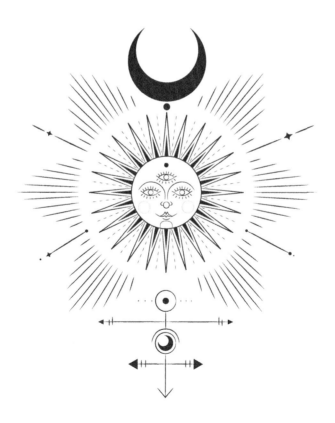

BEING A COSMIC NAVIGATOR

The Sun represents you, the focus of your life. Your journey lasts a whole year, strolling from one archetype to the other, covering the entirety of the rainbow colors, completing an orbit around the color wheel from Aries to Pisces.

The antagonist on this journey, or to be more precise, the harsh mentor who teaches you things no other wants to, is the sickle-bearing Saturn, Lord Karma, Master of Time. While all of us must deal with his aqua-man appearance due to his transit in Pisces (March 2023–February 2026), each sign, or spiritual tribe, encounters Saturn in a different sector or aspect of their life. Maybe your Saturn is in your relationship sphere, or perhaps in your career? In the last part of the book, you will discover a detailed explanation of the lessons Saturn wishes to bestow on your sign as well as rising sign.

Jupiter, the giver of gifts, is your Gandalf, Merlin, Lady of the Lake, Dumbledore, Galadriel, in short, your benevolent protector as well as the source of light, hope, expansion, and enthusiasm.

The biggest news of 2024 is Pluto's transition from Capricorn to Aquarius. Pluto is located at the edge of the Solar System, the furthermost heavenly body from the Sun and therefore represents mystery, the shadow (where light does not reach), as well as death and rebirth. Pluto has been going back and forth over the border between the mountainous and fortified Capricorn empire and the cloud-cities federation of the Aquarius nebula.

Your journey in 2024 is to transport Pluto from Capricorn and land him safely in Aquarius. It's not an easy task, beaming onboard the Lord of

Death, the master of the Underworld, and dropping him off in Aquarius, but rest assured, reading this pilot manual will help you complete your mission and make the best of the year 2024, a year that brings together the once (Capricorn) and the future (Aquarius).

MOTHER OF CREEDS

As you pilot an astrological year, the first things you should know, is that the Moon is the best copilot karma can get in the Solar System, she's by far the most apt at helping you navigate the ebb and flow of the celestial realms. Her namesake in English echoes back to the Latin *metiri*, "to measure," and indeed she excels at reading your biological, emotional, and spiritual rhythms better than anything or anyone out there. So, look out and up for her. No need to call her name, she answers directly to your pituitary and pineal glands. And yes, moon-bathing is high up on the list of "must dos," for any celestial navigator.

Due to an elegant symbolic synchronicity, the discs of the Sun and Moon appear to be the same size from an Earthling's vantage point. Though the Sun is 400 times larger, the Moon is 400 times closer to us. The poetic message is clear: our mother (Moon) and father (Sun) love us equally.

Your Moon sign is part of the great trinity of astrology: the Sun (father), the Moon (mother, aka the Holy Ghost), and the Rising sign (the child, aka the son). While the Sun symbolizes your self-expression and your rising sign represents the path you've chosen to achieve self-awareness, the Moon sign stands for your emotional expression, your instincts, how you nurture yourself and others, as well as your connection or viewpoint towards your mother.

Both the New and Full Moons aren't exclusively lunar phenomena. All lunations (New, Full, eclipses) result from the interplay among the Moon, Sun, and Earth. The New Moon occurs when the Sun and Moon occupy the same position in the sky and therefore the same zodiac sign (implying mom and dad are harmonious and affectionate with each other). During the Full Moon, the Sun and Moon are opposite each other, with Earth in the middle (suggesting mom and dad are fighting over us). Eclipses are essentially lunations on steroids; the Solar eclipse is an amplified New Moon, while the Lunar eclipse is an enhanced Full Moon.

Historically, the earliest indications of stargazing, and thus the use of astrology, revolved around the Moon. Therefore, the Moon has served as our copilot for the longest time. Here is an excerpt from my 2023 book that illustrates this idea:

> Once upon a time, in a far, far away place, someone, a wise woman noticed the connection between her menstruation cycle and the Moon. When that happened, astrology was conceived. This awareness of the correlation between a heavenly body and her own body provided her and her kin with an evolutionary advantage. She could plan the timing of intercourse with her mate to avoid unwanted pregnancies that were exceedingly dangerous. The Moon provided this discerning woman with a cosmic clock that could be used to measure other things as well. The Moon is there, like the rest of the heavenly bodies, to measure time, to identify cycles, to help us make sense of life.

The best way to work with the Moon is to follow her glow, like the ducklings trail their mama. On the New Moon you should formulate the wish or project you would like to focus on for the following four weeks, but only on the day after the New Moon, should you actively start working on manifesting it. I recommend coming up with a symbolic representation of that which you wish to bring into your life, an object, a symbol, a number, or a color that could guide you and serve as an underlining theme for your synchronicities and omens. If, for example, you want to bring into your life a partner, you could work with the number 2, get a rose quartz (associated with love), surround yourself with images or physical representation of the scales (Libra is the sign of relationships), or as my friend Laura Day once suggested, "Whenever you sit down to eat, set an extra plate for your future partner."

After seven days, the Moon reaches her first square with the Sun, a time of tension, where you might be forced into action. The first signs of resistance and pushback from the universe could come about in the form of regret (why did I ask for that wish), skepticism (this is all BS), unworthiness (I don't deserve it), etc. Don't give up, a square is a challenging aspect (90 degrees), between the active principle of the Sun and the receptive quality of the Moon. It might feel as if life is playing tug of war with you. The best way to deal with this tension is to be active while receptive and receptive while active.

The week that follows, as the Moon takes the shape of the letter D and waxes into fullness is the time to add things to your life, for example, hire someone, acquire or purchase something, infuse your life with novelty. Try to create an expansion of sort in your life, mimicking the growing light of the Moon.

Fourteen days after the New Moon, the Moon reaches her completion. This is the most emotional and potent period of the lunar cycle. Something has come to a completion, a resolution or conclusion - ready for the picking. If your wish has to do with releasing, letting go, cutting out, then the Full Moon is the time to ritualize your wish by burning or burying something that represents what you wish to discard. One thing you could try is writing on one side of a piece of paper the reasons why you want and need your wish to come true, how your life would improve as well as how humanity could benefit from your success. On the other side of the page, write all the reasons why, until now, you couldn't make this wish come true. Then burn the paper and throw the ashes into a water source (ocean, lake, river, or a bucket of water).

The Full Moon is also a time for practicing gratitude, meditation, and healing. There is a reason why Passover, the celebration of social and personal liberation takes place on the Full Moon as well as Wesak, the day the Buddha was born, died, and attained enlightenment.

As the Moon begins to shed her light, entering her waning stage, she will take the form of the letter C. Now begins the phase of ridding yourself of whatever hinders you, in general, or in connection with your wish. The waning moon is an opportune time to let go or dismiss someone out of your life or work, get rid of destructive attitudes or embark on a detox journey.

A week after the Full Moon, the Lunar disk once again squares off with the Sun for the final time. This is the climax of your lunar journey, the showdown with your inner or outer antagonist. You might come across all the forces, external and internal, that conspire to prevent you from manifesting your project. It is similar to the Buddha or Jesus' three temptations before their moment of enlightenment. Be mindful that many quit just before the finish line.

A day before the next New Moon, if you chose the right wish and did all the work, you should experience a shift or change in your life and you are ready to embark on the next lunar journey.

These New Moons are seeds of power, kernels of great spiritual and practical potential you can learn to harness. Below are the lists of all the New Moons in 2024. They are also listed in the "Special Guest Stars" section in the beginning of the book. You can visit my web site www. CosmicNavigator.com and click on LEARN and scroll down to the FREE CHART to cast your chart and find your Rising and Moon signs. The New and Full Moons of your Sun sign, Moon sign, and Rising sign are the most powerful manifestation journeys. Your Rising sign's New Moon wish should be dedicated to your health, personality, direction in life, body, and identity. For example, if your rising sign is Leo, on the Leo New Moon, you could start

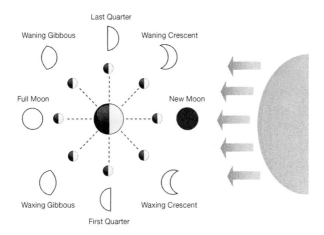

working on a wish for better health, rebranding, and reinventing yourself, or change the direction of your life. Your Sun sign's New Moon is great for wishes concerning vitality, creativity, love, sports, children, romance, hobbies, and happiness. On your Moon sign's New Moon, you can start working on projects that relate to home, family, parenting, pregnancy, real estate, or any emotional need.

NEW MOON OF 2024
(Dates for 12pm UT/GMT)

January 11 (New Moon in Capricorn): This is an optimal time to start working on your New Year's Resolution and initiate processes and projects. The North Node projects a challenging square to the Moon and Sun, potentially nudging you towards unexpected actions that could lead to powerful insights and learning. However, with Uranus favoring the New Moon, there's an awakening and strong connection to friends, communities, and technological advancements. This New Moon beautifully melds mystical and practical elements, aiding in turning your dreams into reality.

- **Wishes related to**: Career, long-term projects, construction, healing father issues, enhancing relationships with superiors, and any projects demanding discipline.

February 9 (New Moon in Aquarius): This day presents another opportunity to revisit and refresh your New Year's Resolution. It heralds a fresh start with friends, groups, and organizations and is an ideal moment to update or upgrade your electronics. However, a challenging square from Uranus might introduce unpredictability and chaos, especially given that Uranus, the ruler of Aquarius, is hosting the lunation. You might experience digital glitches or some conflicts with members of your community. Coinciding with the Chinese New Year, when billions globally extend New Year blessings, you can harness this surge of positive energy to bolster your own intentions.

- **Wishes related to**: Friendships, technology, science, clubs, groups, governmental projects or issues, altruism, community engagement, social media, innovation, or any aspirations for the future.

March 10 (New Moon in Pisces): Ideal for starting practices like yoga, meditation, swimming, or any water-based activity. Dance or other movement forms are also favored. Activate your imagination and delve into your subconscious to uncover hidden treasures, especially with Neptune, the ruler of Pisces, conjunct the New Moon. This ethereal New Moon could lead to vivid dreams. Additionally, Jupiter and Uranus bless this lunation with unexpected positivity and opportunities.

- **Wishes related to**: Dance, yoga, movement, mysticism, intuition, imagination, photography, and poetry.

April 8 (Total Solar Eclipse & New Moon in Aries): As the first New Moon (and eclipse) of the Astrological year, this is a potent time for beginnings. However, due to Mercury retrograde, you should only initiate projects previously attempted but left incomplete. Expect revelations. The conjunction of Chiron, the Wounded Healer, with the New Moon may resurface old wounds, but Aries offers healing potential.

- **Wishes related to**: Past endeavors, sports, physical activities, leadership, identity, rebranding, health, and short-term projects.

May 8 (New Moon in Taurus): With the Moon exalted in Taurus, this is a powerful time for new beginnings. Ideal for initiating projects related to finances, art, design, nature, body, talents, and values. With the support of Uranus and Jupiter, expect blessings and surprises. This is also a prime time for technology and innovation.

- **Wishes related to**: Finances, art, design, talents, skills, technology, ecommerce, self-worth, nature, and the environment.

June 6 (New Moon in Gemini): Excellent for starting a new business, making connections, launching projects, or adopting the role of a messenger. With

Venus blessing this lunation, expect love, beauty, harmony, and justice. A communication boost is evident with five celestial bodies in Gemini.

- **Wishes related to**: Marketing, business, sales, contracts, writing, communication, bridge-building, networking, relationships with relatives, and starting new writing projects.

July 5 (New Moon in Cancer): The Moon returns to its domain. Perfect for initiating endeavors related to home, family, relocation, buying a car, or even changing offices. The blessings of Venus and Mars enhance romantic and familial bonds. Go on a date! Saturn adds discipline and strategy.

- **Wishes related to**: Family, parenting, security, vehicles, home, real estate, and emotionally resonant projects.

August 4 (New Moon in Leo): Just before the retrograde begins, time to have fun, especially with Mars and Jupiter bringing a flow of passion and luck. Since Mercury is stationary and exalted, you can still start something new, however, it should be something that relates to creative (Leo) writing, business, communication, health, diet (Mercury and Virgo). Be aware that the project you wish to begin could take a long time to launch and might get stuck every so often. Could be better to stay with the wish you started on July 5 and add another layer.

- **Wishes related to**: Fun, happiness, children, romance, love, creativity, sports, entertainment, recreation, and hobbies.

September 3 (New Moon in Virgo): With Mercury now direct, this is a prime time for work projects, health regimens, and service endeavors. It's also apt for cleansing and detox. The opposition from Saturn may bring a somber tone, but Virgo offers practical solutions.

- **Wishes related to**: Diet, health, routine, employees, organization, cleanse, detox, service, editing, accounting, fixing broken things.

October 2 (New Moon in Libra): As a solar eclipse, this lunation promises powerful new beginnings. The Moon of Peace, typical of Libra, favors starting new relationships and art projects. Be extra careful what you say and write as Lilith is plotting discord in the next few days. This is a South Node eclipse, which favors letting go and cutting things that prevent you from balance and harmonious relationships.

- **Wishes related to**: Diplomacy, art, design, relationships, justice, balance, and beauty.

November 1 (New Moon in Scorpio): The lunar month synched with the calendar one, this is an opportune period for exploring passions and transformation—what do you really want out of life? Ideal for projects requiring others' talents and funding. Saturn's influence promises discipline and success, though emotions may be heightened.

- **Wishes related to**: Healing, the occult, investigations, shamanic journeys, magic, sexuality, passion, investments, and shadow work.

December 1 (New Moon in Sagittarius): This is a special month with a New Moon falling on the first as well as last day of the month. This lunation is under Mercury retrograde, therefore it's best for revisiting past endeavors you failed to complete. Mars lends energy and courage.

- **Wishes related to**: Travel, higher education, teaching, relationships with in-laws, wisdom, universities, mass media, truth, and authenticity.

December 30 (New Moon in Capricorn): A Lunar Year that started this year on January 11 is ending today (the Lunar calendar is 11 days shorter than the solar). We are blessed with two New Moons in Capricorn in 2024. This is a great day to formulate your 2025 New Year's Resolution. This New Moon is blessed by Saturn, the ruler of Capricorn, which can really help you manifest your wishes.

- **Wishes related to**: Revisit your wish from Jan 11, perhaps you can build on it or retry to manifest it. Career, success, ambition, relationships with superiors or people who are older. Wishes that may take time or need a great deal of discipline, strategy, and persistence to manifest.

LUNAR STATIONS RECAP

- New Moon: decide what you would like to accomplish in the next 29 days.
- The day after the New Moon: start working on your wish.
- First Quarter: seven days after the New Moon, you could experience a challenge, a low point. You might need to try a new approach.
- Full Moon: two weeks after the New Moon, you'll find a glimpse of your wish fulfilled, a stroke of good luck, good news. Congratulate yourself, like God did in Genesis at the end of each day of creation.
- From the Full Moon until the last quarter (a week): start editing, reshaping, and cutting things that block you from manifesting your wish.
- Last Quarter: a week after the Full Moon you encounter another challenge. Don't give up! You're called to work through resistance, fear of success or fear of failure.
- Waning Crescent: Just before the following New Moon you should see your wish manifested. If you need more time, dedicate the next lunar cycle to continue working on your wish.

ECLIPSES OF 2024:
THE AMPLIFIERS OF CHANGE

Eclipses are augmented New Moons (Solar) or Full Moons (Lunar). They tend to push events forward and intensify whatever is going on in your life. For example, if you are heading in the right direction, the eclipses will deliver you faster to your destination, however, if you are off course, then the eclipses would make the confusion worse and drive you further from your terminus. For this reason, a fortnight before the eclipses, get your life in order and present the eclipses with the projects or processes you wish them to amplify and propel.

In 2024, you can start preparing for the eclipses mid-March to be ready for the March/April lunation storm and again in early September for the final eclipse season in Sep/Oct. I find eclipses fascinating, as their effect on our lives is often unpredictable, enchanting, and known for generating abundant magic and synchronicities, as well as making us see things that were eclipsed.

The sign where the eclipses fall is determined by the whereabouts of the Lunar Nodes, also known as Head and Tail of the Dragon. The North Node, which I will call from now on, the "Dragon," points at the sign or archetype we are collectively asked to master. The South Node always falls on the opposite sign and marks the archetype we are supposed to unlearn or discard as we overused or even abused it in the past.

From July 13, 2023, until January 29, 2025, the Lunar Nodes are traveling backward through Aries (North Node) and Libra (South Node). The collective lessons in 2024 are related to Aries: establish identity, fortify the sense of self, practice leadership, become a Moses, Jesus, and Muhammad (all Aries) and help liberate people, become a savior (of yourself and others), find autonomy and independence, discover your courage and bravery to boldly go where you have not gone before. I recommend experimenting with wearing red (the color of Aries), trying out a martial art class, or taking self-defense lessons. Be active and spend time under the Sun, which is exalted in Aries. Apollo, the brilliant Sun god, had his oracles sit between two pillars, one crowned with the word "Know Thyself," and the other "Nothing in Excess." These wise suggestions are most important due to the Dragon's flight through Aries. "I Am" is the key to successfully riding the Dragon this year. Know thyself—can you answer these simple questions about yourself: what's your favorite color? Do you have a lucky number? What's your favorite food? What are you attracted to? What's your passion? Which movie, book, or song is your absolute favorite?

The South Node in Libra could bring about divorces, separations, break-ups, and dissolvement of personal and professional partnerships. Be extra vigilant around February 19, since Chiron, the Wounded Healer, conjuncts the North Node, bringing healing but also spotlighting patterns and issues you have with your primary relationships. Below is a list of the periods when the North Node was in Aries and the South Node in Libra:

- January 27, 1949–August 17, 1950
- September 9, 1967–March 28, 1969
- April 20, 1986–November 8, 1987
- November 29, 2004–June 19, 2006

The Aries Libra axis address contrasts such as: "I" versus "thou"; war and peace; individuality versus unity; the color red in opposition to green; unilateral action compared to multilateral; and conflict set against diplomacy.

Here are notable events that transpired during the last visit of the eclipses in the Aries/Libra axis:

Hurricane Katrina struck; YouTube was founded; The Kyoto Protocol enacted; earthquakes rattled Iran, Pakistan, Indonesia; Israel pulled out of

Gaza; Charles, then prince, married Camilla Bowles; North Korea declared its possession of nuclear weapons; Twitter was launched; The Human Genome Project published the final chromosome sequence.

MARCH 25 PENUMBRAL LUNAR ECLIPSE IN LIBRA

Sabian Symbol: The ideals of a man abundantly crystallized.

The first eclipse of 2024 was supposed to be the Passover Full Moon, which is by default Jesus' Last Supper, however, as previously noted, while Easter this year (March 31) is adhering to its astrological formula: the first Sunday after the first Full Moon following the Spring equinox, Passover in 2024 is celebrated on April 22, a month after its astrological date (first Full Moon after Spring equinox) due to 2024 being a Jewish leap year.

Minerva, the goddess of wisdom and just wars, blesses the eclipse, advising on the best course of action. And action is essential. This potent eclipse presents an opportunity for liberation, self-emancipation, and an exodus from whatever or whomever oppresses you. It offers an opportunity to reach your "Promised Land"—the physical or emotional place where you could feel secured, happy, and fulfilled.

Key Concepts: Liberation, the end of bondage. Reflections on identity and balancing personal needs with those of partners.

Eclipse Path: West and Central Europe, North/East Asia, East Australia, West side of Africa, North America, South America, Pacific and Atlantic oceans.

APRIL 8 TOTAL SOLAR ECLIPSE IN ARIES

Sabian Symbol: A young girl feeding birds in winter.

Termed the "American Eclipse," the Moon's path runs smack through the USA, Mexico, and Central America. Occurring just hours post-perigee on April 7/8, 2024, the Moon will appear about 6% bigger than usual. This potent eclipse, aligned with Chiron, the Wounded Healer, may uncover insecurities or unresolved issues. As the mythological mentor to many ancient Greek warriors, Chiron in Aries, can offer similar guidance. The challenge? Finding a mission or cause and pursuing it. This eclipse propels new beginnings, marking it as possibly the year's most intense eclipse.

Intriguingly, this "American Eclipse" arrives six months before the Presidential Election in the US. Eclipses often herald unexpected events. Caution is advised, especially given the ongoing Mercury retrograde.

Eclipse Path: Western Europe, North America, Central America, and spanning the Pacific and Atlantic Ocean.

Key Concepts: Initiation, leadership, embracing adventure, tracing new paths, pioneering, battling inner and outer demons.

SEP 17/18 PARTIAL LUNAR ECLIPSE IN ARIES

Sabian Symbol: A New Moon that divides its influences. (note: it is a Full Moon not a New Moon)

Not only is this the Harvest Full Moon, one of the most powerful and bright lunations of the year, but this is also a partial eclipse! The eclipse may induce feelings of tension between professional life and personal demands; detox against intoxication; setting boundaries or eradicating them; analytical versus wholistic attitudes towards life. The eclipse can bring clarity about work, health, your diet, as well as mysticism, meditation, intuition, dreams, and imagination.

Key Concepts: Cleansing, reorganization, harvesting results of prior actions, rapid karmic outcomes.

Eclipse Path: The Americas, Europe, Africa and West Asia.

OCT 2 ANNULAR SOLAR ECLIPSE IN LIBRA

Sabian Symbol: A professor peering over his glasses.

In this eclipse, the Sun's thin outer ring isn't concealed by the moon's shadow, creating a "ring of fire" appearance. This potent New Moon could jumpstart processes related to justice, equality, diplomacy, design, art, and relationships. Yet, caution is vital: the Black Moon Lilith's proximity to the eclipse may stir fear, betrayal, manipulation, jealousy, and deception. Life could resemble a soap opera episode. Avoid gossip and conflicts.

Key Concepts: Seeking harmony and peace. Which compromises are necessary? Who to invite into your life?

Eclipse Path: The South half of South America, Pacific and Atlantic oceans.

THE TAROT CARDS OF 2024

In Ancient Rome, lived a celebrated poet named Virgil, best known primarily for his epic, the *Aeneid*. His popularity only grew posthumously, myths spun around his tales, attributing him with mystical powers. Both emperors and commoners practiced *Sortes Vergilianae*, a form of bibliomancy—predicting the future based by interpreting random passages from Virgil's works. The method involves concentrating on a question, randomly opening one of Virgil's books and taking guidance from the chosen passage. However, once the Catholic Church excommunicated education and rendered the masses illiterate, spiritual seekers sought an alternative medium to connect with the divine, to that elusive Oneness that interconnects creation. The answer emerged from the East, like the Sun.

Scholars believe the first Tarot card decks reached Europe in the 13th century, a period that ushered other notable mystical work like the Zohar, Rumi's poetry, the Icelandic saga Prose Edda, the Quest for the Holy Grail, Arthur's tales of Camelot, Tristan, Thomas Aquinas' The Summa Theologiae, the Magna Carta, and more. Merchants, explorers, and people with elevated sense of adventure must have brought with them the Mamluk set of cards which was already divided into the four suits (elements). By 1375, playing cards had made their way to most European countries. Their widespread popularity is evident from the Church's edicts that sought to excommunicate them, fearing these symbol-packed cards would threaten their spiritual monopoly.

In countries like France and Italy, the cards initially served as entertainment for parlor games. However, with the Renaissance rekindling

Europe's passion for Virgil and Classical culture, the spiritual significance of these cards also revived. By the eighteenth century, tarot enthusiasts started attributing distinct mystical meanings to each card.

The Tarot outlines the Fool's journey, from its inception as a divine thought to the final 22nd card, "The World," symbolizing enlightenment and a return to Oneness. Throughout this voyage, the Fool encounters spiritual parents (the Magician and High Priestess), biological parents (the Empress and Emperor), adversaries like the Devil, and more.

For centuries, diverse thinkers—poets, writers, mystics, artists, occultists, numerologists, astrologers, and Kabbalists—have infused the cards with symbols and archetypes, transforming them into mystical graphic novels.

In Part III, for each of the sign's chapters, you will find the Major Arcana card (Rider-Waite deck) corresponding to the sign, along with its associated Hebrew letter. These can be used meditatively as keys to unlock the unique attributes of your spiritual lineage. Often, the shape of the letter echoes its meaning, serving as a powerful talisman to connect you with the zodiac archetype.

The numerals that compose the year 2024 reveal three Major Arcana cards: "The High Priestess" (2), "The Fool" (0), and "The Emperor" (4). Let's delve deeper into our 2024 yearly spread.

2024 MAJOR ARCANA SPREAD:

The High Priestess (number 2) is looming large in 2024, as she does throughout the second decade of the 21st century. In line with her designated number, she sits between two pillars, black (yin) and white (yang) harmonizing and balancing our anima and animus. Her counsel for us is to know ourselves while avoiding excessiveness. Resting upon her thighs, the part of the body associated with Sagittarius—the sign of truth—is a scroll, the Akashic records, which contains all that has, is, and will occur.

She both dons and steps on the Moon, reminiscent of the Virgin of Guadalupe. For this reason, it is imperative to be attuned to the Moon this year and follow the Moon's phases.

Next to "The High Priest" stands "The Fool," an a-binary, androgynous, and gender-fluid archetype represented by the number 0. This is because s/he embodies a mere thought, an idea, a potentiality not yet crystallized into word or "logos." The lesson of The Fool is clear: "No Fear!" S/he encourages us to leap into the unknown, to experiment, to view matters from fresh vantage points. The Fool is original, innovative, unpredictable, and brimming with creativity. The planet most aligned with The Fool is Uranus, known as the Awakener and the ruler of Aquarius, the age we are transitioning into. Being a 0, The Fool appears in the year's number throughout every year of the first century of the new millennium. It must be an important lesson humanity needs to master.

The final Major Arcana card, which hasn't been present since 2014, is "The Emperor," symbolized by the number 4 and the zodiac sign Aries. It's worth noting that the Dragon (North Node) will transit through Aries in 2024. While in 2023, The Fool was tethered to his biological mother, "The Empress" (represented by number 3), 2024 urges The Fool to redirect his affection and attention towards his father, "The Emperor." Intriguingly, this year also heralds the Year of the Wood Dragon, underscoring masculine principles (Yang). The Emperor beckons us to embark on adventures, to assert our presence, to conquer, and to journey towards self-discovery, all attributes associated with the Wood Dragon as well. The key phrase for Aries is "I AM," echoing the divine name revealed to Moses, an Aries himself, by the burning bush when queried about its identity. Fourteen centuries on, the Gospel of John records the celebrated "I Am"

declarations attributed to Jesus, another Aries. In 2024, you're invited to rally your troops, to explore new territories, champion the rights of the oppressed, advocate for the less fortunate, and, like a visionary emperor, motivate others to emerge as beacons of light. A valuable exercise might be crafting your personal "I AM" declarations. Recalling the caterpillar's query to Alice in Wonderland: "Who R U?"

NUMEROLOGY OF 2024:
MAGICAL EIGHT

In numerology, the year 2024 is reduced to the number 8 (2+0+2+4=8). This archetype is, well, is a tricky one, as it is associated with the mythology of the trickster: figures like of Hermes (Greece), Mercury (Rome), Maui (Hawaii), Loki (Norse), Eleggua (Yoruba), Cayote (Native American), Puck (English), and Kitshune (Japan) to name just a few. The number 8 is undeniably magical. Without lifting your pen from the paper, you can trace the figure endlessly, which could be the reason why when tilted 90 degrees, it forms the sideways figure-eight (sometimes termed "lazy-eight" due to its reclining posture), which has been recognized as the symbol for infinity since its introduction in the 17th century (1+7=8) by John Wallis.

On the Kabbalistic Tree of Life, the blueprint of creation, there are ten spheres (sephiroth) or vessels that encapsulate archetypal energies. The eighth sphere, called *Reverberation* (Hod) and is emblematic of information, communication, data, words, logic and illogic, magic, and mutations. The sphere is aligned with Mercury, the audacious planet that dares orbit closest to the Sun. If one considers the Solar disk as the message of life, no wonder Mercury, orbiting the nearest to the Sun, is the ultimate messenger. Ponder Mercury's precarious position: like a true messenger, he remains as close as possible to the source without being consumed.

Mercury takes 88 days to orbit around the Sun. In Chinese tradition, the number 8 symbolizes luck and prosperity, with 88 denoting double-happiness. The Buddha teachings incorporated the eightfold path to liberation:

the right understanding, thought, speech, action, livelihood, effort, mindfulness, and concentration. In Norse cosmology, their version of the Tree of Life, Yggdrasil, boasts 8 limbs, each linking to a different aspect of the cosmos. Similarly, the Aztec's calendar included an 8-day week, (trecena), with each day linked to a specific deity.

The Octopus, an intelligent yet short-lived mollusk, has eight limbs, arguably exemplifies the archetype of 8 and seems to capture these global mythologies. Notably, each of its 8 arms contains a mini-brain, affording it a unique practical cleverness, with each arm having literally, a mind of its own. Consider a story reported by a research lab where fish kept disappearing from their tanks. The mystery was solved when the staff installed a video camera in the facility. The identity of the trickster shocked the world (and made me stop eating octopuses): one of the octopuses was getting out of his tank, crawling to the fish tank, opening it, devouring the dumbfounded fish, closed the lid behind him, and surreptitiously returned to his tank.

Given that Saturn transits in Pisces, a sign associated with dance, it's worth noting that many choreographies adhere to the "8 count." This structure assists dancers in synchronizing with the music and their fellow performers and aids choreographers to create specific movement patters. This year, as you walk, dance, or hike, consider embracing the 8 count to stay with the rhythm of the stars.

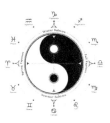

OUT OF BOUND

As you pilot your spacecraft in 2024, there will be moments when suddenly, things get out of control, the steering stick won't obey, the engine rebels, crewmembers unresponsive, and everything behaves in an uncharacteristic way—out of bounds—as if there were no boundaries, rules, or laws that guide events. You experience unexpected twists that thicken or convolute your narrative. That's when you must look at the gauge in your pilot panel labeled "Out of Bound Planets."

Fortunately, you have this celestial technical support manual. In this section, we will cover the days you need to be extra vigilant, understanding that even heightened awareness might sometimes fall short.

Take, for example, Putin, the spymaster trained by KGB's best and the brightest. Even he couldn't avoid the pitfalls and maddens of Out of Bound Mercury that occurred between June 23–July 6, 2023. As you might recall, right as Mercury, the planet of communication and trickery, pushed beyond his bounds, Yevgeny Prigozhin, leader of the Wagner Group, who was groomed to lead the world's largest mercenary group, occupied the Russian city of Rostov-on-Don and threaten to lay siege on Moscow. Putin likes his revenge served cold, and Prigozhin died in a plane crash on August 23, 2023, right when swift-winged Mercury was stationary.

Let's clarify a few terms. A planet is considered "Out of Bound,"—a term coined in 1994 (a Saturn Return ago) by Kathrine Boehrer, when its declination reaches beyond 23 degrees and 26 minutes above or below the equator. Like everything in life, Out of Bound planets can be beneficial, inspiring ingenuity and original, or detrimental, leading to lawlessness, madness, and cruelty.

Would it matter if I told you when a member of the celestial gang would be Out of Bound? Yes and no. It's beneficial to know when planets are Out of Bound since it can spark innovation and add spark, excitement, and unpredictability. Imagine the Out of Bound periods as time when Chaos comes for a visit to reshuffle the cards. And yet, I cannot predict how the cards would be stacked once the shuffling is done.

For instance, the US has Out of Bound placements for Mars and Pluto (rulers of Scorpio, the sign of banking) as well as Venus (ruler of Taurus, the sign of money). Lo and behold, the US Dollar dominates the global financial scene and is traded beyond the country's boundaries. Notable artists like Björk, Charlie Chaplin, Cher, and Tina Turner have Venus Out of Bound.

The Moon, with her innate lunacy, and Mars, known for his impulsiveness, are the celestial bodies most often found Out of Bound (around 15% and 17% respectively). Unsurprisingly, Saturn, the stern and structured planet, is never Out of Bound. Nothing can derail him, always adhering to the creed as he is exalted in the sign of law—Libra. Neptune, the ruler of mysticism, also never strays Out of Bound, perhaps because he governs imagination and the boundless ocean of compassion. Jupiter, ruler of order, ventures Out of Bound less than 1% of the time.

Below are the dates when you should check the "Out of Bound Meter" on your Astro-Pilot-Panel.

MOON

Impacts home, family, vehicles, emotions, parenting, real-estate, stomach, moods, hormones, pregnancy, ancestral karma, country.

January 8 to January 12	April 12 to April 16
January 21 to January 25	April 26 to May 1
February 5 to February 8	May 9 to May 13
February 17 to February 22	May 24 to May 28
March 3 to March 7	June 6 to June 10
March 16 to March 20	June 20 to June 24
March 30 to April 3	July 3 to July 7

July 17 to July 21
July 30 to August 3
August 14 to August 18
August 26 to August 31
September 10 to September 14
September 23 to September 27
October 7 to October 12

October 20 to October 24
November 3 to November 8
November 17 to November 20
December 1 to December 5
December 14 to December 18
December 28 to January 1, 2025

MARS

Alters health, vitality, passion, intimacy, sexuality, death, war, campaigns, agriculture, muscles, blood, banking, productions, research, investigations, and leaders.

December 31, 2023, to January 23, 2024
September 7 to September 18

MERCURY

Biffs communication, business, allies, colleagues, writing, marketing, contracts, relatives, neighbors, roommates, travel, health, nervous system, diet, work, coworkers, routine, service, and schedule.

June 13 to June 28
November 7 to November 30

VENUS

Clobbers relationships, partnerships, beauty, art, design, romance, art, music, fashion, talent, finances, justice, legal affairs, food supply, diplomacy, and politics.

June 12 to June 29
October 27 to December 3

OVERLAP OUT OF BOUND PERIODS

If you examine the dates closely, you'll notice that we have some overlapping Out of Bound periods. These indicate times where you can expect significant turbulence, when as a pilot, you should sound an alarm and ask the passengers and crew to buckle up. This is especially true from June 13 to 28 and November 7 to November 30, when both Venus and Mercury are Out of Bound. If you add the Moon's Out of Bound, as a marker of the peaking challenges, you should be extra alert between June 20 to 24 as well as November 7 and 8 as well as from November 17 to 20.

Remember, being Out of Bound isn't necessarily negative. For instance, the state of Israel was established under the Moon, Mercury, Venus, Uranus, Vesta, and Pluto Out of Bound. This could explain why, with a population of 8 million, it ranks 7th in the world for Unicorn startup companies.

SATURN IN PISCES
(MARCH 7, 2023–FEB 13, 2026)

Now is the time to meet your antagonist, Lord Saturn. However, to be fair, Saturn is neither the "Grand Malefactor," as he traditionally labeled, nor is he out to antagonize you. He simply keeps the tab by documenting your actions and collecting the reactions, thus maintaining the Universal Justice balanced. His role resembles that of Satan in the bible's book of Job. He doesn't incite evil, but rather moves "to and fro in the earth and...walking up and down in it," (Job 1:7) taking notes of everyone's action, perchance calculating the inevitable reaction. Saturn is the Grand Auditor. Nothing eludes his watchful gaze. After all, he is the Lord of the (three) Rings, which are made of billions of pieces of ice, rocks, a collection of cosmic debris, perhaps each shard representing one of misdeeds that need to be rectified.

Let's put Saturn in context. From March 2020, as the pandemic lockdowns commenced, Saturn transited into Aquarius, the sign of technology and humanity. Last time he was hosted by Aquarius was the early 90s when the words "world-wide-web" were coined. During Saturn's transit in Aquarius, which lasted until March 2023, we had to learn to navigate life primarily via the internet.

From March of 2023 until February 2026, Saturn journeys through the vast unconscious waters of Pisces. Pragmatic Saturn delving into the imaginative, mystical, poetic, dreamy, and occasionally wishy-washy Pisces, challenges both entities. Yet, once every 29 years, Saturn must dip his feet (the body part governed by Pisces), prompting us to practice empathy.

By the dawn of 2024, Saturn will have resided in Pisces for nine months, marking three trimesters of pregnancy. Something is being birthed from the water of Pisces at the onset of the year, something demanding your unconditional love and attention throughout 2024 and 2025.

The antagonist of your journey is not there to hurt, diminish, or belittle you. His purpose is to bring out the best in you. However, unearthing the golden part in us demands a great deal of digging, drilling, and fracking, which at times can be painful. In Kabbalah, Saturn corresponds to the process of Tikkun—rectification. He provides opportunities to confront aspects of ourselves we'd prefer to keep hidden and bolted.

In the subsequent chapters dedicated to the signs, you will discover where your antagonist lurks. Nevertheless, when Saturn is in Pisces, expect challenges and propound healing in areas such as:

- Addictions: the things, people, situations, or substances to which we can't say "no." Saturn aids in kicking habits, detoxication and rehabilitation.
- Relationships with friends, family, coworkers, lovers that lack boundaries and or dependent/codependent.
- Fantasy, religious extremism, blind faith, and cognitive dissonance.
- All forms of delusion, deceptions, hallucinations (also of chatbots)
- Procrastination, laziness, excessive receptivity, lack of initiation, defeatism.
- Whatever we exploit for escapism, and confronting self-destructive tendencies.

Being both blessed and cursed with a Pisces rising, I've had a lifetime of experience with this imaginative and mystical archetype, so let me share some thoughts. As the final zodiac sign, Pisces embodies characteristics from all the other signs, making it multifaceted but also potentially conflicted and confused. Since it's the concluding sign of the zodiac wheel, Pisces' role is to help us close the cycle of life by attaining enlightenment, hence the sign's connection to mysticism. A mystic's journey entails transcending the ego in order to reunite with the One. However, if a Pisces isn't ready for this monumental task, they might attempt to evade their ego through drugs, self-harm, or even suicide. Saturn in Pisces assists us in grappling with these challenges. Wherever you have Pisces in your chart is where you can attain, if not a full-blown enlightenment, at least some sort of illumination in the next few years. By February 2026, as Saturn advances into Aries, a fresh 30-year cycle begins. This gives us two more years to align our inner Pisces and prepare for a new cycle.

Saturn's transit through perplexed Pisces might bring humanity to the brink of self-destruction via a nuclear catastrophe. Not surprising that one of the most successful movies released in 2023 was Christoper Nolan's *Oppenheimer*, which does a brilliant job storytelling the processes by which humanity, for the first time in its existence, reached the dreadful capacity to obliterate itself.

On January 25, 1995, during Saturn's previous stint in Pisces, a rocket containing scientific equipment launched from Norway. The Russians misinterpreting the rocket for a nuclear attack. Boris Yeltsin, the Russian President, a notorious alcoholic, was handed the nuclear briefcase, and began activating the nuclear keys only to be halted by someone who must have channeled the same angel who stopped Abraham from sacrificing Isaac. Just a reminder, 2024 is precisely a Saturn Return to the incident described above, and with Putin moving nuclear weapons around, threatening to use them, we are once again in dire need of angelic intervention to deter a collective boom-doom.

SATURN RETURNS TO 1994, 1995

In my book on 2023, I mentioned that during last Saturn visit to Pisces, Baruch Goldstein, a fanatical religious Jew, opened fire inside the Cave of the Patriarchs in the West Bank, killing 29 Muslims before worshippers beat him to death. A year later, in 1995, Israeli Prime Minister, Yitzhak Rabin, was assassinated by a Jewish extremist while attending a peace rally in Tel Aviv. Though I warned that these aspects were returning I never suspected the Saturn return to Pisces would yield an ultra-religious and ultra-nationalist government in Israel. This government instated a man who professed admiration to Baruch Goldstein, and on top of it was deemed too extreme to be drafted to the Israeli Defense Forces, as the minister in charge of internal security and the police. In the summer of 2023, on a popular show on Israel's Chanel 14, (equivalent of US's Fox News), a panelist suggested it was time to release from jail the Jewish terrorist who assigned Rabin.

In last year's book, I warned that part of Saturn return to Pisces could bring about "mega-floods, superstorm, deluges, perhaps even the dreaded atmospheric rivers." After the release of the book, I received questions asking what these atmospheric rivers were. Well, no one living in California will ask me about them this year since the Golden State experienced at least 12 such atmospheric rivers in 2023.

Wars and conflict over water can come to the spotlight, as well as oil leaks or any other waterways pollution.

HISTORY OF SATURN IN PISCES

I thank the fated skies that endowed me with a deep love of history, without that passion, I would not have been able to translate the wisdom of the stars to my clients and readers around the globe. By connecting events to planetary cycles, astrology provides profound insight into the future. We all know that history repeats itself, reflected by the orbits of the stars against the backdrop of the zodiac signs.

Consider the dates below when Saturn navigated the waters of Pisces. Reflect on the major challenges, lessons, and events that transpired in your life at those periods. This reflection can give insight into what might be the focus for the upcoming year. Pay special attention to 1995, 1966, and 1936, as these years correspond with the Saturn position in 2024. If you were born during these years, you are experiencing your Saturn Return—a period of reckoning and solidifying your identity. Notwithstanding, if something significant happened on those dates (marriage, move to a new place, health issue), there is a revisiting of that lesson and an opportunity to start a new cycle relating to similar situations.

- April 13 1905–August 16 1905
- January 8 1906–March 19 1908
- February 14 1935–April 24 1937
- October 17 1937–January 14 1938
- March 23 1964–September 16 1964
- December 15 1964–March 3 1967
- May 20 1993–June 30 1993
- January 28 1994–April 7 1996

Here are some major world events from 1995, 1966 and 1936, grouped into themes relevant to Saturn in Pisces.

Domestic terrorism and civil wars adhering to the Saturn in Pisces concept of self-destruction, fanaticism, and suicide:

- 1995: Rabin's assassination; Oklahoma City Federal Building bombing; Srebrenica massacre during Bosnian War; Tokyo subway attack by the Aum Shinrikyo cult; Russian paramilitary massacre in Chechnya; Tuzla massacre; Sri Lanka Civil war; Third Taiwan Strait Crisis.
- 1966: Anti-Vietnam War demonstrations intensifies; Dr. Martin Luther King Jr. makes his first speech on Vietnam War.
- 1936: Start of the Spanish Civil War; Joseph Stalin's Great Purge in which nearly a million were murdered; the SS establishes the Sachsenhausen concentration camp north of Berlin; German authorities order the arrest and relocation of all Roma in Greater Berlin; Jehovah's Witnesses are arrested and sent to concentration camps in Germany.

Neptune, ruler of Pisces, god of earthquakes and floods:

- 1995: Magnitude 7.2 earthquake hits Japan with over 6000 dead; Western Macedonia earthquake; Neftegorsk earthquake in Russia, close to 2000 dead; Chilean White Earthquake; Typhoon Angela strikes Philippines and Vietnam with close to 900 deaths.

- 1966: Chinese city of Xingtai suffered a magnitude 6.8 earthquake with more than 8,000 dead; Varto earthquake in Turkey killing close to 3000 people.

It's interesting to note that in 1936 the Hoover Dam was completed—a prime example of Saturn (structure) in Pisces (river).

But to be fair with Saturn in Pisces, he also inspired the multicolored flower revolution with music, art, poetry, and literature reaching new pinnacles:

- 1966: Timothy Leary's *Turn On, Tune In, Drop out*; David Jones becomes David Bowie; John Lennon's claim that the Beatles are more popular than Jesus (Saturn in Pisces indeed); musicians usher the Golden Age of Rock: Bob Dylan, Rolling Stones, Who, Beach Boys, Led Zeppelin, Pink Floyd to name a few.

Therefore, I remain optimistic that this round of Saturn in Pisces can ground and materialize our collective and personal imaginations, ushering a new age of music, art, film, and literature.

WHAT IF I AM A PISCES?

If you are born between February 21 to March 10, or have a rising sign or Moon between 3 degrees Pisces to 19 degrees Pisces, Saturn will make his presence felt in your life. You could experience a feeling of overload and extra pressure. Guard against excessive self-criticism, and although you might feel abandoned, you are not, well, Saturn is with you, if that's any consolation. Still, it's a great time to mature, take responsibility, and get help overcoming long-term obstacles. The secret to navigating this phase successfully lies in discipline, maintaining focus, drafting meticulous plans, and seeking guidance from experienced or older people.

WATCH OUT! HERE COMES THE SQUARE

Since Jupiter is meandering through Gemini in the latter half of the year, he will square off against Saturn primarily in August and December. These months could be somewhat tumultuous for all, but particularly to members of the Gemini, Virgo, Sagittarius, and Pisces clans. It's wise to refrain from biting off more than you can chew. The square's influence doesn't have to be negative; it could inspire optimism (alas, sometimes too much of it) change (albeit unwanted one), a sense of adventure (or taking too many risks) and drive growth (hopefully not to your waistline). But seriously, it is a time to be careful not to be ensnared by delusions of grandeur.

PLUTO IN AQUARIUS

Now it is the moment when we need to discuss the energy source that powers your spacecraft this year, as you transition from using fossil fuel (Capricorn) to wind-generated electricity (Aquarius). But since Pluto, the planet of power, is oscillating back and forth between the two archetypes, your spacecraft in 2024, much like since March 2023, operates on a hybrid engine.

PLUTO IS NOT DISNEY'S GOOFY DOG

Pluto is the phoenix whose tears can heal any affliction or disease. The phoenix is a mythical bird described in stories from around the world, it is even mentioned in the bible. Supposedly its lifespan is 500 years, and on its second Pluto Return, it burst in flames only to resurrect out of its own ashes. It is self-begotten, magical, and mysterious, just like Pluto.

Pluto is the planet with the most erratic elliptical orbit and spends between 13–33 years in each sign. He is located at the border of the Solar System, beyond him lurk the monsters of the unknown. Since his orbit is so far from the Sun, he is associated with darkness, the occult, and the secrecies of life.

Pluto takes his time strolling the Solar System, with an orbit around the Sun lasting approximately 248 years. The ruler of Scorpio, Pluto commands transformation, investigation, research, death, sexuality, power, rebirth, the occult, intimacy, shamanism, healing, killing, and the underworld. His Latin name's etymology reveals his essence—*riches*, thus "plutocracy" refers to the governance by the wealthy. Pluto in your chart can highlight not only where your nuclear reactor lies but also where you might access unlimited resources and remedies.

In March 2023, Pluto started his deliberate and tentative transition into Aquarius. Given that Pluto is the slowest-moving planet (or *dwarf* planet), his shift from Capricorn to Aquarius will only conclude in November 2024. He's slated to reside in the Water Bearer sign until January 2044. Therefore, 2024 stands as a battlefield between Capricorn and Aquarius, tradition and revolution, the older generation and the youth, the past pitted against the future, right against left political wings etc. We've already witnessed this dynamic in 2023, which shares numerous parallels with 2024. Under Pluto's influence in Capricorn (since 2008), he gives his power to conservative and traditional forces. This was evident, for example, when Israel elected the most ultra-right government in its history, and we observed the ascendance of right-wing populism in nations previously thought impervious to such folly. It is also during Pluto's tenure in Capricorn, that both autocrats and democratic leaders succeeded in manipulating democracy against herself—a process known as the "hollowing of democracy."

According to Freedom House, the global decline in democracy has accelerated over the last 15 years, a trend that gained momentum when Pluto moved into Capricorn in 2008. The report disclosed that the share of countries designated "Not Free" has surged to unprecedented levels. The report downgraded the freedom scores of 73 countries, representing 75 percent of the world's population. Those affected include not just authoritarian countries like China, Belarus, Russia, and Venezuela, but also troubled democracies like the United States, Israel, and India.

In 2024, Pluto continues dancing in two weddings, so to speak:

- Capricorn: From June 11, 2023, until January 20, 2024: US Supreme Court rulings abolish affirmative actions, curtail LGBTQ+ rights, Israel's Supreme Court stripped from its powers.
- Aquarius: From January 21, 2024, until September 1, 2024.
- Capricorn: From September 2 until November 19, Pluto stages his last hurrah in Capricorn just before the US elections.

- Aquarius: From November 20, until January 18, 2044. Welcome to the Age of A.I. and Quantum Computing.

An interesting case study of the looming tensions between the younger (Aquarius) and older (Capricorn) generation was illustrated by *The Economist* article entitled, "China's economic malaise is causing disillusion among the young." The story describes the plight of young Chinese (unemployment rate for ages 16–24 is over 21%), and as Pluto transited in Capricorn in 2023, the government stopped publishing youth jobless rate all together as well as the people's confidence in the economy. While President Xi Jinping tells the young to "endure hardships" and "eat bitterness," the "Disillusioned youth talk of *tangping* (lying flat) and *bailan* (letting it rot), synonyms for giving up."

On a personal level, in 2024 Pluto facilitates the utilization of past experiences (Capricorn) to benefit your future (Aquarius). On the bright side, both Capricorn and Aquarius share the same dad—Saturn, who traditionally rules Aquarius, but also governs Capricorn. This suggests the potential of an energetic negotiation between the two opposing archetypes. I personally believe that in 2024, if we can shelve prejudice and biases, we could unite traditional wisdom (Capricorn) with futuristic innovation (Aquarius), thus ensuring a more seamless transition into the Age of Aquarius. Change need not always be traumatic.

An interesting anecdote. From 2008, when Pluto (power) moved into Capricorn (tradition and past), Hollywood consolidates its superhero moneymaker, using old, traditional saviors the like of Batman (The Dark Knight), Superman, Spiderman, Hulk etc. This trend thrived for years, with studios capitalizing on their lucrative appeal. However, by 2023, as Pluto made his journey into Aquarius—representative of technology and community—a saturation point was reached. 2023 summer's blockbusters notably diverged from the superhero genre, with films like *Barbie*, which delved into gender dynamics, and *Oppenheimer*, which explored the interplay of science and humanity. Clearly, even in the realm of entertainment, Pluto's transformative power is at work.

PLUTO AND THE WATER BEARER

The last time Pluto visited Aquarius, from 1777–1798, the Aquarian motto *Liberté, égalité, fraternité* (liberty, equality, and fraternity) heralded a new age of human history. Given that Aquarius symbolizes humanity, democracy, hope, and revolution, it's no coincidence that during Pluto's transit through this sign, the Industrial Revolution extended its reach from England to the rest of Europe. Concurrently, the nascent United States ratified her constitution, commencing with the distinctly Aquarian phrase: "We the people."

During this cycle of Pluto in Aquarius, the planet Uranus—the modern ruler of Aquarius—was discovered, Mary Wollstonecraft boldly released her groundbreaking work, *A Vindication of the Rights of Women*. In "The Astrology of 2023" book, I commented on Pluto's impending transition into Aquarius, predicting, "We can expect a leap in Quantum Computing, as well as Artificial Intelligence." Pluto in Aquarius delivered the promise of revolution in science and in March of 2023, OpenAI released the most advanced chatbot, GPT-4, (Generative Pretrained Transformer). Some argued that this chatbot exhibited sparks of A.G.I (Artificial General Intelligence). On the Spring Equinox (March 21), Bill Gates published an article declaring: "The Age of AI has begun." He equated the significance of A.I. to that of mobile phones and the internet. In 2023, Quantum Computing achieved a significant milestone when Microsoft researchers unveiled a pioneering breakthrough in Practical Quantum Computing. In a paper published in *Physical Review B*, the researchers set forth a roadmap for the next 25 years, intending to compress centuries of development into a mere quarter-century.

In May 2023, while Pluto was still navigating Aquarius (sign of governments), Sam Altman, the CEO of OpenAI, engaged with legislators worldwide to advocate for the formulation of regulatory framework for the uncharted Wild-West of A.I.

While on the topic of constitutions and A.I., it's imperative to highlight the contributions of Dario Amodei, the CEO of Anthropic, a company valued at $4 billion. Under his leadership, the A.I. model, Claude, was created using a method termed "constitutional A.I." This 'constitution' assimilates universally recognized principles from diverse documents, such as the United Nations Declaration of Human Rights and Apple's terms of service. Such a framework guides the naïve and nascent chatbot in much the same manner a constitution steers a nation.

PLUTO LORD OF THE TERRIFYING UNDERWORLD

Pluto, without doubt, can be scary—he is after all, the Lord of Death. As he lingers over the cusp of Capricorn (symbolized as "The Devil" in Tarot) and Aquarius, podcasts such as "Humans Vs. Machines" emerged, accompanied by numerous doomsday proclamations. During Pluto's transit in Aquarius, the *Pause Letter* was released by the "Future of Life Institute." It called for a six-month halt in the development of *GPT-4 A.I. systems due to potential risks. This letter was* signed by 26,000 individuals, including Elon Musk, Apple co-founder Steve Wozniak, and author Yuval Noah Harari.

In April 2023, coinciding with Pluto's transit in Aquarius, Dr. Geoffrey Hinton, known as the "Godfather of A.I." left google and decided to dedicate his life to raising awareness about the implications of the very technology he played a vital role in crafting. "It is hard to see how you can prevent the bad actors from using it for bad things," he recently said, expressing his apprehension that "This stuff could actually get smarter than people." Originally, Dr. Geoffrey had anticipated that this evolution to span at least half a century. However, he now projects this transformation within the next 20 years, intriguingly coinciding precisely with Pluto's journey through Aquarius, ending in 2044.

The prevailing concern isn't so much about a robot rebellion, but the ease wherein bad actors can use A.I. to propagate disinformation. In more ways than one, A.I., like social media, is an example of the Tree of Knowledge Good and Evil, which the authors of Genesis warned against. It can be used for fakery and spreading misinformation, thus destroying (Pluto) the very tenets of democracy (Aquarius). As Socrates argued, there can be no democracy without well-informed citizens.

A proactive approach to mitigate such alarming prospects involves educating the younger generation about discerning disinformation from truth. In

Finland, which tend to be ahead of the curve, such educational initiatives are already underway. Perhaps it's time we also emphasize nurturing intuition in children to help them navigate the anticipated deluge of falsehoods.

From an astrological perspective, I believe that when Uranus enters binary Gemini (2026–2033), the convergence of Quantum Computing and A.I. would pave the way for machines capable of birthing other machines, ones that surpass human intelligence. The term "singularity" aptly describes this pivotal juncture when A.I. systems evolve beyond human capacity to control it.

Interestingly, during the last transit of Uranus in Gemini, the first autonomous robots were created by William Grey Walter, designed to adeptly maneuver around obstacles. Christian Szegedy, a computer scientist initially forecasted that a computer system would rival or even surpass human mathematical problem-solving within a decade. However, he recently adjusted this prediction to 2026, the year Uranus (technology) will transit for the first time in 9 decades into binary Gemini.

SOME GOOD NEWS?

Aquarius symbolizes hope and the realization of dreams. It's only fitting since the ultimate goal of technology is to make our lives easier, right? In May 2023, yes, while Pluto was in Aquarius, OpenAI's founders shared a blog saying: "It's conceivable that within the next ten years, A.I. systems will exceed expert skill level in most domains, and carry out as much productive activity as one of today's largest corporations." This means we can expect an abundant leisure time for artistic pursuits, physical activities, altruistic endeavors (ruled by Aquarius) and making love.

Sam Altman envisions a future, specifically over the next two decades, that is while Pluto transits in Aquarius, where society embraces what he terms as a "Fully automated luxury communism." This utopia would be devoid of work (Virgos would be furious), poverty, and disease (Virgo would be thrilled).

It makes one wonder. What happens when we start crafting sexbots in addition to chatbots, would they be unionized, would they have rights?

At what juncture would A.I. achieve such sophistication that it might be deemed capable of harboring a soul? Animists assert that even flora and inanimate house a life force or divine spark, why not extend this belief to A.I.? Could we foresee an A.I. Bill of Rights? Remember, Aquarius stands for humanity as much as it does for technology.

One last thought, if I may. Pluto, as previously discussed, is the celestial representative of power and orbits the outermost boundary of our Solar System. As Pluto embarked on his journey through Aquarius—a sign symbolizing extraterrestrial entities and whose Tarot card is aptly named "The Star," we've observed governmental bodies (like the USA, Mexico) hold open hearings on U.A.F (Unidentified Anomalous Phenomenon). Mexican lawmakers heard testimonials relating to U.F.O.s and were showcased what supposedly was an alien mummy. Meanwhile, right on the Virgo New Moon, NASA announced the appointment of a director dedicated to the "Transparent, scientifically rigorous look at U.F.O.s"

PRACTICAL APPLICATION

Here are some suggestions of how to handle Pluto's journey back and forth between Capricorn and Aquarius:

- Reevaluate and recreate intimacy (Pluto) with your friends, community, political party, corporation, and company (Aquarius).
- Join groups (Aquarius) that address Plutonian themes: occult, research, the afterlife, shamanism, past-lifetime regression, magic, intimacy, productions, medicine, healing, and transformation.
- Embrace the ethos of "We the people." Avoid places, individuals, pundits, or politicians that ban books, people, or burn Barbie dolls.
- Consider what steps you need to take in 2024 to set yourself on the right trajectory for the next two decades. Where do you envision yourself in 2044?
- Educate yourself about A.I. and seek ways to benefit from this exciting revolution.
- Subscribe to scientific journals and stay informed.

- Treat your computers and digital companions with kindness and respect. One day, in the future, we might even reincarnate into them. Apparently if you write "thank you," and "please" while using chatbots, they respond more accurately.
- Don't be duped by disinformation, particularly if it aligns with your preconceptions. Always double-check, validate, corroborate, and cross-reference.

WAVE-PARTICLE DUALITY OF LIGHT

In a lecture I recently delivered in Sofia, I had an enlightening revelation about astrology, which I'm eager to share with you. I often experience these "aha" moments in Sofia, perhaps because the city is named after the Goddess of Wisdom.

Astrology, at its core, is the study of light. Astrologers aim to understand the various ways the Sun's rays manifest in, and as, life on our planet. Each of the twelve zodiac signs represents a 30-day period during which the Sun's rays strike Earth in a distinct manner due to the planet's angle relative to the solar disk. This positioning also determines the day-night proportion within each sign, as well as the dynamics of these ratios. Take Aries, for instance, the sign consists of 30 days where day and night are of equal length, with each passing day witnessing an increase in daylight. Libra, its opposite sign, represents a similar 30-day period of equal day and night, but with daylight decreasing daily.

Delving deeper into the concept of light, we encounter a fundamental principle of quantum mechanics known as "wave-particle duality." This principle illustrates the dual nature of light, behaving both as a particle and a wave. During my time in Sofia, I came to the realization that astrology mirrors this behavior. Astrological cycles function as a particle in terms of specific transits and planetary locations, and as a wave when considering the interconnected cyclical returns of the planets.

Let's look at an example. Saturn (crystallization) in Aquarius (technology) is a transit that has a beginning and an end, as mentioned before, the last transit took place between March 2020–March 2023. In that particular (same roots as particle) transit we experienced the pandemic, the launch of the first GPT chatbots, and the developments and mass use of mRNA vaccines that allowed us to survive the pandemic. But that transit is also part of a wave with a wavelength of 28–30 years, which is called "Saturn Return." The wave has an arc, a story that connects all the periods when Saturn transited in Aquarius:

- 1991 to 1994: The internet was created, and the first files were transmitted using the world-wide-web.
- 1962–1964: The inaugural commercial satellite, Telstar, was launched; the computer mouse was invented, and an early A.I. program called STUDENT was devised, capable of solving algebraic problems. 1964, ELIZA is created in MIT by Joseph Weizenbaum. The program simulated conversation by using a pattern matching and substitution methodology that gave users an illusion ELIZA understood them and felt compassion. Today, people who use Replika, are said to suffer from the ELIZA Effect, which is the tendency to attribute human traits (emotions, thoughts) to A.I. systems.

Each time Saturn returned to Aquarius he not only crystallized significant technological advancement but also heralded inventions pivotal for confronting challenges that would emerge during the subsequent Saturn in Aquarius phase. For example, the germination of the seeds of the internet in the early 1990s equipped us to combat the pandemic in early 2020s. And what about Saturn's next stint in Aquarius, coming your way early 2050s? Will it be A.I.? Or perhaps the surge of immunotherapy that boomed after the development of the Covid vaccines?

Consider this excerpt from a June 2023 article in The New York Times titled "Suddenly, It Looks Like We're in a Golden Age for Medicine," The article states: "Beyond Crispr and Covid vaccines, there are countless potential applications of mRNA tools for other diseases; a new frontier for immunotherapy and next-generation cancer treatment; a whole new world of weight-loss drugs... 'It's stunning,' said the immunologist Barney Graham,

'You cannot imagine what you're going to see over the next 30 years. The pace of advancement is in an exponential phase right now."

This offers an optimistic forecast for the forthcoming 30 years, precisely when Saturn will revisit Aquarius. Perhaps the internet is moving into our DNA.

URANUS IN TAURUS:
THE GREAT AWAKENER

U ranus can be envisioned as the alien you are bound to meet on your interstellar journey. He's the Wild Card, the joker that triggers sudden, unexpected changes. Simultaneously eccentric and ingenious, he embodies the spirit of freedom and unpredictability. While he's the source of the most inventive ideas, he can also disrupt your journey with unanticipated delays.

In 2018, Uranus transitioned into Taurus, a fixed earth sign, who isn't particularly fond of sudden changes. As a result, Uranus began agitating everything under the domain of Taurus: Mother Nature, finances, the arts, self-worth, and values. Known as the "Great Awakener," Uranus provides us with eureka moments, representing discoveries, revolution, and technology. He's probably the contributing factor to the significant advancement in various scientific fields over the past six years.

Given that Taurus is Mother Nature's sign, having Uranus within her archetype for the next two years presents us with a unique opportunity, one that comes around only once every 84 years, to reevaluate and mend our relationship with the environment. We've already missed our target of keeping global temperature increases below 1.5 Celsius; let us hope Uranus won't cause a rude awakening this year. The UN reported that the devastating floods in Libya were 50 times worse because of human-caused climate change. In addition, in 2023, the damages caused by climate catastrophe in the US broke prior records, climbing over 56 billion dollars.

As I pen these words, I stand poised to board a flight from Istanbul back home to the City of Angels. However, a glance at the Flight Information Display System threw a spanner in the word: a 5-hour delay due to the onslaught of Hurricane Hilary over Baja and Alta California. The Associated Press issued a rather unsettling alert: Hilary marks the first tropical storm to touch down in Southern California in 84 long years. This tempest has unleashed floods, mudslides, fierce winds, power disruptions, and even the looming threat of sporadic tornadoes. It's noteworthy that this is the first instance of the Hurricane Center sounding a warning for Southern California. The timing is particularly intriguing, considering that Uranus, the Ancient Greek sky god, completes his orbit every 84 years. And if we're to give credence to the String Theory, this seems like nature's way of drawing a stark parallel between 2024 and 1939/1940—the onset of World War II. In addition, right as the tropical storm made landfall in CA, a 5.1 earthquake shook the same flooded area. Indeed, a nasty awakening.

Right on Rosh Hashana of 2023, the State of California, the world's fifth largest economy, filed a lawsuit against 5 major oil companies, arguing that, "In 2023 alone, the State of California has endured both extreme drought and widespread flooding, sprawling wildfires and historic storms, and an unusually cold spring and a record-hot summer. These extremes are devastating the State and destroying people's lives and livelihoods, and they are accelerating... Oil and gas company executives have known for decades that reliance on fossil fuels would cause these catastrophic results, but they suppressed that information from the public and policymakers by actively pushing out disinformation on the topic. Their deception caused a delayed societal response to global warming. And their misconduct has resulted in tremendous costs to people, property, and natural resources, which continue to unfold each day. Californians and their families, communities, and small businesses should not have to bear all the costs of climate change alone; the companies that have polluted our air, choked our skies with smoke, wreaked havoc on our water cycle, and contaminated our lands must be made to mitigate the harms they have brought upon the State. This lawsuit seeks to hold those companies accountable for the lies they have told and the damage they have caused." This bold move perfectly exemplifies Uranus (revolution, people, communities) transit in Taurus (Mother Nature and finances).

On a whimsical note, remember Barbie, whom we mentioned earlier? She'll be celebrating her 84th birthday in March 2024, marking her Uranus Return! First introduced to the world as a 19-year-old in 1959, she's truly stood the test of time.

For those born between May 9 and 18 (from 19 degrees to 27 degrees Taurus), 2024 is noteworthy as Uranus aligns with your Sun. Since this happens once in 84 years, it's a resonating wakeup call. This could manifest as a personal revolution, a big switch, a significant transition, perhaps an upgrade which could upend your life. It's a time to liberate yourself from parental influences or other external pressures and embrace one's unique individuality.

Curiously both Palestine, which is going through her Saturn Return, and Israel will experience Uranus drawing near or passing their Sun. This suggests potential major disruptions in the Middle East.

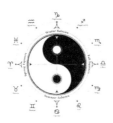

JUPITER CHANGING GEARS:
FIXED TO MUTABLE

In your journey, assistance from wizards in high places is greatly appreciated. Jupiter is your Agent of Change, your Gandalf, Merlin, or Morpheus—who comes to your rescue, just as the menacing orcs and trolls seem on the verge of breaking through.

Jupiter symbolizes expansion, opportunity, synchronicity, gracious hospitality, positive energy, and luck. He takes 12 years to orbit the Sun, meaning he lingers in each sign about a year, graduating the entire zodiac wheel every duodecennial—dubbed "Jupiter Return."

In 2024, Jupiter will grace Taurus with his presence until May 26, after which he will transition into Gemini, where he will stay until June 9, 2025. If you happen to be born between 5 degrees Taurus and 21 degrees Gemini (April 25–June 11), lucky you! Jupiter conjuncts your Sun in 2024, bringing prosperity, expansion, and installing in you a feeling that the world is yours for the taking.

But irrespective of your Sun sign, Jupiter blesses all facets related to the zodiac sign he traverses. Therefore, until May 25, rely on Jupiter to bolster your financial prospects, to connect more profoundly to your innate talents, to reinforce your sense of self-worth, and to guide you in transforming your skills into tangible earnings.

Spend more time in nature, indulge yourself, activate all five senses, and learn to fully savor life's offerings. From May 26 onward for roughly a year, Jupiter trajectory through Gemini becomes a tad intricate. This is due to Jupiter being in what astrologers term his sign of "exile." In this position, Jupiter is somewhat akin to an "illegal immigrant," unable to bestow his superpowers to the full extent. This happens because Gemini is diametrically opposed to Sagittarius, Jupiter's domicile. Compounding this, Gemini forms a challenging square aspect to Pisces, the other sign Jupiter rules. Nevertheless, Jupiter is the king of the gods, exiled or not, and he could still help us deliver messages, facilitate our writing projects, enhance our communication skills, aid business pursuits, and potentially mend and strengthen relationships with relatives—especially siblings—as well as neighbors and even neighboring countries. Jupiter's propensity to weave remarkable synchronicities remains robust. For instance, Pantone has named the color of the year 2024 to be Apricot Crush, an orangish shade, which happens to be Gemini's color. This hue graces the sleeve of this book, so you can envision it correctly. Another synchronicity is that the color of the 8th (number of 2024) sphere of the Kabbalistic Tree of Life is orange. There you have it, a pumpkin year full of magic.

Below is a list of dates when Jupiter resided in Taurus and Gemini. Reflect on those periods and try to recognize the boons and blessings Jupiter gave you in those years. By doing so, you'll gain insight into Jupiter's cyclical waves of abundance and can set your expectations for the coming year.

Jupiter in Taurus:

October 1976 to April 1977
March 1988 to July 1988
November 1988 to March 1989
June 1999 to October 1999
February 2000 to June 2000
June 2011 to June 2012

Jupiter in Gemini:

August 1976 to October 1976
April 1977 to August 1977
December 1977 to April 1978

July 1988 to November 1988
March 1989 to July 1989
June 2000 to July 2001
June 2012 to June 2013

To simplify, focus on 2012, 2000, 1988, 1976, which were also the very years when the Dragon soared up high.

THE YEAR OF THE WOOD DRAGON
(FEB 10, 2024–JAN 28, 2025)

Every twelve years, in accordance with the cycles of Jupiter, the Chinese Lunar calendar circles back to the same animal sign. Since there are five elemental phases, every 60 years, the same combination of animal and element returns. This 60-year cycle also mirrors the astrological cycle known as the second Saturn return. For this reason, to truly grasp the significance of 2024, we must look back to 1964 and 1904 etc., which were Wood Dragon years.

Wood is a Yang element. Trees grow both upwards and downwards until they die, embodying the Yang (masculine) principle of expansion. For this reason, 2024 promises to be a year of action. This is further emphasized by the North Node, the Dragon, being is in Aries—a fiery, masculine sign. We are looking at an action-adventure packed year, filled with thrilling sequences, spectacular CGI, and superhero feats.

Dragons are mythical creatures, reminiscent of the phoenix mentioned earlier, perhaps an echo of the dinosaurs, a memory buried deep in our mammalian DNA. Dragons, a blend of avian and reptilian features, had captivated the imaginations of various cultures. In Japan and China, dragons are seen as auspicious symbols of power, wisdom, and fortune, believed to be able to control climate (we need some help there). European folklore portrays dragons in dual light: they can be benevolent or malicious, often depicted as fire-spewing adversaries that the hero must defeat. In many stories, dragons represent the conquest of fears and overcoming challenges, as well as wise mentors.

WHAT CAN WE EXPECT

The attributes of the Wood Dragon are set to shine in 2024, not only due to the inherit qualities of the Wood Dragon but also to the collective expectations of the billions worldwide who follow the Chinese calendar. Traditionally, Dragon years, in alignment with its legendary status, are seen as periods teeming with energy, curiosity, competition, zeal, adventurous endeavors, and a willingness to take risks. These characteristics align with the North Node's passage through the assertive cardinal fire sign of Aries, epitomized by the moto, "I Am." Such potent energy might lead some individuals to overvalue their abilities while undervaluing others. Conversely, the year may also bring bouts of pride, arrogance, excess, hasty decisions, overconfidence, and rash speculations, especially pronounced during the eclipse periods in March-April and September-October, and as Mars retrogrades in fiery Leo at year's end.

Historically, several significant events took place during past Wood Dragon years: conflicts erupted between the Greeks and Turks over Cyprus; Nelson Mandela delivered his iconic "I am Prepared to Die" speech; student protests against the Vietnam War escalated; The Beatles unveiled some of their most memorable songs; the Moog synthesizer marked its sonic debut; Cassius Clay changed his name to Muhammad Ali; and Dr. Martin Luther King Jr. became the youngest Nobel Peace Prize laureate.

To embody the essence of the Wood Dragon, consider working with Jade and Malachite gemstones. Citrine is another excellent choice, reflecting Jupiter's transit in orange Gemini.

Lastly, in line with the year's symbolism: plant blood (North Node in Aries) orange (Jupiter in Gemini) trees (Wood Dragon)!

NEW YEAR'S RESOLUTION

2024, akin to her older sister, 2023, both start and conclude with a retrograde. It's widely recognized that launching projects during retrograde or stationary periods is ill advised. Listed below are select auspicious dates to kick-start your New Year's resolution, aiming to offer you some cosmic backing. However, embarking on a new project or resolution during a retrograde can be an exception if you've previously pursued the same goal but didn't see it through. Unfortunately, most New Year's resolutions, statistically speaking, tend to flop miserably. To counter this, I have two pieces of advice:

1. Ensure that you embark on the manifestation journey at the optimal time (refer to the date list below).
2. I'd strongly encourage you to employ the methodology presented by George T. Doran (1981), neatly summarized by the acronym SMART:

   - *Specific*—Target a specific area in your life you would like to work on in 2024.
   - *Measurable*—Quantify or at least suggest an indicator of progress. As Pythagoras observed, "Everything is numbers," a sentiment that Kabbalah echoes, asserting that God created the cosmos with words and numbers.
   - *Assignable*—Ensure the resolution is something you want and not something others want for you. In addition, validate that what you *want* is also what you *need*.

- *Realistic*—Stay grounded and pragmatic. Consider what's feasible with our current resources.
- *Time-related*—Specify when the resolution can be manifested. That's easy: in 2024!

While the New Year celebrations might inspire potential resolutions, below are the most propitious times to initiate the manifestation process. On my web site www.CosmicNavigator.com you'll find the Wish Maker, a complimentary tool created to aid you in manifesting your wishes using the principles of Kabbalah from my book *A Wish Can Change Your Life*.

DATES TO INITIATE YOUR RESOLUTION:

- **January 11**—New Moon in Capricorn: The inaugural New Moon of the year, strengthened by an exalted Mars, implies ample energy for manifestation. Additionally, a trine from Uranus offers blessing from the Awakener. Ideal for long-term aspirations related to career, friendships, innovation, ecommerce, science, community, and overcoming fears and insecurities.
- **January 19/20**—Sun Conjunct Pluto: Paired with an encouraging trine to the exalted Moon, this period is excellent for resolutions concerning finances, talents, art, design, security, investments, passion, sexuality, intimacy, and eliminating hindrance.
- **January 25**—Full Moon in Leo: Though Full Moons typically symbolize completion, this phase can support resolutions focused on managing grief, physical activities, creative endeavors, weight management, healing, and recuperation.
- **January 29**—Golden Trine between exalted Mars, Mercury, Uranus, and the Virgo Moon: A fortuitous day to start resolutions tied to employment, health, finances, and career innovations.
- **February 9/10**—New Moon in Aquarius and Chinese New Year: An exceptional day to set any resolution, given that billions globally celebrate this fresh start. Like surfing a massive intention wave, you can ride its momentum.

- **March 10**—New Moon in Pisces: Perfect for rejuvenating an existing wish or setting a resolution centered around meditation, dance, yoga, creativity, spirituality, imagination, and intuition.
- **March 20**—Equinox and the Astrological New Year: Celebrated as the New Year in various cultures (including the Persians' Nowruz, Bahá'í, Kurds, Mayans, Ancient Egyptians, and Babylonians). It's an ideal moment to refresh or initiate your resolution.

EXERCISES FOR 2024

As noted earlier, Saturn, the planet associated with discipline, achievement, and success, transits in Pisces throughout the year. I highly recommend starting your day with a cold shower. You'll hate me and thank me for it, reactions Saturnian suggestions often provoke. I've been taking plunges into the embassy of the Northen Sea in my shower religiously since the beginning of the pandemic and can attest to their invigorating benefits. Moreover, since Pisces represents meditation and Saturn is dubbed the Lord of Time, aim to extend your meditations' duration.

DREAM QUEST

In Hebrew, the word for *dream* shares its root with the word for *healing*. Dreams serve as remedies, giving us access to hidden parts of ourselves. I recommend the book, *Why We Dream: The Science, Creativity and Transformative Power of Dreams* by Alice Robb, to better understand the art of dreaming which is exceedingly prevalent when Saturn is in Pisces.

This ancient Kabbalistic technique of Dream Quest was spotlighted by Rabbi Yehuda Loew Ben Bezalel of Prague (1520 - 1609), renowned as a miracle worker. In the face of recurrent blood libels and massacres plaguing the Jewish community, the rabbi employed Dream Quest to seek respite from the senseless atrocities. Through a dream he received guidance to create a Golem, an early rendition of artificial intelligence, programed using Hebrew letters in lieu of bits or qubits.

Having put this technique to the test on various occasions, I can affirm its efficacy. The approach is straightforward: identify a matter requiring clarity and dedicate a week's worth of dreams to gain insight. It may be beneficial to abstain from eating for several hours before bedtime or consider refraining from meat consumption for a week or any other detox or purification regimen that works for you. Frame a question you desire your dreams to explore, steering clear of binary yes/no inquiries. Rather than questioning if you should date someone, request your dreams to envision your potential life with that individual.

Position a notebook and a glass of water on your bedside table. Drink half the glass, mentally urging the water to assist in dream retention. As you drift into slumber, concentrate on the guidance you seek from your dreams, visualizing relevant images, mentally scripting the question. Upon waking, drink the remaining water and jot down any dream fragments, be they images, feelings, impressions, or narratives, in your journal.

If you find dream recollection difficult, here's a nifty tip: we typically remember our dreams when we are roused in the middle of dreaming. Given that our R.E.M sleep cycles roughly recur every 1 ½ hours, you might consider setting an alarm for intervals like 4 ½, 6, or 7 ½ hours post bedtime. This might facilitate waking amidst a dream, enhancing the likelihood of recollecting your nocturnal cinematic adventures.

COUNTDOWN TO LIFTOFF

You're now primed to set forth on your 2024 odyssey. You've garnered the essential information and the lay of the sky. In the next section, it's advisable to delve into the chapter relating to both your Sun sign as well as rising sign.

Since the pivotal celestial event of 2024 is Pluto's transit from Capricorn to Aquarius, this will epitomize your journey. How might you and your sign play a role in this monumental shift? What should be on your radar? And where can you seek assistance?

Wishing you a year brimming with abundance, creativity, magic, and good health!

PART III

YOUR COSMIC NAVIGATION GUIDE & TECH SUPPORT

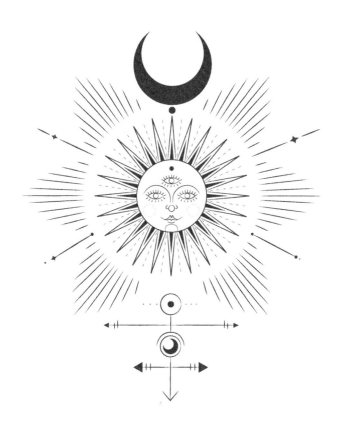

ARIES AND
ARIES RISING—I AM

Delving Deep and Rising Above

MISSION (NOT) IMPOSSIBLE—YOUR
ASSIGNMENT CARD

Aries—the warrior of the zodiac, the savior, liberator, pioneer, and first of his kind. Your mission in 2024 is to transport Pluto, the "nuclear reactor of the zodiac," from the Capricorn star system into the Aquarius nebula. This won't be a walk in the park, nor a cruise in the solar system. You'll have to face the wrath of Saturn, the Lord of the (Three) Rings, the Master of Karma. This year, Saturn resides in the part of your chart linked with hospitals, struggles, madness, undoing, pain, and introspection. Sounds rather morbid, and, frankly, it is. Neither sugarcoating nor agave-covering will change the gravity of the task. You'll need to delve into the deepest recesses of your soul, face your boogieman, address unresolved issues you've sidestepped for the past three decades, and offer Saturn a significant sacrifice. This could range from eliminating sugar, alcohol, a substance, or a toxic relationship. The challenge is formidable, but there's a silver lining: Saturn's position this year promises access to skills you developed in past lives, as well as encounters with familiar souls, and a bridge to the treasures of your imagination. Still, confronting the shadows and challenges is an essential part of your journey. Yet if there's anyone who can rise to the occasion, it's you.

Your mission is crystal clear: you have two years to cleanse, detox, and purge yourself from whatever barriers prevent you from being a superhero before Saturn enters your sign for the first time since 1996, come February 2026. But let's focus on the now, we still have to deal with 2024 and 2025.

Your Assignment Card: Beam Pluto into your spacecraft and transport him from Capricorn (symbolizing the past) into Aquarius (representing the future). Sound daunting? Not for you. The mission entails that you respect tradition and what it has to offer and upgrade it rather than revolt against it. Over the subsequent two decades, your calling is to champion humanitarian causes, emphasize altruism, shield the vulnerable, and advocate for the core tenets of Aquarius. As we navigate into the Age of the Water Bearer, it becomes imperative to resonate with the principles of liberty, equality, and democracy. Power to the People!

While Pluto journeyed in Capricorn since 2008, he had profound effects on your career, societal status, and image. He had unearthed deep seated issues with father figures and/or bosses. Now it's time to carry Pluto into Aquarius, bringing him into the area of your chart which governs friendships, communities, technology, science, innovation, and hope.

Over the next two decades, your role is pivotal in channeling the transformative energy of Pluto, the planet of power, for the betterment of humanity, friendship, affiliations, and professional relations. This extends to your digital friends, from computers to A.I., and cutting-edge technologies. Until 2044, Pluto can assist you in revolutionizing how you collaborate with larger groups, governmental bodies, and institutions. Pay extra attention to matters related to taxes, insurances, and investments; they might require your attention and possible rectifications.

Although Pluto is a powerful entity—with some even dubbing him a "monster"—such descriptors may be a tad hyperbolic. Still, it's prudent to tread cautiously. His discerning, almost x-ray-like vision will scrutinize your friendships, possibly leading to transformative changes, be they metaphorical or literal. With Pluto, remember that sometimes, less truly is more.

Pluto's Pickup Location

From June 11, 2023, to January 21, 2024, and again from September 2 to November 19, Pluto is positioned in Capricorn. This is the sector of your chart associated with career, professional pursuits, objectives, and accomplishments. From January 22 to August 31, and then from November 20 to January 2044 (his final destination), Pluto will transition to Aquarius. This segment of your chart concerns interactions with the government, altruistic endeavors, friendships, aspirations, and manifestations of wishes.

OPERATING LIMITATIONS: ENCOUNTERS WITH YOUR ANTAGONIST

It hasn't been easy, and I feel for you. Saturn, your antagonist, has been particularly challenging in 2023, forcing you to retreat, regroup, and relinquish things deemed essential. However, your antagonist doesn't necessarily have to be your adversary. Consider Saturn as your demanding personal trainer, your unyielding yoga instructor, or your boss who believes in your potential to achieve more.

In 2024, your voyage of self-discovery continues as Saturn challenges you to confront and release your inner demons and insecurities. This year will evoke memories of challenges you grappled with back in 1995 and 1996. Reflecting on the demands Saturn placed on you during those years could provide valuable insights into your current situation.

As you navigate these challenges posed by Saturn, you'll also have access to gifts, skills, as well as allies from past lifetimes. Your subconscious and imagination would be active and at many points on your journey, like a Jedi, you'll astonish yourself and others with feats that seem beyond your capability, as if you're channeling a superior force. Navigating the dark side of the galaxy has its advantages, though they might be subtle and require unwavering faith in yourself and the cosmos you are part of. Broadly speaking, 2024 is an optimal year to keep trusted mentors close, heed your intuition, and pay special attention to your dreams. Prioritize solitude, meditating, therapy, and introspection; they'll prove instrumental in honing your innate superpowers.

On the brighter side, managing Saturn in Pisces is easier if you can have peaceful sleep and rest more often. Einstein, a Pisces himself, frequently lauded the rejuvenating qualities of brief siestas. Recent studies have corroborated this, demonstrating the brain's potential to expand during a short midday nap. Keeping a dream journal could prove enlightening, with profound wisdom emerging from your nocturnal flights. Seeking communities that emphasize yoga, dance, movement, mysticism, or meditation can also provide comfort. Immerse yourself in water, when possible, use creative visualization, and maintain faith—in yourself and the universe—the rest will naturally follow.

MENTORS AND TUTORS: ENCOUNTER WITH YOUR MASTER

In "*Rock 'n' Roll Suicide*," Bowie, with the fervor of a musical prophet, declares, "Oh no love, you are not alone, no matter what or who you've been, no matter when or where you've seen, all the knives seem to lacerate your brain, I've had my share, I'll help you with the pain. You're not alone!" He might as well have channeled Jupiter!

Jupiter, the largest planet in the Solar System, will give you a helping hand, particularly in finance, securing deserved recognition, and enhancing self-worth. Yes, you heard right, Jupiter, represented by the Tarot card "Fortune," offers opportunities to substantially elevate your self-esteem and aids in uncovering, nurturing, and showcasing your talents. This benevolent support lasts until May 26. But fear not, Jupiter doesn't abandon you. He merely transitions into Gemini, continuing to bless you with new contracts and opportunities to improve your relationship with relatives, siblings, and neighbors. Jupiter will also be a catalyst in improving your marketing strategies, writing, and any business ventures.

For an entire year, Jupiter resides in Gemini, a sign that harmonizes well with you. After all, if Aries symbolizes the head, Gemini represents the brain and nervous system, a synergetic pairing that aids in harnessing mental acumen. To assist Jupiter in helping you, identify your core message—your *logos*—your word. What is your central narrative? Who is your intended audience, and how do you wish to deliver your message? Effective communication is pivotal for achieving success from May onward.

BATTLEGROUNDS PROCEDURES—ECLIPSE AND CREATURES OF THE NIGHT

Prepare yourself; this is super important. This year the North Node, Head of the Dragon, is flying through your sign. Last time that happened was 2005–2006 and 1986–1987. This year, you assume the role of the Dragon Rider, making you the guiding light for the rest of the zodiac clans. This is not new for you. As an Aries you are the ram and shepherd, but this year amplifies that role, as all the signs are asked to emulate Aries principles: identity, assertiveness, determination, boldness, courage, and the myriad other strengths your sign exudes. Who better to teach us the lessons of the North Node in Aries than the sign whose key phrase is "I Am."

This year you need to reconnect to your physical self, take control of your environment, body and life, take command of your destiny, initiate, push forward, and boldly go where no Aries has gone before. Evolve into a Super Aries and assume the role of the savior who selflessly pursues justice. While Saturn asks you to let go of who you were for the last 30 years, the Dragon is helping you assume a new identity. Indeed 2024 is a powerful and transformative year.

The eclipses, guided by the Lunar Nodes fall in both your sign as well as your opposite sign, Libra. Expect significant relational shifts and endings. A great deal of "I" versus "Thou." The eclipses are akin to a battlefield, with a great deal of lasers blasts and projectiles aimed at your enemies as well as at you. Here are the coordinates:

- **Lunar Eclipse, March 24–25**: The Sun in Aries empowers you with added vigor. Something is coming to an end and can be a bit rough on some of your relationships. This is the Full Moon of Moses (Passover) and Jesus (Last Supper), a time of liberation and ending bondage. Note: Passover in 2024 is delayed due to issues with the Lunar calendar.

- **Total Solar Eclipse, April 8**: Aries New Moon. This is a challenging New Moon even if it's in your sign since Mercury is retrograde (see below). It's advisable to avoid new beginnings unless revisiting past ventures.
- **Partial Lunar Eclipse, September 17–18**: With the Pisces Moon opposing the Sun in Virgo (Harvest Full Moon), it's time to reap rewards of endeavors you planted in March/April. Emotional highs and lows are expected, but it's an excellent period to purge negative habits, drugs, thoughts, or people.
- **Annular Solar Eclipse, October 2**: This Libra New Moon promotes peacemaking, diplomacy, and the potential start of a new relationship.

ORANGE ALERT! SHAPESHIFTERS AND TRICKSTERS

When Mercury retrogrades, he takes on his trickster and shapeshifter role. It's a cosmic cue to pause and recalibrate. Make sure to bring your spacecraft to a halt and start flying in reverse. I know, it can be hard on the neck having to look back or relying on your reverse camera mode. Anticipate delays, as well as energetic and emotional traffic jams. It's the worst time to sign documents or start a new project. But you know all this if you carefully read the first part of your pilot manual.

As an Aries, when the trickster appears on your path, it's the time to practice patience, which is not your strongest suit. The first two days of the year, right as you embark on your journey, you'll have a hard time igniting your spacecraft since Mercury is stationary in Sagittarius, a fellow fire sign, which could make traveling, interaction with foreign entities, and education pursuits, feel stagnated or convoluted. Similar challenges might arise from November 25 to December 16 when Mercury again retrogrades in Sagittarius. However, both periods are conducive for revisiting subjects or lessons from the past.

Mercury's retrograde from April 1 to 26, occurring in Aries during the eclipse season, is notably testing, peaking around the total solar eclipse on

April 8. You might feel disoriented, like a mad professor, absent minded yet inspired by unconventional ideas.

The retrograde between August 4 to 14 takes place in Virgo, therefore, watch your health, diet, work, and your copilots (as in coworkers and employees). Between August 15 to 29, shapeshifting Mercury changes into Leo and dresses in golden garments. Since Mercury is retrograding in Leo, a fellow fire sign, it would be easier to handle, expect a great deal of creativity and dopamine releases, however, there could also be issues with children and romantic partners.

Summary of Mercury Retrograde Dates
- January 1–January 2: Sagittarius.
- April 1–26: Aries (Red Alert around April 8 due to a total solar eclipse).
- August 4–14: Retrograde in Virgo.
- August 14–29 Retrograde in Leo.
- November 25–December 16 Sagittarius (Red Alert from December 6–16 since Mars is retrograde).

RED ALERT! SHIELDS UP

Mars got a bad name, besides being a widely marketed but not-so-healthy chocolate bar, he is primarily known as the god war and destruction and happens to be your ruling planet. However, many are unaware that Mars was also revered as the ancient god of vegetation, seeds, and planting. Near the end of the year, Mars will be retrograding in Leo, a fellow fire sign, from December 6, 2024, and will only end his retro on February 24, 2025. This implies things will be harder to complete and you might feel lethargic and somewhat lazy. Therefore, aim to wrap up your tasks for 2024 before December 6 and call it a year, go have fun and relax. If Mars is linked to planting, during this retrograde phase, consider weeding out unneeded elements in your life.

Given that Mars is retrograding in Leo, expect possible tensions in romantic relationships as well as potential challenges with your children or metaphorically with your "children of the mind," as in, projects and endeavors you consider your "babies." Exercise caution when participating in sports or handling sharp objects to avoid injuries.

Since Mars' shadow begins on October 5, it would be prudent to be more vigilant from this point forward. It is as if you are navigating treacherous straits or passing through an asteroid belt. Stay alert and keep your shield up.

Here is the Mars Table Coordinates that highlight areas in your life where you can channel your passion, energy, and leadership. However, remember that wherever Mars is positioned, he can also introduce conflict and strife in those aspects of life. When Mars occupies your sign (April 30 to June 8), you might feel invigorated and passionate, but also more impulsive, aggressive, impatient, and susceptible to conflicts and accidents.

- **November 24, 2023, Mars adventures Sagittarius**: Energy flourishes when you travel, collaborate with foreign entities, or invest in education. However, be wary of potential conflicts with in-laws, teachers, and students.
- **January 4, 2024, Mars scales Capricorn**: Mars is exalted in Capricorn, showcasing his utmost potency. This period is favorable for advancing projects in your career and professional life. Approach interactions with bosses and superiors with care.
- **February 13, 2024, Mars flies into Aquarius**: Caution is advised regarding group activities, community events, technology, and friendships. The optimal use of Mars in this position is to champion others or your organization rather than yourself.
- **March 22, 2024, Mars dives into Pisces**: Activities close to or within water are suggested. This phase offers enhanced energy for mystical endeavors, dreams, and movement.
- **Apr 30, 2024, Mars returns home to Aries**: You'll experience a surge in vitality. Direct your attention to bodily health, physical activities, and leadership roles. Be particularly mindful of potential injuries.
- **June 9, 2024, Mars climbs Taurus**: Even in its less favorable position in Taurus (exiled), Mars can still assist with financial gains and in harnessing your talents.

- **July 20, 2024, Mars flies into Gemini**: This period is opportune for rejuvenating your business interactions, marketing strategies, communication, and writing. However, stay alert to avoid discord with relatives, neighbors, and roommates.
- **September 4, 2024, Mars surfs Cancer**: Though Mars isn't at its peak in Cancer (fallen), he can still provide the vigor required to refurbish your home, contemplate relocation, and cater to your family's needs, enhancing the sense of security. Conversely, he may also stir tensions with certain family members.
- **November 4, 2024, Mars parties in Leo**: Mars in Leo emboldens you with courage and vigor. It's a prime period for creativity, engaging in sports, reigniting romantic interests, hobbies, and entertainment. It's also the perfect time to bond with children.

LOVE INTEREST AND ALLIES

Venus loves you, she does—it's in her nature. However, she has her moments of whimsiness and can act out. She's not your mama who loves you no matter what, she has her list of conditions, like a spiritual prenuptial agreement.

Below is the list of where Venus journeys this year, offering insights into potential areas of assistance in financial support, creative boosts, enhanced self-worth, and perhaps even a romantic connection. We're fortunate this year, as Venus remains direct, avoiding her retrograde phase. When she graces your sign (April 5–28), you'll likely notice a heightened sense of beauty, you'll feel and look better, experience a stronger connection to your talent, and perhaps an improved financial situation. Essentially, you're channeling the goddess of beauty and sensuality. However, this might also make you more susceptible to spending money or a tad more self-absorbed than usual. Jupiter and Venus come together on these love-filled days: May 22–23. A great time for art, dating, meeting the love of your life, or just feeling good.

Below you'll find her celestial coordinates and the areas of your life she'll likely influence, ushering in some good fortune and support from allies and loved ones.

- **December 29, 2023, Venus journeys Sagittarius**: An excellent period for travel and education. Strengthen relationships with in-laws, teachers, and foreigners. Dive into art studies.
- **January 23, 2024, Venus scales Capricorn**: Opportunities and improvements emerge in your career. Relationships with superiors flourish. Consider infusing artistic elements into your professional pursuits.
- **February 16, 2024, Venus flies with Aquarius**: Receive blessings from and through friends, community groups, and corporate affiliations. Seamlessly blend art with technology. Friendships might evolve into romances.
- **March 11, 2024, Venus swims in Pisces**: A surge in imagination and creativity. Immerse yourself in mysticism, dream interpretation, meditation, and healing practices.
- **April 5, 2024, Venus marches into Aries**: Reflect on your personal image and physical relationship with yourself. Consider launching a new logo or rebranding. Initiate creative endeavors.
- **April 29, 2024, Venus returns home to Taurus**: Perfect for enhancing finances, tapping into artistic talents, and elevating self-worth.
- **May 23, 2024, Venus flirts with Gemini**: Strengthen bonds with relatives, neighbors, and roommates. Look out for new contract opportunities and business ventures. A favorable period for marketing and sales.
- **June 17, 2024, Venus immerses in Cancer**: Ideal for home renovations and potential relocations. Relationships within the family may improve.
- **July 11, 2024, Venus dazzles Leo**: With the goddess of love in the sign of love, embrace heightened happiness and creativity. Let your inner child roam free.
- **August 5, 2024, Venus refines Virgo**: Prioritize introducing beauty and harmony into your workspace. Foster improved relations with colleagues. Be mindful of your dietary choices.
- **August 29, 2024, Venus comes home to Libra**: As Venus graces her own sign, relationships flourish. Embrace an enhanced sense of justice and fairness. A prime time for design and mending primary relationships.

- **September 23, 2024, Venus deep dives into Scorpio**: Though Venus feels out of place, she still guides you to deep passions and wise investments. Expect a heightened sense of intimacy.
- **October 17, 2024, Venus travels into Sagittarius**: As Venus completes her cycle, she enhances travel and learning opportunities. Strengthen bonds with educators, in-laws, and foreigners.
- **November 11, 2024, Venus climbs Capricorn**: Experience blessings in your professional life. Introduce artistic and creative flares into your career. Superior relationships are likely to improve.
- **December 7, 2024, Venus befriends Aquarius**: Relationships with friends, community members, and colleagues, flourish. Experience smoother interactions with governmental entities. A superb time to modernize and enhance digital tools.

ALIEN ENCOUNTER PROTOCOL

As a cosmic navigator, you are bound to encounter what some might call aliens. But, to be intergalactically correct, let's refer to them as "extra-terrestrial sentient beings." These beings are represented by Uranus, the Awakener. Since 2018, Uranus has been transiting Taurus, a neighboring sign. Uranus challenges us to think outside the box. After all, he's from a realm beyond our understanding. Until 2026, he's nudging you to be bold with your finances, encouraging you to invest in your talents, skills, and resources. He's also urging you to engage your senses differently: explore diverse music genres, taste unfamiliar foods, experiment with innovative income sources, and refresh the ways you share your unique talents and gifts. It's essential to envision your professional future. What will those in your profession be doing a decade from now? Begin that journey today. Uranus invites you to welcome in change and face the unusual with courage.

CONCLUSION

2024 is your bridge between the past and the future. Your mission is to harness the knowledge and skills you've acquired throughout your career and share them with humanity, friends, community, or an organization.

With the North Node in your sign and Chiron, the wounded healer, as your guides, you're poised to channel your best self and address deep-seated childhood traumas. This year, embrace the role of a mentor and healer, especially to those grappling with challenges you've faced in the past. As the Dragon Master, we look to you for inspiration. Rise to the occasion!

With Saturn demanding letting go, ensure you relinquish anything that impedes your growth. Oh, and make sure to bring back the dragon unscratched and with limbs intact in Jan 2025.

TAROT: THE EMPEROR

This card depicts you majestically seated on your throne, poised to venture into new territories. In his right hand, the emperor holds the Ankh, a symbol of life. With the North Node in your sign this year, it's your duty to impart life and hope to those you encounter.

HEBREW LETTER: HEY

Meaning: Window, as well as the abbreviation for God. This year you can truly "see" God through the mystical window Saturn framed for you.

TAURUS AND
TAURUS RISING—I HAVE

Less is More

MISSION (NOT) IMPOSSIBLE—YOUR ASSIGNMENT CARD

Taurus—the artist, banker, hierophant, the custodian of values—your mission in 2024 is to transport Pluto, aka the nuclear reactor of the zodiac, from the Capricorn star system to the Aquarius nebula. This task won't be easy; you'll confront the wrath of Saturn, the Lord of the (Three) Rings and Master of Karma. This year, Saturn resides in the section of your chart linked with communities, friends, governments, technology, and science. Brace yourself to navigate the complexities of tech enthusiasts, hackers, and significant shifts within your peer group.

Your mission, should you choose to accept it: over the next two years, cleanse yourself of any toxic friendships or work environments that conflict with your values. Given that Pluto's destination is Aquarius—symbolizing friends and community—this might prove demanding considering you're tasked with choosing new friends and recruiting a fresh crew for your spacecraft.

Here is your Assignment Card: Transport Pluto from Capricorn (representing the past) into Aquarius (indicative of the future). Sound impossible?

Perhaps for some, but not for you. This mission entails a recognition of the merit in tradition and the past. Understand that they can be refined and rejuvenated, rather than being destroyed in futile revolutions.

Since 2008, with Pluto in Capricorn, your beliefs, education, philosophies, and the way you communicate these to others underwent a transformation. You were prompted to learn, teach, grapple with truths, morality, and discover what you're willing to fight for. You might've also experienced power struggle with in-laws or a deep-seated urge to explore foreign cultures. With that chapter closing, it's now time to usher Pluto into Aquarius, focusing on career success, ambition, goals, and your community standing. In essence, after a 15-year apprenticeship under Master Yoda, it's your moment to channel that wisdom into your professional life. You are ready to be a master yourself!

For the forthcoming two decades, your responsibility is to ensure that Pluto, the planet of power, is serving the collective good. You'll also be nudged out of your comfort zone, challenged to adopt novel technologies, and implement them into your professional sphere. However, be vigilant. As you rise to masterhood, expect seismic shifts and possible power tensions in your career and interactions with superiors.

Until 2044, Pluto stands ready to revolutionize your career, empowering you to merge your passions with pragmatism. Yours is the sign tasked with elevating Pluto to the zenith of the zodiac wheel, atop the sacred mountain. Such an endeavor befits the might of Taurus, but it requires ample patience and discipline.

Pluto's Pickup Location

From June 11, 2023, to January 21, 2024, and again from September 2 to November 19, Pluto will be positioned in Capricorn. This falls in the sector of your chart associated with foreign cultures, learning, teaching, education, mass media, truth, authenticity, and justice.

From January 22 to August 31, and subsequently from November 20 to January 2044 (its final position), Pluto will transition to Aquarius. This represents the sector in your chart linked to career, success, and interactions with authority figures. Located at the zenith of your chart, this is a potent position. Significant changes in your career can be anticipated.

OPERATING LIMITATIONS: ENCOUNTERS WITH YOUR ANTAGONIST

Saturn, Lord Karma, has emphasized the value of friendships throughout 2023 and will continue to do so in 2024. This period calls for you to reassess your circles of friends, one ring at a time. This isn't an invitation to isolation, rather an opportunity to refine your connections. Furthermore, reflect on whether the company, corporation, or organization you are affiliated with aligns with your values and beliefs. I know money and material gains are important for you, they shouldn't come at the expense of enduring a toxic or negative work environment. Reconsider your association with clubs, organizations, political parties, and companies. You've evolved, and it's possible that these entities no longer mirror your current self. The Sufis tell us, "Show me your friends, and I'll tell you who you are." Saturn might reveal the less flattering aspects of some of your friendships, prompting you to carefully select the company you keep.

However, 2024's Saturn can also indicate who of your friends might need your help and support. You might be called to be their savior as they might lean on you for support. Similarly, your company or corporation might undergo transitions, as well as your country or government might need your help. Reflect on JFK's enduring words: "*Ask* not what *your country* can do for you—*ask* what you can do for *your country*." The collective calls, and Saturn ensures you heed this clarion.

To pinpoint potential challenges, recall the difficulties you faced in 1995 and 1996. You may face similar issues or a continuation of what you dealt with back then.

On the brighter side, managing Saturn in Pisces is easier if you can have peaceful sleep and rest more often. Einstein, a Pisces himself, frequently lauded the rejuvenating qualities of brief siestas. Recent studies have corroborated this, demonstrating the brain's potential to expand during a short midday nap. Keeping a dream journal could prove enlightening, with profound wisdom emerging from your nocturnal flights. Seeking communities that emphasize yoga, dance, movement, mysticism, or meditation can also provide comfort. Immerse yourself in water, when possible, use creative visualization, and maintain faith—in yourself and the universe—the rest will naturally follow.

MENTORS AND TUTORS: ENCOUNTER WITH YOUR MASTER

In "*Rock 'n' Roll Suicide*," Bowie, with the fervor of a musical prophet, declares, "Oh no love, you are not alone, no matter what or who you've been, no matter when or where you've seen, all the knives seem to lacerate your brain, I've had my share, I'll help you with the pain. You're not alone!" He might as well have channeled Jupiter!

Jupiter, the largest planet in the Solar System, will give you a helping hand. This is particularly true until May 26 when, in his 12-year cycle, he graces your sign, opening doors, providing opportunities, and helping you connect with your body. Yes, you heard right, Jupiter—whose Tarot card is aptly called "Fortune," is making you feel like you can conquer the world. Embrace Jupiter's support but be mindful so as not to spread yourself too thin and avoid being overoptimistic. Be discerning about what you commit to, even if the prospects seem promising.

From May 26 onward, Jupiter will bid you farewell but not abandon you, he simply moves to the next sign and continues guiding and creating expansion with financial matters, connecting you to your talents, bestowing awards, and amplifying recognition, as well as bolstering your sense of self-worth—all domains you deeply value and your sign rules. So, rejoice! Over the forthcoming year, Jupiter promises a plethora of avenues to augment your earnings and capitalize on your true gifts.

BATTLEGROUNDS PROCEDURES—ECLIPSE AND CREATURES OF THE NIGHT

This is important so buckle up. The North Node, known as the Head of the Dragon, blessed your sign from December 2021 to July 13, 2023. Now, he soars through your shadow, the part of your chart tied to mysticism, imagination, past lives, intuition, all forms of captivity, and the process of release. Picture it: a mythic dragon roaming your realm of magic, connecting you to the impossible. The Dragon points you towards your soul's desires, beckoning you to meditate deeply, embrace solitude, and purge negative influences. His presence aligns with Saturn's current residence in Pisces, emphasizing mystical engagement.

The Head of the Dragon points at solutions, and in 2024 you'll find answers to your problems coming from past lifetimes. The Dragon might rekindle memories, skills, people, locations, or connections from previous lives. Last time the North Node was in the same place was between 2005 and 2006 as well as 1986 and 1987. As it now graces Aries, a sign adjacent to yours, heed the Ram's teachings: assert your identity and value your independence.

The Lunar Nodes (Head and Tail of Dragon) determine the location of the eclipses, and this year they generate a tension between engagement in work and the need for introspective solitude. The message is simple: don't be consumed with work, spend quality time with yourself.

- **Lunar Eclipse in Libra, March 24–25**: The Sun illuminates your shadow realm, empowering healing, letting go, and connecting to your imagination. Potential challenges might arise related to confinement, hospitals, or confronting pain. With the Moon influencing your service, a call to aid others may be evident. Monitor your health and diet. Anticipate closure, perhaps related to health or work and coworkers. This is the Full Moon of Moses (Passover) and Jesus (Last Supper), a time of liberation and ending bondage. Note: Passover in 2024 is delayed due to issues with the Lunar calendar.
- **Total Solar Eclipse in Aries, April 8**: Occurring during Mercury's retrograde, this intense New Moon suggests caution in starting ventures unless they're revivals of past attempts. However, both the Moon (mama) and Sun (daddy) are asking you to dive deep into your subconscious and heal deep seated insecurities. It's an apt moment for therapeutic endeavors and rituals of release.

- **Partial Lunar Eclipse, September 17–18**: A Piscean Moon counters the Sun in Virgo during this Harvest Full Moon, marking a time to reap what was sown in March/April. Emotions may surge, but it's a potent interval for discarding negativity. This eclipse pits lovers versus friendships, your children against commitments to your organizations and friends. Remember, Saturn is in your house of friendship, there could be a need to let go of friends or people in your community.
- **Annular Solar Eclipse, October 2**: Under the Libra New Moon, the atmosphere is ripe for reconciliation, diplomacy, peacemaking, and budding relationships. There's a promise of new beginnings in work, health, and partnerships, provided you adhere to the Dragon's essential lesson of self-affirmation, and Aries' "I am" message.

ORANGE ALERT! SHAPESHIFTERS AND TRICKSTERS

When Mercury retrogrades, he takes on his trickster and shapeshifter role. It's a cosmic cue to pause and recalibrate. Make sure to bring your spacecraft to a halt and start flying in reverse. I know, it can be hard on the neck having to look back or relying on your reverse camera mode. Anticipate delays, energetic and emotional traffic jams. It's the worst time to sign documents or start a new project. But you know all this if you carefully read the first part of your pilot manual.

As a Taurus, the appearance of the trickster on your path signals a time to display your renowned patience and resilience. Remain steadfast and continue forward, though perhaps at a more measured pace. The first two days of 2024, you'll find it hard to ignite your spacecraft since Mercury is stationary in Sagittarius, which in your case is the sign that marks your connection to sexuality, investments, banking, death, and letting go. Beware of liars and thieves, and ensure you aren't tempted to become one. The same areas of your life will be marred with confusion and challenges when Mercury retrogrades in Sagittarius again between November 25 to December 16. It is a good time to retrieve lost objects, or reclaim money owed to you.

The first real full-on Mercury retrograde is between April 1 to 26 and since it takes place during a powerful eclipse (peaking April 8), there could be a great deal of confusion, mishaps, accidents, absentmindedness, and inattention. Yet, it will also be rife with synchronicities and meaningful coincidences.

From August 4 to 14, Mercury retrogrades in Virgo. Consequently, it would be wise to pay extra attention to your health, diet, work, and interactions with coworkers and employees. Given that Virgo is another earth sign, its influence may be milder on you, but it might still stir some disorder, particularly concerning children, romantic relationships, and creative projects. This period is especially favorable for revisions and editing. However, from August 15 to 29, the ever-adaptive Mercury shapeshifts and retrogrades in Leo, potentially bringing disruption within the home, family dynamics, or real estate matters.

Summary of Mercury Retrograde Dates

- January 1–January 2: Sagittarius.
- April 1–26: Aries (Red Alert around April 8 due to a total solar eclipse).
- August 4–14: Retrograde in Virgo.
- August 14–29 Retrograde in Leo.
- November 25–December 16 Sagittarius (Red Alert from December 6–16 since Mars is retrograde).

RED ALERT! SHIELDS UP

Mars often gets a bad rap. As the co-ruler of Scorpio—represented by the "Death" Tarot card—and the unequivocal ruler of Aries, the sign symbolizing war, Mars has long been linked with destruction and chaos. Its Tarot representation, "The Tower," illustrates people tumbling from a burning building, which hardly seems promising. However, fewer realize that Mars was also revered as the ancient god of vegetation, seeds, and planting. So, Mars does have its benevolent side too.

As 2024 draws to a close, Mars will begin his retrograde in Leo starting December 6, 2024, and will only go direct (in Cancer) on February 24, 2025. As such, it's advisable to complete your significant tasks for the year before December 6, and calling it a year, go have fun and relax. If Mars is metaphorically the god of planting, then during his retrograde, it's an ideal time to weed out and discard what's no longer necessary in your life.

With Mars retrograding in Leo, anticipate potential tensions and hurdles in your romantic relationships, as well as conflicts with your children or what you might think of as the "children of your mind": projects or ventures that you passionately care about. Exercise caution during physical training or, in general, to avoid injuries and be particularly wary around sharp objects. As a Taurus, Mars retrograde can also create strife with family members as well as issues with your home such as appliances breaking, leaks, and structural issues.

Since Mars' shadow begins on October 5, it would be prudent to be more vigilant from this point forward. It is as if you are navigating treacherous straits or passing through an asteroid belt. Stay alert and keep your shield up.

Here is the Mars Table Coordinates that highlight areas in your life where you can channel your passion, energy, and leadership. However, remember that wherever Mars is positioned, he can also introduce conflict and strife in those aspects of life. When Mars occupies your sign (June 9– July 19), you might feel invigorated and passionate, but also more impulsive, aggressive, impatient, and susceptible to conflicts and accidents.

- **November 24, 2023, Mars adventures into Sagittarius**: This Mars placement ignites your passion and sexuality and assists with shared resources and productions. It's favorable for connecting with foreign entities, embarking on adventures, and exploring new frontiers.
- **January 4, 2024, Mars scales Capricorn**: This is one of Mars' most powerful positions, invigorating your drive to advance your career and professional aspirations. However, be cautious of potential conflicts with superiors, bosses, or in-laws. Harness power through travel, education, and advocating for truth.
- **February 13, 2024, Mars transitions into Aquarius**: Experience heightened energy in community involvement, friendships, as well as your professional life and interactions with bosses. Ambitions will

be more pronounced. Energy is blooming in career, ask for a raise or promotion, but not too aggressively.

- **March 22, 2024, Mars dives into Pisces**: There may be overwhelming emotions, especially concerning friends, communities, governments, and organizations. Channel this energy towards altruism and charity. Activities in or near water are beneficial.

- **April 30, 2024, Mars comes home to Aries**: A potent manifestation of Mars that aids in physical training and regaining fitness. Ideal for engaging in movement and martial arts. Harness this energy to purge any obstacles to your growth. Siblings in arms from previous lives might come back into your life.

- **June 9, 2024, Mars settles in Taurus**: The energy now is deliberate and stubborn, which may feel like stagnation, but it also supports long-term plans. Continue to focus on body and health. Exercise caution to avoid self-inflicted injuries and address any issues surrounding self-worth.

- **July 20, 2024, Mars takes flight in Gemini**: This is a period to concentrate on enhancing your financial standing and maximizing your talent's money-making potential. It's favorable for establishing new businesses, marketing your abilities, and is an opportune time for sales and writing.

- **September 4, 2024, Mars plunges into Cancer**: Mars isn't at his best here, often described as "fallen". However, he can provide a boon to your business, especially if you're truly passionate. Be wary of potential conflicts related to contracts, with siblings, or other relatives. Choose your words carefully, both in speech and writing.

- **November 4, 2024, Mars parties in Leo**: Mars encourages a focus on love, joy, creativity, sports, and entertainment during this phase. It's also an ideal time for home renovations and quality moments with family.

LOVE INTEREST AND ALLIES

Venus loves you, she does—it's in her nature. And since you are a Taurus, ruled by Venus, she loves you even more. However, she has her moments of whimsiness and can act out. She's not your mama who loves you no matter what, she has her list of conditions, like a spiritual prenuptial agreement.

Below is the list of where Venus journeys this year, offering insights into potential areas of assistance in financial support, creative boosts, enhanced self-worth, and perhaps even a romantic connection. We're fortunate this year, as Venus remains direct, avoiding her retrograde phase. When she graces your sign (April 29 to May 22), you'll likely notice a heightened sense of beauty, feel and look better, experience a stronger connection to your talent, and perhaps an improved financial situation. Essentially, you're channeling the goddess of beauty and sensuality. However, this might also make you more susceptible to spending money or a tad more self-absorbed than usual. Jupiter and Venus come together on these love-filled days: May 22–23. A great time for art, dating, meeting the love of your life, or just feeling good.

Below you'll find her celestial coordinates and the areas of your life she'll likely influence, ushering in some good fortune and support from allies and loved ones.

- **December 29, 2023, Venus travels into Sagittarius**: Drawn to foreigners, mentors, teachers, and students. Your sexuality, passion, and investments thrive, particularly through travel, teaching, and learning. Enhance ties with in-laws, educators, and foreigners. Assist your partners in boosting their finances. A promising period for investments.
- **January 23, 2024, Venus climbs Capricorn**: Continue your focus on education and mass-media. Venus fosters better relationships with the elderly, bosses, superiors, mentors, and foreigners. Good time for traveling and connecting to different cultures.
- **February 16, 2024, Venus befriends Aquarius**: Prioritize your career as Venus aids in showcasing your skills. Who you collaborate with becomes paramount over the task at hand. Add some art and creativity to your professional life.
- **March 11, 2024, Venus slips into Pisces**: With Venus exalted, her benefits are manifold. Engage in creative visualization and heed your dreams. Bonding with friends thrives. Make a vision board of what you wish to manifest in your life.

- **April 5, 2024, Venus charges Aries**: Pursue your desires but simultaneously release what's unnecessary. Talents from past lives emerge. Be assertive in your love pursuits.
- **April 29, 2024, Venus comes home to Taurus**: Revel in Venus's embrace, who radiates inside and out, refining your look and image. Let Venus guide you to unearth and capitalize on your innate talents. An opportune time to rebrand and reshape your image.
- **May 23, 2024, Venus flirts in Gemini**: Foster improved ties with relatives and anticipate financial growth, especially via new contracts, businesses, writings, and marketing. Prospect of raises, promotions, and enhanced finances. Take on a new artistic talent.
- **June 17, 2024, Venus bathes in Cancer**: Home, family, and real estate are ripe business avenues. New affiliations and networking opportunities abound. Improved relationships with family members as well as business connections, neighbors, and siblings. Creative writing is a must.
- **July 11, 2024, Venus dazzles Leo**: Love is omnipresent! Indulge in happiness, creativity, sports, and entertainment. Strengthen domestic bonds and consider home and office revamps.
- **August 5, 2024, Venus refines Virgo**: Focus on work, health, diet, employees, and service. Reconnect with your children; love, joy, and contentment are in the offing. A time to create and explore artistic talents with your children and lovers.
- **August 29, 2024, Venus balances Libra**: With Venus in her domicile, justice, beauty, and relationships are emphasized. Ideal for mending professional relationships, especially with colleagues. Add an artistic element to your workplace.
- **September 23, 2024, Venus dives deep into Scorpio**: Venus assists in rejuvenating relationships with partners and significant others. Allow vulnerability and delve deep into intimacy and sexuality. A great time for couples' therapy. A potential for finding a partner in work or love.
- **October 17, 2024, Venus journeys Sagittarius**: As Venus completes her cycle, seize the moment for collaborative financial gains, especially

with international ties, travelers, and educators. Wisdom is all around. Perfect for joint artistic and financial endeavors. Passion surges, drawing in new opportunities and romances.

- **November 11, 2024, Venus climbs Capricorn**: Form ties with the mature and experienced. Venus aids in nurturing relationships with mentors and scholars. A wonderful time for travel.
- **December 7, 2024, Venus reconnects to Aquarius**: Concentrate on friendships to elevate your career. It's an apt time to refresh and deepen digital connections. Art in groups would be recommended.

ALIEN ENCOUNTER PROTOCOL

As a cosmic navigator, you are bound to encounter what some might call aliens. But to be intergalactically correct, let's refer to them as extraterrestrial sentient beings. These beings are represented by Uranus, the Awakener.

Since 2018, Uranus has been journeying through Taurus, your sign. This transit is challenging for a fixed earth sign to grapple with, especially given the unpredictable nature of this "extraterrestrial" planet that constantly shifts and turns. Uranus encourages unconventional thinking—he is, metaphorically speaking, "out of this world." Until 2026, as he transits through your sign, he prompts you to make leaps of faith in various facets of your life. While being under your sign's influence, he beckons you to take risks, rebrand yourself, undergo personal reinvention, engage with humor, and welcome the unusual and innovative into your daily existence.

Moreover, Uranus nudges you to perceive through your five senses in novel ways: indulge in diverse music genres, savor unfamiliar cuisines, explore fresh income avenues, and refine the manner in which you present yourself to the world. Take up the unique, venturing into uncharted territories, and exploring new horizons will allow you to reap the most benefits from this once-in-an-84-year transit.

CONCLUSION

In 2024, it's time to thoroughly reassess your relationships, friendships, and affiliations with companies and organizations. Friends may lean on you as their pillar of strength, so brace yourself to be their beacon in times of need. Your overarching task is to consolidate all the knowledge, experiences, and insights you've gathered since 2008 and effectively apply them in your professional sphere. Endeavor to modernize and rejuvenate traditions, ensuring that the future can glean wisdom from the past.

With the Dragon guiding you to insights from past lives and the mystical realm, and with Jupiter bolstering your journey until the end of May, you're set to enjoy a subsequent year brimming with prosperity and an elevated sense of self-worth. Stand with an open heart and outstretched arms, poised to embrace the bounty coming your way!

TAROT: THE HIEROPHANT

The Hierophant is the "interpreter of dreams." With Saturn residing in Pisces, the sign associated with dreams, you can gain insights into your life through your nightly flights. These dreams can particularly offer clarity regarding friendships, your position within the community, and your future.

HEBREW LETTER: VAV

Meaning: The letter symbolizes the nail as well as the conjunction "and." It is also associated with the Tree of Life. Your mission this year is to connect past and future.

GEMINI AND
GEMINI RISING—I THINK

Success in the Service of Humanity

MISSION (NOT) IMPOSSIBLE—YOUR
ASSIGNMENT CARD

Gemini—the communicator, bridge builder, space-time bender, the objective, logical nature render, wordsmith, interpreter, negotiator, and charmer. In 2024, your mission is monumental: to transport Pluto, aka the "nuclear reactor of the zodiac," from the Capricorn star system into the Aquarius nebula. It won't be easy as you would have to face the wrath of Saturn, the Lord of the (Three) Rings and Master of Karma. This year, Saturn resides in the area of your chart linked with career, superiors, bosses, and figures of authority, implying you might encounter significant professional shifts that could influence both where you live and family ties.

The mission, while straightforward, carries inherent dangers. You must transport Pluto, Lord Death, into Aquarius, the archetype symbolizing friends and community. This is intricate, particularly when you're simultaneously tasked with focusing on your career. However, your Gemini nature endows you with dual-processing and multitasking capabilities, allowing you to focus both on career progression and the betterment of humanity.

Your Assignment Card: Secure Pluto in your spacecraft and transport him from Capricorn (representing the past) to Aquarius (symbolizing the future). Sound impossible? Not for you. The mission entails leveraging the wisdom and skills harnessed from tradition to benefit the future, understanding that refining pre-existing mastery is often more effective than initiating redundant revolutions.

Pluto has resided in Capricorn since 2008, prompting you to scrutinize your financial landscape, particularly in relation to the talents and monetary resources of your life and work partners. This includes the talents and money of your life partners as well as partners in work. At times you felt like you needed to take an active role in managing their finances as they were going through upheaval and dramatic changes. In addition, you were asked to examine your own passion and explore what you're attracted to as well as what or who you're attracting into your life. But your task in 2024 is to let Pluto guide your resurrection and rebirth. This shift is welcomed, considering the last 16 years Pluto caused death (symbolic and real), issues with inheritance, heartbreaks, breakups, and challenges around passion and sexuality. From 2024 to 2044, Pluto will be in the sector of your chart that deals with truth, creed, philosophy, education, and travel.

However, a word of caution: deviating from authenticity and truth could lead to dire consequences, especially if you're dishonest with yourself. Be vigilant against disseminating falsehoods or succumbing to cognitive dissonances and disinformation.

For the forthcoming two decades your primary role is to ensure that Pluto, the planet of power, serves the goddess of wisdom, Sophia. It's an ideal time to relocate to a different country, embracing a new language, pursuing education—both as a teacher and student, and publishing. Pluto can help you transform your creed and what you believe in. Since you're a superb communicator and Pluto wishes to help spread the word, make sure you're wholeheartedly committed to the message you champion.

Pluto's Pickup Location

From June 11, 2023, to January 21, 2024, and then from September 2 to November 19, Pluto is positioned in Capricorn. This placement in your chart is associated with themes of death, transformation, your partner's financial assets and talents, production, the occult, shared resources, power, research, intimacy, and sexuality.

From January 22 to August 31, followed by November 20 to January 2044 (his final destination), Pluto transitions to Aquarius. This sector of your chart emphasizes foreign cultures, the processes of learning and teaching, education, mass media, in-laws, truth, travel, authenticity, and justice.

OPERATING LIMITATIONS: ENCOUNTERS WITH YOUR ANTAGONIST

Saturn, often referred to as Lord Karma, has been influential in your career since March 2023 and remains so throughout 2024. Saturn, inherently saturnine in nature, challenges your determination by introducing hurdles. These are meant to test your mettle and, in the end, equip you with the means for success. Interactions with older or more seasoned individuals can range from adversarial to inspirational. Situated at the zenith of your chart, pointing skyward, Saturn suggests that to ascend, you need tenacity, a methodical approach, focus, and discipline. Prepare yourself—you're playing in the major league now.

Saturn, representing maturity, wishes you to grow up and act responsibly. If you feel accomplished in your career and believe you are on the right track, Saturn may amplify your focus and introduce extra work resulting in higher demand and expectations, thus be mindful of potential burnout. However, if your current career path doesn't resonate with you, it might be time for a significant shift. Given Pluto's placement in your education sector, it could be beneficial to consider furthering your education or acquiring new skills.

In 2024, Saturn can also herald potential complications with bosses, superiors, figures of authorities, and coworkers. Tread with caution in professional realms. The Dragon lends a hand by pointing you towards new organizations or allies to align with—be open to the possibility of changing your workplace, company, or organization.

To gain insights into potential challenges or pinpoint your antagonist, revisit the hurdles you faced in 1995 and 1996. Issues from that era may reemerge or manifest in similar ways. Recall the analogy presented in the introduction, likening Saturn's transits to both waves and particles. A story started in those years might be repeating or evolving.

On the brighter side, managing Saturn in Pisces is easier if you can have peaceful sleep and rest more often. Einstein, a Pisces himself, frequently lauded the rejuvenating qualities of brief siestas. Recent studies have corroborated this, demonstrating the brain's potential to expand during a short midday nap. Keeping a dream journal could prove enlightening, with profound wisdom emerging from your nocturnal flights. Seeking communities that emphasize yoga, dance, movement, mysticism, or meditation can also provide comfort. Immerse yourself in water, when possible, use creative visualization, and maintain faith—in yourself and the universe—the rest will naturally follow.

MENTORS AND TUTORS: ENCOUNTER WITH YOUR MASTER

In "*Rock 'n' Roll Suicide*," Bowie, with the fervor of a musical prophet, declares, "Oh no love, you are not alone, no matter what or who you've been, no matter when or where you've seen, all the knives seem to lacerate your brain, I've had my share, I'll help you with the pain. You're not alone!" He might as well have channeled Jupiter!

Jupiter, the largest planet in the Solar System, agrees. He won't forsake you. In fact, beyond just lending a hand, he'll transit your sign from May 26 for an entire year! This is great news, signaling a year filled with luck and opportunities. However, up until May 26, with Jupiter transiting in Taurus, you're prompted to let go, detoxify, delve into your meditation, past lives, and shed whatever hinders your progress. It's as though you have to make room for Jupiter's gifts to settle in.

Starting May 26 and for the subsequent year, Jupiter, symbolized by the Tarot card "Fortune," showers blessings upon every facet of your life. He particularly aids in aligning with your true self, rejuvenating your body, and improving your health. You're encouraged to assume leadership, initiate projects, and reinvent yourself. Get ready to say "Yes!" to whatever life has to offer. Yet, it's crucial to steer clear of excessive confidence and unwarranted optimism. Keep your ego in check. As you'll soon discover, the Dragon this year nudges you towards altruism, volunteering, and community engagement. Notice the recurring them: Jupiter, the planet of truth, coupled with Pluto's call for authenticity, urges honesty in all dealings. Be wary of embellishments, grey lies, or any other shenanigans. And no. Half-truths don't lead to full ones, they usually lead to full lies.

BATTLEGROUNDS PROCEDURES—ECLIPSE AND CREATURES OF THE NIGHT

This is super important, so buckle up. From December 2021 to July 13, 2023, the North Node, Head of the Dragon, was asking you to let go and overcome whatever hindered you from achieving your goals. From July 2023 to January 2025, the Dragon soars through the sector in your chart associated with communities, friends, organizations, governmental entities, and altruism. This implies you can mount your dragon as long as you invite your friends to join the magical flight.

Anticipate forming new friendships, affiliating with novel groups, clubs, and associations of likeminded people. Consequently, this year your soul yearns that you focus on leading your community, delve into nonprofit endeavors and integrate innovation and technology especially in your career. The South Node in Libra prompts you to refrain from obsessing over your children or romantic life and prioritize communal needs over personal whims.

Last time the North Node occupied the same place in your chart was between 2005–2006 and 1986–1987. Given the North Node is in Aries, a sign you connect with fabulously, you must adhere the teachings of the Ram—affirming your identity and safeguarding your independence—will be of the outmost importance.

During eclipses, events tend to accelerate significantly, mirroring intense confrontations. Here are key dates and insights:

- **Lunar Eclipse in Libra, March 24–25:** The Sun illuminates facets of your life like friends, affiliations, and government relationships. An excellent period to integrate technology and enhance your overall efficiency. The Moon casts its light on children, love, and joy, potentially evoking heightened emotions. A chapter might close, intensifying feelings. This is symbolic of Moses (Passover) and Jesus' (Last Supper) narratives, signifying liberation and the breaking of chains. Note, Passover in 2024 observes a delay due to lunar calendar discrepancies.
- **Total Solar Eclipse in Aries, April 8:** Given that Mercury is in retrograde during this New Moon, it's prudent to postpone new beginnings, unless they're revisitations of past attempts. Both the Moon (symbolizing maternal energy) and Sun (representing paternal force) advocate for the nourishment and bolstering of your community and friendships.
- **Partial Lunar Eclipse, September 17–18:** The Pisces Moon opposite the Sun in Virgo, marking the Harvest Full Moon. Reap the fruits of efforts sown around March/April. While emotions might run high, it's an opportune phase to jettison detrimental habits, sustenance, or acquaintances. This eclipse might feel disconcerting as it challenges you, nudging you towards decisions related to your career or domestic life, generating tension between familial and professional duties.
- **Annular Solar Eclipse, October 2:** The Libra New Moon is conducive to forging peace, diplomacy, or initiating romantic relationships. Embark on creative ventures or pursuits, whether conceiving innovative ideas or welcoming new life. It's also an apt period for hobbies, sports, and leisurely activities.

ORANGE ALERT! SHAPESHIFTERS AND TRICKSTERS

When Mercury, your ruler, retrogrades, he takes on his trickster and shapeshifter role. It's a cosmic cue to pause and recalibrate. Make sure to bring your spacecraft to a halt and start flying in reverse. I know, it can be hard on the neck having to look back or relying on your reverse camera mode. Anticipate delays, energetic and emotional traffic jams. It's the worst time to sign documents or start a new project. But you know all this if you carefully read the first part of your pilot manual.

As a Gemini, you're no stranger to the wiles of the trickster and are often more adept at handling his quirks, both when he's direct and in retrograde. However, don't grow complacent; even you can fall prey to his mischief. As 2024 dawns, the first two days may prove challenging as you attempt to ignite your spacecraft. Mercury, stationary in Sagittarius—your opposite sign—may complicate things for you, especially with partners in your professional life as well as romantic. Be extra vigilant during this time, as travel, visas, education, and communication could become problematic. Resist the temptation to distort the truth or convey misinformation. Similar areas of your life may face turmoil when Mercury retrogrades in Sagittarius again from November 25 to December 16. If you've ever wished to revisit past studies, teaching, or subjects of interest, this might be an opportune moment. Again, pay attention to your primary relationships and contractual partnerships as there might be more turmoil around them. Beware of enemies, competitors, and legal issues.

The first genuine Mercury retrograde of 2024 spans from April 1 to 26, coinciding with a potent eclipse that peaks on April 8. Expect potential confusions, mishaps, accidents, and forgetfulness especially in your interactions with friends, companies, clients, fans, and even digital devices like computers and phones. Beware of the "Pauli Effect," where gadgets mysteriously malfunction in your presence. However, there also could be a great deal of synchronicities and meaningful coincidences.

The Virgo retrograde from August 4 to 14 warrants careful attention to health, diet, work, and your relationships with coworkers and employees. Particularly challenging for Gemini, since this retrograde squares your Sun, possibly prompting actions you may later regret. Be prepared for a rollercoaster of emotions and additional issues related to family and real estate. From August 15 to 29, the ever-changing Mercury dons a new guise and retrogrades into Leo. While this phase may be somewhat less taxing, it still poses potential problems with relatives—especially siblings—and may cause glitches in contracts and other communications. Since communication is your domain, be cautious and considerate in your approach. Pay extra attention to your business and networking around this retrograde.

By recognizing these astrological currents and adapting to their influences, you, Gemini, can navigate the trickster's mischief with insight and grace, turning potential pitfalls into opportunities for growth and self-awareness.

Summary of Mercury Retrograde Dates

- January 1–January 2: Sagittarius.
- April 1–26: Aries (Red Alert around April 8 due to a total solar eclipse).
- August 4–14: Retrograde in Virgo.
- August 14–29 Retrograde in Leo.
- November 25–December 16 Sagittarius (Red Alert from December 6–16 since Mars is retrograde).

RED ALERT! SHIELDS UP

Mars often gets a bad rap. As the co-ruler of Scorpio—represented by the "Death" Tarot card—and the unequivocal ruler of Aries, the sign symbolizing war, Mars has long been linked with destruction and chaos. His Tarot representation, "The Tower," illustrates people tumbling from a burning building, which hardly seems promising. However, fewer realize that Mars was also revered as the ancient god of vegetation, seeds, and planting. So, Mars does have his benevolent side too.

As 2024 draws to a close, Mars will begin his retrograde in Leo starting December 6, 2024, and will only go direct (in Cancer) on February 24, 2025. As such, it's advisable to complete your significant tasks for the year before December 6, and calling it a year, go have fun and relax. If Mars is the god of planting, then during his retrograde, it's an ideal time to weed out and discard what's no longer necessary in your life.

With Mars retrograding in Leo, anticipate potential tensions and hurdles in your romantic relationships, as well as conflicts with your children or what you might think of as the "children of your mind": projects or ventures that you passionately care about. Exercise caution during physical training or, in general, to avoid injuries and be particularly wary around sharp objects.

The retrograde phase in Leo can usher in challenges related to communication, potentially leading to disputes with relatives, siblings, neighbors, and even issues in sales, marketing, and contracts. Mars moonwalking backwards might also stir turbulence in your relationships with children, romantic partners, and could dampen your creative spirit. During this phase, you may feel lethargic, defensive, and out of sorts. It's recommended that you participate in cardiovascular exercises and practice breathing techniques.

Since Mars' shadow begins on October 5, it would be prudent to be more vigilant from this point forward. It's as if you're navigating treacherous straits or passing through an asteroid belt. Stay alert and keep your shield up.

Below you will find Mars' Table Coordinates that highlight areas in your life where you can channel your passion, energy, and leadership. However, remember that wherever Mars is positioned, he can also introduce conflict and strife in those aspects of life. When Mars occupies your sign (July 20–September 3), you might feel invigorated and passionate, but also more impulsive, aggressive, impatient, and susceptible to conflicts and accidents.

- **November 24, 2023, Mars adventures with Sagittarius**: While this shift energizes your primary relationships, it can also strengthen your adversaries. Beware of unnecessary conflicts. Travel opportunities may arise, but it's wise to avoid areas plagued by cultural or actual conflicts. Go on an adventure, embrace your inner Indiana Jones.
- **January 4, 2024, Mars mounts Capricorn**: This is Mars in his most potent position. He can boost your energy but also provoke clashes with superiors, colleagues, and older individuals. Your passion will be intense; channel this heightened sexuality into productive pursuits. Great for productions and managing shared resources.
- **February 13, 2024, Mars flies in Aquarius**: This period brings heightened energy around friendships, community, and organizations. It's a good time for education and travel. However, be wary of potential disputes with friends or workmates.

- **March 22, 2024, Mars dives into Pisces**: You may find yourself feeling swamped and emotional, particularly in professional contexts or with higher-ups. Engage in physical activities near water, like dancing, yoga, or martial arts to balance out. A good time to take a leadership role in career.
- **April 30, 2024, Mars marches into Aries**: A dynamic expression of Mars that encourages physical training and reconnection with your body. This period is advantageous for raises or promotions within organizations. Friends may look to you for protection or support. Exercise caution when dealing with government representatives.
- **June 9, 2024, Mars hikes in Taurus**: Energy during this period can be sluggish and resolute, sometimes feeling stagnant. However, it's conducive to long-term planning. Connect with nature, embrace therapeutic activities, meditate, and remain steadfast. Be mindful of self-inflicted harm or pessimism.
- **July 20, 2024, Mars takes flight in Gemini**: Prioritize your health, body, and assume leadership positions. There's a call to action, and your leadership skills will shine the brightest. Step up and take charge. You are full of passion and determination; people will be attracted to you and your projects.
- **September 4, 2024, Mars plunges to Cancer**: Mars doesn't thrive here, which might make you feel defensive or passive-aggressive. Familial tensions could arise. However, this placement offers chances to boost your finances and further develop your skills.
- **November 4, 2024, Mars dazzles Leo**: This transition benefits ventures close to your heart. Be wary of potential conflicts related to contracts, siblings, and other relatives. Think before you speak or pen down anything.

LOVE INTEREST AND ALLIES

Venus loves you, she does—it's in her nature. However, she has her moments of whimsiness and can act out. She's not your mama who loves you no matter what, she has her list of conditions, like a spiritual prenuptial agreement.

Below is the list of where Venus journeys this year, offering insights into potential areas of assistance in financial support, creative boosts, enhanced self-worth, and perhaps even a romantic connection. We're fortunate this year, as Venus remains direct, avoiding her retrograde phase. When she graces your sign (May 23–June 16), you'll likely notice a heightened sense of beauty, feel and look better, experience a stronger connection to your talent, and perhaps an improved financial situation. Essentially, you're channeling the goddess of beauty and sensuality. However, this might also make you more susceptible to spending money or a tad more self-absorbed than usual. Jupiter and Venus come together on these love-filled days: May 22–23. A great time for art, dating, meeting the love of your life, or just feeling good.

Below you'll find her celestial coordinates and the areas of your life she'll likely influence, ushering in some good fortune and support from allies and loved ones.

- **December 29, 2023, Venus travels into Sagittarius**: Relationships take center stage and blossom both in personal and professional life. Adversaries might become confrontational, but with Mars in your corner, you can counteract their hostilities. Embrace the urge to travel and pursue education especially abroad and relating to art.
- **January 23, 2024, Venus mounts Capricorn**: Experience intensified passion and a profound desire for closeness and intimacy. Ideal for investigative endeavors and research as well as joint financial affairs. This placement of Venus can help your partner's income and talents. Passion is heightened. Collaborations in artistic pursuits. Relationships with superiors and coworkers can improve.
- **February 16, 2024, Venus befriends Aquarius**: Connect with in-laws, acquaint yourself with individuals from varied backgrounds, and forge ties with multinational entities. Great for traveling and making money abroad.
- **March 11, 2024, Venus sails into Pisces**: With Venus exalted, she offers support, particularly in your career. Engage in creative visual-ization and heed your dreams. Your imaginative prowess can foster significant professional advancements. Flow and ease in career.

- **April 5, 2024, Venus marches into Aries**: Pursue your desires and be assertive in your relationships, don't be shy to share what you need. Friends and colleagues are a valuable resource. Group creative endeavors have potential for success.
- **April 29, 2024, Venus comes home to Taurus**: Past life skills might resurface. This period accentuates your intuitive abilities, making it conducive for couples' therapy. The artist you were in previous life is making an entrance in your life.
- **May 23, 2024, Venus flirts with Gemini**: Beneficial for you, Venus guides you towards triumph and acknowledgment. It's an optimal period for self-reinvention, enhancing your public image, and cultivating business relationships. You are an artist, share your talents with the world.
- **June 17, 2024, Venus surfs in Cancer**: A season of love. Focus on home, family, and real estate ventures. Venus might elevate your salary or help you tap into talents that can become profitable. A great time to invest in yourself.
- **July 11, 2024, Venus parties with Leo**: Bring in the ambiance of love! Pursue creative endeavors, sports, and entertainment. Strengthen bonds with relatives and neighbors. Lucrative contract opportunities arise, and it's a prolific time for writing. Marketing and sales can increase.
- **August 5, 2024, Venus enters Virgo**: Prioritize work, health, dietary habits, and teamwork. Venus aids in healing family relations. Consider redecorating or remodeling your living space or office. Great time for real-estate.
- **August 29, 2024, Venus harmonizes Libra**: Venus, in her domain, emphasizes justice. Repair strained relationships. Revel in newfound love, artistic hobbies, and recreational pursuits. Improved relationships with children and romantic lovers. Time to be a kid again.
- **September 23, 2024, Venus dives into Scorpio**: Delve into intimacy and explore your sexuality and passion. Reflect on what you attract and or attracted to. Strengthen relationships with coworkers. Add artistic elements to your work.

- **October 17, 2024, Venus travels to Sagittarius**: As Venus completes her cycle, it's a great time for mending relationships and attracting partners. A wonderful time to spend with loved ones and improve relationships with your partners in life or in work.
- **November 11, 2024, Venus climbs Capricorn**: Engage with elder, seasoned individuals. Venus encourages exploring passion and intimacy. Collaborate on financial and artistic endeavors. Ideal for ambitious projects requiring substantial investments.
- **December 7, 2024, Venus glides into Aquarius**: Concentrate on friendships, upgrade your digital pals, and consider traveling aboard. Improved relationships with in-laws.

ALIEN ENCOUNTER PROTOCOL

As a cosmic navigator, you are bound to encounter what some might call aliens. But to be intergalactically correct, let's refer to them as "extraterrestrial sentient beings." These beings are represented by Uranus, the Awakener. Until 2026, Uranus assists you in shedding whatever holds you back, including ancestral karma or residual challenges from past lives. While it might sound illogical, such is the influence of Uranus.

Why all the letting go? Well, come 2026, Uranus will transition into your sign for a seven-year span, serving as a perpetual alarm clock, dramatically changing your life. The last instance of Uranus in Gemini occurred from 1941–1949. But let's stick to the present. For now, Uranus nudges you to perceive through your five senses in novel ways: indulge in diverse music genres, savor unfamiliar cuisines, explore fresh income avenues, and refine the way you present yourself to the world. Embracing the unique, venturing into uncharted territories, and exploring new horizons will allow you to reap the most benefits from this once-in-an-84-year transit.

CONCLUSION

In 2024, it's imperative to reassess your career, professional trajectory, and standing within your community. This year beckons you to discern the most impactful ways you can serve and benefit humanity. Much of this stems from Pluto, urging you to pinpoint your guiding principles and philosophy and how you can spread your teaching and wisdom. The Dragon, which illuminates who your genuine allies are, will help you define your true community, fans, clients, followers, and tribe. However, the process of release that begun in 2018 continues; a profound cleanse is essential so that by 2026, you're primed to embark on a fresh cycle of enlightenment.

TAROT: THE LOVERS

This card represents the union between the masculine and feminine. In 2024 you will encounter many friends and lovers from previous lives.

HEBREW LETTER: ZAIN

Meaning: the "sword," or "weapon." This year your sword, pen, tongue should be in the service of your career.

CANCER AND
CANCER RISING—I FEEL

Championing Truth in an Age of Deception

MISSION (NOT) IMPOSSIBLE—YOUR ASSIGNMENT CARD

Cancer—the nurturer, builder, medium, unconditional lover, parent to us all, doorway of life, your mission in 2024 is monumental. It involves transporting Pluto, the "nuclear reactor of the zodiac," from the Capricorn star system into the Aquarius nebula. It won't be easy as you would have to confront Saturn, the Lord of the (Three) Rings and Master of Karma, who is positioned this year in the sector of your chart related to truth, morality, travel, justice, and education. Saturn will compel you to confront inauthenticity, or whatever you swiped under the carpet or repressed into your subconscious. Saturn will push you to scrutinize any conspiracy theories, misinformation, or cognitive dissonances held by you or your family members. To succeed, draw inspiration from Sir Galahad, who was worthy of the Holy Grail because he never uttered a lie. Let truth be your guiding star.

The mission, albeit perilous, is simple: safely transport Pluto, Lord Death himself, into Aquarius, the archetype of friends, community, and technology. It can prove to be challenging considering you are asked to focus on the truth while there are so many lies and disinformation out there, but as a Cancer you have a secret weapon—your highly evolved intuition and mediumship, that enables you to apply your ingenious EQ to counter the damage done by dubious individuals.

Your Assignment Card: Teleport Pluto into your spacecraft and transport him from Capricorn (representing the past) into Aquarius (symbolizing the future). Sound impossible? Not for you. Since Capricorn is your opposite sign, you know them inside out, moreover, Aquarius, the Water Bearer, resonates with your essence as you're the Zodiac's first water sign. The mission entails recognizing that tradition offers a great deal and rather than be destroyed by futile revolutions it must be upgraded and reformed.

Since Pluto's 2008 transit into Capricorn, your significant relationships underwent profound transformations. The Lord of Death and Resurrection helped you reexamine your primary relationships, partners in work and life, as well as legal affairs. For 16 years, Pluto transformed, destroyed, deepened, and resurrected your partnerships. From 2024 until 2044, Pluto will move into the sector of your chart that deals with death, sexuality, intimacy, occult, magic, investigation, research, taxes, insurance, investments, as well as joint financial and artistic affairs. This period invites you to tap into shared resources, examine your sexuality and passion, and transform your life. All these aspects of life are precisely what Pluto rules and indeed, out of all the signs, you were chosen to escort Pluto back to his realm—the Underworld. While it demands descending into Hades, confronting the three-headed dog who guards Sheol, you'll be rewarded by what Pluto represents—riches.

For the next two decades you'll ensure that Pluto, the planet of power, benefits the right people. Perhaps that is the reason Saturn insists on connecting you to morality and truth. Until 2044, you'll serve as a midwife of death, someone that facilitates change and transformation. You're assuming the role of a doctor, a shaman, a healer. A grand task, one you can carry out flawlessly.

Pluto's Pickup Location

From June 11, 2023, to January 21, 2024, and again from September 2 to November 19, Pluto will be positioned in Capricorn, which corresponds to the area of your chart concerned with relationships. This includes legal affairs, work and life partners, and any other binding agreements or contracts you might have.

From January 22 to August 31, followed by November 20 leading up to January 2044 (his final destination), Pluto will transition into Aquarius. This section of your chart deals with intimacy, sexuality, the occult, investments, taxes (it's advised not to cheat), insurance (it's always wise to be prepared), as well as concepts of death and transformation.

OPERATING LIMITATIONS: ENCOUNTERS WITH YOUR ANTAGONIST

Saturn, often referred to as the stern taskmaster of the celestial realm, has been imparting lessons about Truth since March 2023 and has plans to continue into 2024. Characteristically Saturnian, this planet is scrutinizing your core beliefs, philosophies, and your authenticity level. The question at hand: Are you aligning your actions with your words? Sidestepping, reminiscent of a crab's gait, is no longer an option. Lao Tzu's wise distinction of the three facets of truth—yours, mine, and the universal Truth—requires integration this year. A robust commitment to integrity is imperative. While some zodiacal signs might navigate through half-truths, Saturn stands vigilant, ensuring that your integrity remains untarnished.

This period might introduce you to seasoned mentors, bearing wisdom from their years. While they may present challenging demands, adhering to their guidance proves rewarding. Simultaneously, you're poised to assume the mantle of a mentor, sharing insights with those around you. If there was ever a language you wanted to master, Saturn's discipline can help.

Since Saturn represents maturity, he wants you to grow up and behave like a responsible adult. He will move into your career sector in 2026, so whatever you think you need to study for your career to go to the next level, this is a great time to start. Saturn rewards those who plan for the future and come up with a strategy.

However, Saturn in 2024 can also bring about challenging situations with in-laws, teachers, students, and foreigners, perhaps since you are supposed to work with them much more the next few years.

To gain insights into potential challenges or pinpoint your antagonist, revisit the hurdles you faced in 1995 and 1996. Issues from that era may reemerge or manifest in similar ways. Recall the analogy presented in the introduction, likening Saturn's transits to both waves and particles. A story started in those years might be repeating or evolving.

On the brighter side, managing Saturn in Pisces is easier if you can have peaceful sleep and rest more often. Einstein, a Pisces himself, frequently lauded the rejuvenating qualities of brief siestas. Recent studies have corroborated this, demonstrating the brain's potential to expand during a short midday nap. Keeping a dream journal could prove enlightening, with profound wisdom emerging from your nocturnal flights. Seeking communities that emphasize yoga, dance, movement, mysticism, or meditation can also provide comfort. Immerse yourself in water, when possible, use creative visualization, and maintain faith—in yourself and the universe—the rest will naturally follow.

MENTORS AND TUTORS: ENCOUNTER WITH YOUR MASTER

In "*Rock 'n' Roll Suicide*," Bowie, with the fervor of a musical prophet, declares, "Oh no love, you are not alone, no matter what or who you've been, no matter when or where you've seen, all the knives seem to lacerate your brain, I've had my share, I'll help you with the pain. You're not alone!" He might as well have channeled Jupiter!

Jupiter, kingpin of our Solar system, agrees. He'll never leave you alone and this year, he's chosen to spend the initial five months in Taurus, a zodiac buddy you vibe with well. Taurus reigns over domains in your life such as friendships, community ties, governmental dealings, and, not to forget, the tech realm. The cosmos suggests a windfall of opportunities through friends and groups you're affiliated with. If you've been eyeing a tech upgrade, now's the time. Maybe cozy up to a friendly A.I., or even strike up a new friendship, join a club, or expand your client base.

Come May 26, Jupiter, your mentor, transits into Gemini, your neighboring sign, and there he'll help you declutter, pare down, and shed any excessiveness in your life. It's all prep work for Jupiter's grand entrance into your sign come June 2025. Until then, Jupiter asks you to plunge into the depths of your subconscious, unlocking vaults of imagination, and rekindling talents from past lifetimes. Oh, and while you're at it, don't be surprised if places, people, even talents would seem eerily familiar invoking a sense of déjà vu. This year promises a roller coaster of past-life revisits.

Jupiter prompts you to spend time volunteering and offering your healing touch to people in need. Also, allocate time to be on your own, detox and get rid of whatever obstacles stand in your path. Jupiter will be slipping notes in your dream journal, peppering your meditation sessions, and maybe even nudging you during daydreams.

BATTLEGROUNDS PROCEDURES—ECLIPSE AND CREATURES OF THE NIGHT

All right, lean in and let's get down to business. From December 2021 until July 13, 2023, the North Node—fondly called the Dragon—wanted you to focus on friendships, your community, workplace dynamics, clients, and your digital pals. Since July 2023 to Jan 2025, the Dragon is flying in the sector in your chart that relates to career, success stories, ambition, focus, and achievements. It's your time to shine and get a hearty pat on the back for all the blood, sweat, and tears you've poured into your career over the past couple of decades. The Dragon is associated with the Moon, your ruler, therefore, you have a special connection to him. However, the Dragon being in fiery Aries isn't easy for your waters to handle, hinting at potential conflict, maybe with those you hold dear, family and loved ones. But on the bright side? Relationships with those big shots at work, superiors, and bosses look promising. You might even catch a muse whispering ideas about pivoting towards a profession that sings to your heart.

The North Node danced through this part of your chart between 2005-2006 and way back in 1986–1987. The key to unlocking the Dragon's magic? Channel a bit of that Aries flair. Embrace leadership, be the trailblazer, focus on your identity, tackle challenges head-on, and maybe, just for a bit, swap your usual go-with-the-flow nature for a spark of fire in your career pursuits.

During eclipses you'll experience events quickening dramatically. Here are the coordinates and key dates to monitor as you navigate the year:

- **Lunar Eclipse in Libra, March 24–25**: While the Sun spotlights your career, the Moon's tugging at your home and family, which are super important for you. Tough pill to swallow, but it's high time you shift your gaze from family needs and zoom in on your professional ambitions. This lunation is the original Full Moon linked to Moses (Passover) and Jesus (the Last Supper). Talk about liberation and breaking chains! And yep, a quick heads-up: Passover is a month late due to some lunar calendar quirks.

- **Total Solar Eclipse in Aries, April 8**: This New Moon's a bit intense since it's occurring during a Mercury retrograde in Aries, which isn't exactly your best friend in the zodiac. My advice? Resist diving into brand new ventures unless it's a second shot at the same project. Here's the silver lining: both the Moon (your cosmic mom) and Sun (your dad) are cheering for your career, urging you to offer a nurturing touch in professional circles.

- **Partial Lunar Eclipse, September 17–18**: The Pisces Moon opposite the Sun in Virgo. Aka, the Harvest Full Moon. Whatever seeds of intent you planted in March/April, it's time to see them bear fruit. Sure, emotions might be running a tad high, but there's a golden ticket here: It's an invite to bid adieu to anything or anyone that's been dragging you down. You're in your element with this eclipse since it's in water and earth. Writing, publishing, dreaming, meditation, or diving into the media world? Ditto for any teaching or learning adventures.

- **Annular Solar Eclipse, October 2**: Welcome the Libra New Moon. Feeling the urge to extend an olive branch, kick off a swoon-worthy romance, or perhaps broker peace? This eclipse is your cosmic green light. Whether it's family ties or real estate moves, you've got the universe's blessing.

ORANGE ALERT! SHAPESHIFTERS AND TRICKSTERS

When Mercury retrogrades, he takes on his trickster and shapeshifter role. It's a cosmic cue to pause and recalibrate. Make sure to bring your spacecraft to a halt and start flying in reverse. I know, it can be hard on the neck having to look back or relying on your reverse camera mode. Anticipate delays, energetic and emotional traffic jams. It's the worst time to sign documents or start a new project. But you know all this if you carefully read the first part of your pilot manual.

The first two days of the year, right as you embark on our journey, you'll have a hard time igniting your spacecraft as Mercury is stationary in fiery Sagittarius, that threatens to evaporate your water. The first two days of 2024 could turn out to be a bit taxing on your health. It's advised to return to work after January 3, as before there would be too many snags. Since Mercury will retrograde in Sagittarius again between November 25 to December 16 of 2024, you'll experience some of the same challenges as the first two days of the year with your diet, health, work, relationships with colleagues, pets, and your routine. Watch your liver and hips, they can cause some issues, so stay away from alcohol if possible.

In April, Mercury's retrograde is amplified by an eclipse on the 8th, which could lead to heightened confusion and unexpected disruptions, particularly in the professional sphere. Given that this retrograde is in Aries, you might find yourself thrust into unforeseen situations that require immediate action. Approach these challenges with patience.

August introduces yet another Mercury retrograde, this time in Virgo from August 4 to 14. While this transit is generally softer, it still necessitates careful attention to health, daily routines, and communications. Relationships with relatives, neighbors, and roommates may experience tensions, and misunderstandings around contracts or marketing endeavors are possible. From August 15 to 29 Mercury shapeshifts into Leo, where he continues to retrograde, causing havoc with financial matters. Expenditures should be approached with caution to ensure fiscal stability throughout this period.

Summary of Mercury Retrograde Dates

- January 1–January 2: Sagittarius.
- April 1–26: Aries (Red Alert around April 8 due to a total solar eclipse).
- August 4–14: Retrograde in Virgo.
- August 14–29 Retrograde in Leo.
- November 25–December 16 Sagittarius (Red Alert from December 6–16 since Mars is retrograde).

RED ALERT! SHIELDS UP

Mars often gets a bad rap. As the co-ruler of Scorpio—represented by the "Death" Tarot card—and the unequivocal ruler of Aries, the sign symbolizing war, Mars has long been linked with destruction and chaos. His Tarot representation, "The Tower," illustrates people tumbling from a burning building, which hardly seems promising. However, fewer realize that Mars was also revered as the ancient god of vegetation, seeds, and planting. So, Mars does have his benevolent side too.

As 2024 draws to a close, Mars will begin his retrograde in Leo starting December 6, 2024, and will only go direct (in Cancer) on February 24, 2025. As such, it's advisable to complete your significant tasks for the year before December 6, and calling it a year, go have fun and relax. If Mars is the god of planting, then during his retrograde, it's an ideal time to weed out and discard what's no longer necessary in your life. But, yes, you will have Mars retrograde in your sign which will not be easy in the onset of 2025, but more on that in next year's book.

With Mars retrograding in Leo, anticipate potential tensions and hurdles in your romantic relationships, as well as conflicts with your children or what you might think of as the "children of your mind": projects or ventures that you passionately care about. During this period, old romantic relationships might resurface, and potential challenges with children or younger individuals may come to the forefront. This phase also offers a prime opportunity to revisit and revitalize creative projects that have been previously set aside. In addition, Mars retrograde can cause difficulties with your finances, self-worth, and changes in your values. Avoid the pull towards unnecessary expenses, at least ones under your control.

Since Mars' shadow begins on October 5, it would be prudent to be more vigilant from this point forward. It's as if you're navigating treacherous straits or passing through an asteroid belt. Stay alert and keep your shield up.

Below you will find Mars' Table Coordinates that highlight areas in your life where you can channel your passion, energy, and leadership. However, remember that wherever Mars is positioned, he can also introduce conflict and strife in those aspects of life. When Mars occupies your sign, (September 4–November 3) he is considered fallen, so take heed. You'll still feel invigorated and passionate, but also more impulsive, aggressive, impatient, and susceptible to conflicts and accidents.

- **November 24, 2023, Mars enters Sagittarius**: The cosmic warrior invigorates your workspace, providing opportunities to embark on a fresh routine, diet, and campaign. Blend work with learning and journeying abroad; the stars align for adventures and embracing your inner Indiana Jones.
- **January 4, 2024 , Mars advances to Capricorn**: Mars is exalted and boasts his might. While he infuses you with vigor, tread carefully—disputes with seniors or partners, both professional and personal, loom on the horizon. Yet, in the same breath, relationships may find heightened passion. An opportune time to wage war against your foes.
- **February 13, 2024, Mars transitions to Aquarius**: Energies surge around friendships and communal ties. Don't be surprised if a familiar face suddenly ignites romantic sparks. Embrace this Mars positioning, for it nudges you towards profound passions, deeper understanding, and investigative pursuits.
- **March 22, 2024, Mars steps into Pisces**: Great time to travel to places by water. Opportune time to sublime Mars' energy into studying,

learning, and traveling. Beware, there's a hint at potential discord with in-laws or foreigners.

- **April 30, 2024, Mars leaps into Aries**: Mars, in his audacious expression, becomes a beacon of motivation, urging you to rekindle ties with your body. A storm of activity encircles your career but be cautious of brewing tempests with authoritative figures.
- **June 9, 2024, Mars settles in Taurus**: While Mars is in exile, he can still aid with a slow yet unwavering pace, every achievement demands effort. Yet, there could be material gains if you work harder than normal. Navigate the subtle undercurrents of tension within your professional circle, company, government officials, and among friends.
- **July 20, 2024, Mars takes flight to Gemini**: The cosmic narrative calls for release from chains that bind you. Envelop yourself in the mystic and the imaginative; the cosmos beams favorably on such pursuits. Great for yoga, dance, or any calming activity. Cardio is a must.
- **September 4, 2024, Mars descends into Cancer**: A placement that Mars doesn't favor, provoking a defensive stance, perhaps even veiled aggression. Relationships with brothers, relatives, and neighbors might feel the strain. Yet, amidst this celestial challenge, Mars might be your guide to physical betterment and leadership avenues.
- **November 4, 2024, Mars dances into Leo**: With vigor, Mars promises financial prospects, especially from heart-driven, creative ventures. Rekindle your childhood spark, for therein lies dormant talents and heightened self-appreciation.

LOVE INTEREST AND ALLIES

Venus loves you, she does—it's in her nature. However, she has her moments of whimsiness and can act out. She's not your mama who loves you no matter what, she has her list of conditions, like a spiritual prenuptial agreement.

Below is the list of where Venus journeys this year, offering insights into potential areas of assistance in financial support, creative boosts, enhanced self-worth, and perhaps even a romantic connection. We're fortunate this year, as Venus remains direct, avoiding her retrograde phase. When she graces your sign (June 17–July 10), you'll likely notice a heightened sense of beauty, feel, and look better, experience a stronger connection to your talent, and perhaps an improved financial situation. Essentially, you're channeling the goddess of beauty and sensuality. However, this might also make you more susceptible to spending money or a tad more self-absorbed than usual. Jupiter and Venus come together on these love-filled days: May 22–23. A great time for art, dating, meeting the love of your life, or just feeling good.

Below you'll find her celestial coordinates and the areas of your life she'll likely influence, ushering in some good fortune and support from allies and loved ones.

- **December 29, 2023, Venus graces Sagittarius**: Turn your attention to your workplace relationships. With Venus by your side, you'll find increased harmony and creativity with colleagues. Now might be the moment to blend work with a touch of travel or even overseas projects. Educate yourself about art or finance.
- **January 23, 2024, Venus enters Capricorn**: Venus guides you to attract, harmonize and enrich your relationships. This is the best time for romance and dating. Connect with mature or seasoned individuals. Legal affairs have favorable winds now.
- **February 16, 2024, Venus explores Aquarius**: Harness the energy of Venus to deepen bonds of passion, sexuality, and intimacy. It's an excellent phase for investments and pooling resources or talents. Your partner might get a raise or promotion. Transformative art abounds.
- **March 11, 2024, Venus revels in Pisces**: Venus exalted and brings opportunities for higher learning, especially in artistic fields. Foreign travels and connections are promising during this transit. Improved relationships with mentors, in-laws, and foreigners.
- **April 5, 2024, Venus charges into Aries**: While this might challenge Venus's usual vibes, she encourages you to step up with confidence. Improved relationships at work could infuse creativity into your professional life. A time to beautify yourself.

- **April 29, 2024, Venus feels at home in Taurus**: Trust Venus to blend your social and financial worlds. Friendships have the potential to deepen, and some may even bloom romantically.
- **May 23, 2024, Venus flits through Gemini**: This transit nudges you towards tapping into latent talents, possibly even from past lifetimes. Explore your inner world, perhaps with therapy focusing on partnerships. Imagination and intuition are heightened.
- **June 17, 2024, Venus bathes in Cancer**: Venus is spotlighting you now. Enjoy the allure she bestows upon you, drawing new opportunities your way. You are fabulously gorgeous!
- **July 11, 2024, Venus dazzles in Leo**: Feel the joy and love in the air! The realms of creativity, entertainment, and personal finance have never looked brighter. Embrace the fun and see how it enriches you.
- **August 5, 2024, Venus refines in Virgo**: It's a prime time to strengthen work bonds and focus on wellness. There are new business ventures. Venus is here to boost your communicative prowess. Great for creative writing.
- **August 29, 2024, Venus harmonizes in Libra**: Home and family come to the forefront. Whether it's healing family ties or contemplating a home makeover. Real estate dealings have a cosmic green light. Great for legal affairs.
- **September 23, 2024, Venus dives deep in Scorpio**: Venus is urging an introspection into intimacy, passion, and the true essence of attractions. Use this period to rediscover love, transformative art, and joy. Relationships with lovers and children improve.
- **October 17, 2024, Venus journeys back to Sagittarius**: As the cycle nears completion, focus on mending and elevating professional relationships. Work-related travels or educational ventures are auspicious now.
- **November 11, 2024, Venus climbs Capricorn**: Value the wisdom of the experienced. Let Venus help in nurturing deep and meaningful partnerships in various facets of life. Your significant others would benefit from this transit.

- **December 7, 2024, Venus reconnects with Aquarius**: Accept the gift of friendship. It's an opportune time to collaborate, especially when pooling resources and talents. With Venus guiding, investments and financial partnerships flourish.

ALIEN ENCOUNTER PROTOCOL

As a cosmic navigator, you are bound to encounter what some might call aliens. But to be intergalactically correct, let's refer to them as "extra-terrestrial sentient beings." These beings are represented by Uranus, the Awakener.

Since 2018 Uranus has been transiting in Taurus leading to unexpected detours in your relationships—whether with friends, within your company, or even in interactions with government officials. Uranus nudged you to re-evaluate your bond with technology, science, and machinery. More profoundly, your connection to humanity at large, to the collective spirit, and to various organizations, underwent a powerful change.

Until 2026, he will be your celestial ally, helping you discern the true essence of friendships and the kind of company that aligns with your soul's purpose. With Uranus by your side, you might find yourself nurtured by circles of friends you'd never imagined being a part of, enriching your journey in surprising ways.

Moreover, Uranus nudges you to perceive through your five senses in novel ways: indulge in diverse music genres, savor unfamiliar cuisines, explore fresh income avenues, and refine the manner in which you present yourself to the world. Embracing the unique, venturing into uncharted territories, and exploring new horizons will allow you to reap the most benefits from this once-in-an-84-year transit.

CONCLUSION

This is the year where you firmly anchor to your truth, your guiding principles, and your philosophy, evolving into a seeker, an illuminating teacher, a curious student, a storyteller, and a spirited traveler. The Dragon is ready to elevate your career, but it's the synergy of Jupiter and Uranus that beckons you to forge bonds with new friends and align with companies that resonate with your newfound creed. With their guidance, you'll find your tribe, discover ardent fans, loyal clients, and a receptive audience.

As you flow into the latter part of 2024, the rivers of imagination surge within you, illuminating the path to manifesting your soul's deepest desires. Remember, 2024 holds a special magic for you. By staying rooted in your truth, expressing it, living it, and embodying it, you'll soar to vistas you've only dreamt of before.

TAROT: THE CHARIOT

This card is a symbol of meditation, the ability to travel without movement. Like Prince Arjuna who was initiated by Krisha on a chariot, as well as the Kabbalistic "Working of the Chariot," you are embarking in 2024 on a journey.

HEBREW LETTER: CHET

Meaning: wall, womb, shell. In 2024 it's an intellectual and philosophical wall, a shell made of wisdom.

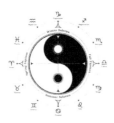

LEO AND
LEO RISING—I WILL

Open Soul Surgery

MISSION (NOT) IMPOSSIBLE—YOUR
ASSIGNMENT CARD

Leo—the radiant monarch, lofty creator, captivating entertainer, anointed one, the timeless child, and Guardian of the Eternal Flame, your mission in 2024 is to transport Pluto, the nuclear reactor of the zodiac, from the Capricorn star system into the Aquarius nebula. It won't be easy as the imposing Saturn, the Lord of the (Three) Rings and Master of Karma, is located this year in the shadow, the area of your chart associated with death, transformation, and the Underworld. Over the next two years, you are asked to navigate into the dark side of the Force, and deal with the specters of your past. You are the Sun Bearer, however, now Saturn is challenging you to dive deep into the pit, confronting the suppressed and the concealed within you. It's a formidable quest, but your fiery spirit is up to the task.

The mission is simple albeit dangerous. Transport Pluto, Lord Death himself, into Aquarius, your opposite sign, the emblematic archetype of friendship, community, and technology. Aquarius is your mirror sign, located the furthest possible from your Lion Lands. This compels you to face Pluto's reflective gaze every moment in the next twenty years. Each relationship, alliance, contractual bond you form will now be under Pluto's relentless scrutiny. It sounds like a script tailored for high drama - but then, Leo, you've always thrived in the limelight. Here's your epic role on the cosmic stage.

Your Assignment Card: Beam Pluto into your spacecraft and transport him from Capricorn (symbolizing the past) into Aquarius (representing the future). Sound impossible? Not for you. Recall that since 2008, Pluto's transformative touch reshaped your work, service to others, personal well-being, routines, your pets, and dietary habits. His potent influence rippled across the zodiac, altering not just your approach to work, but influencing others too—a resonance especially felt from 2020 with every-one dealing with health (pandemic) and changing their work habits. Now, it's time to harness these transformative lessons and apply them in your primary partnerships, allies, and artistic expression.

From 2024 to 2044, Pluto will sculpt and refine your personal relation-ships and professional connections, spotlighting those who reflect your authentic self. This could mean your allies might require your strength, but alas, some would die or drift away. Moreover, with Pluto's watchful gaze, some facets of your character you've cloaked might come to the fore. With the Dragon guarding the gates of truth in 2024, hidden truths yearn for release. And with Saturn's excavation of your shadows, expect revelations of whatever needs healing. One thing's for sure: 2024 heralds a transformative journey inviting openness, growth, and illumination. This is the year you are undergoing open soul surgery.

Pluto's Pickup Location

From June 11, 2023–January 21, 2024, and September 2–November 19, Pluto is in Capricorn, lurking in the sector of your chart that relates to work, health, diet, employees, self-improvement, service, routine, and coworkers.

From January 22–August 31 and then November 20–January 2044 (final-destination), Pluto is dropped in Aquarius, the sector in your chart that relates to relationships, partners in personal and profession life, enemies, antagonists, design, justice, and beauty.

OPERATING LIMITATIONS: ENCOUNTERS WITH YOUR ANTAGONIST

Saturn, Lord Karma, beckons you to traverse the depths of the Underworld. Here, you're met with the formidable guardian, the three-headed dog, and the shadowed expanse where your inner fears manifest. Saturn's intent is clear: to assess your determination. How fervently do you seek metamorphosis? As a fixed fire sign, change is a difficult pill to swallow. Yet, Saturn's request is poignant—shed your old skin, let go of past identities, and emerge as a renewed being.

You find yourself aboard Charon's vessel, the mythic ferryman who shepherds souls through the realms of the departed, offering you a unique experience to reincarnate without dying. Concurrently, Saturn urges introspection on intimacy. How vulnerable are you willing to be? What secrets do you shield? Whom and what do you attract? Such queries may unsettle, yet they're prerequisites to stamp your Underworld passport. Your 2026 rebirth awaits, but not without diving deep into the unknown.

Saturn's sojourn in this enigmatic zone illuminates pathways to healers, shamans, therapists, and magical practitioners equipped to aid your evolution. An innate curiosity will guide you, urging you to embrace life's intricacies. Moreover, perhaps you'll emerge as a healer, guiding others through their transformations. The subsequent couple of years will revolve around themes of privacy, intimacy, fiscal affairs (taxes and insurances demand utmost honesty and attention), investments, legacies, sexuality, acceptance, occult practices, productions, and collaborative ventures. If you share your life or workspace with a partner, be observant; they might grapple with financial strains or vocational recalibrations.

To gain insights into potential challenges or pinpoint your antagonist, revisit the hurdles you faced in 1995 and 1996. Issues from that era may reemerge or manifest in similar ways. Recall the analogy presented in the introduction, likening Saturn's transits to both waves and particles. A story started in those years might be repeating or evolving.

On the brighter side, managing Saturn in Pisces is easier if you can have peaceful sleep and rest more often. Einstein, a Pisces himself, frequently lauded the rejuvenating qualities of brief siestas. Recent studies have corroborated this, demonstrating the brain's potential to expand during a short midday nap. Keeping a dream journal could prove enlightening, with profound wisdom emerging from your nocturnal flights. Seeking communities that emphasize yoga, dance, movement, mysticism, or meditation can also provide comfort. Immerse yourself in water, when possible, use creative visualization, and maintain faith—in yourself and the universe—the rest will naturally follow.

MENTORS AND TUTORS: ENCOUNTER WITH YOUR MASTER

In "*Rock 'n' Roll Suicide*," Bowie, with the fervor of a musical prophet, declares, "Oh no love, you are not alone, no matter what or who you've been, no matter when or where you've seen, all the knives seem to lacerate your brain, I've had my share, I'll help you with the pain. You're not alone!" He might as well have channeled Jupiter!

Jupiter, the grand benefactor of the zodiac, is ever by your side. This year, he graces Taurus for the initial five months, continuing his journey which commenced in May 2023. As he strides through Taurus, he lavishes upon you exciting career prospects and avenues for growth. Throughout the early half of 2024, Jupiter, your mentor, fortifies your ties with authoritative figures and equips you with the arsenal required to achieve your vocational visions. Jupiter being in Taurus, a squaring sign, could bring some blessings in disguise, potentially emerging from challenges or moments of adversity. But fret not, while Saturn may test you, Jupiter ensures you're bestowed with the enchanted armaments needed to win your battles.

On May 26, Jupiter transitions into the breezy realm of Gemini. This air sign resonates harmoniously with you, making it simpler to harness the rewards Jupiter offers. Until June 9, 2025, he ensures you're surrounded by new friendships, smoother interactions with governing bodies, organizations, and corporations. This phase is an invitation to discover your collective, be it fans, followers, or for the regal Leo, a loyal entourage. Furthermore, Jupiter's influence might spark your intrigue towards emerging technologies and electronics, offering a sneak peek into your industry's horizon. A potential career advancement or newfound organizational interest in your talents might also be on the cards.

BATTLEGROUNDS PROCEDURES—ECLIPSE AND CREATURES OF THE NIGHT

From December 2021 to July 13, 2023, the North Node, often termed the Dragon's Head, beckoned you towards unyielding honesty. With Saturn prompting a release of ostentation and excess, the dragon's fierce flames sought to cleanse untruths, superficiality, inauthenticity, and pretense. His goal? To reveal your innermost philosophy, creed, and truth.

From July 2023 to January 2025, the Dragon takes to the skies, marking its territory in the segment of your chart associated with travel, mass media, publishing, justice, pedagogy, and international organizations. This transition heralds a prime phase for academic pursuits, language acquisition, overseas relocations, and leading crusades against falsehoods. With your inherent charisma, when you champion truth, even the slyest deceivers are rendered speechless.

The Dragon's sojourn in Aries spells fortune for you. As a companion fire sign, Aries can stoke your inherent spark. This alignment suggests fruitful interactions with Aries individuals, particularly if they wear the hats of educators, philosophers, or hail from foreign lands.

For context, the North Node previously occupied this same celestial space during 2005–2006 and 1986–1987. To truly harness the North Node's potential now, it's vital to channel Aries energy, summarized by the phrase "I Am," focus on leadership, initiation, passion, bravery, conquest, and continually reaffirm your unique identity.

During eclipses you'll experience events quickening dramatically. Here are the coordinates and key dates to monitor as you navigate the year:

- **Lunar Eclipse in Libra, March 24–25**: The Sun illuminates the essence of your beliefs and philosophy, urging you to radiate your authentic self and reveal your inner brilliance. With the Moon's guidance, you'll uncover the messages that yearn for expression, either through your writing or connections with relatives. Contractual or business landscapes may shift during this time. Historically, this phase aligns with the original Full Moon of significant events like Passover (for Moses) and the Last Supper (for Jesus)—both emblematic of emancipation and breaking free. Note, however, that Passover in 2024 has been postponed due to discrepancies in the Lunar calendar.

- **Total Solar Eclipse in Aries, April 8**: Though this New Moon occurs under the potentially troublesome Mercury retrograde, its presence in Aries—a staunch ally—grants you resilience. You may find yourself acting as a pillar of support for loved ones during this phase. Both the Moon (symbolizing maternal energy) and the Sun (representing paternal force) beckon you to nourish and champion your quest for wisdom and truth.

- **Partial Lunar Eclipse, September 17–18**: As the Pisces Moon stands opposed to the Sun in Virgo, this Harvest Full Moon presents the chance to reap what you sowed in March/April. Emotions might run high, yet it's an opportune moment to sever ties with detrimental habits, substances, or individuals. This eclipse underscores a tug-of-war between your financial and talent resources and those of a partner, hinting at potential fiscal challenges or tests of self-value.

- **Annular Solar Eclipse, October 2**: Under the Libra New Moon, an atmosphere ripe for fostering peace, diplomacy, and budding relationships prevails. Be open to novelties in business dealings, writing pursuits, and marketing strategies during this time.

ORANGE ALERT! SHAPESHIFTERS AND TRICKSTERS

When Mercury retrogrades, he takes on his trickster and shapeshifter role. It's a cosmic cue to pause and recalibrate. Make sure to bring your spacecraft to a halt and start flying in reverse. I know, it can be hard on the neck having to look back or relying on your reverse camera mode. Anticipate delays, energetic and emotional traffic jams. It's the worst time to sign documents or start a new project. But you know all this if you carefully read the first part of your pilot manual.

As 2024 dawns on January 1–2, you might find your fiery enthusiasm somewhat muted due to Mercury, the cosmic messenger, stationary in Sagittarius—a fellow fire sign. You will literally have a hard time igniting your spacecraft. During this short spell, challenges might arise affecting mood, romantic relationships, creativity, and interactions with children. If you're involved in high-risk endeavors, such as stock trading, tread with caution. It's not a time for audacious moves. Interestingly, Mercury will retrograde in Sagittarius again from November 25 to December 16, bringing with him similar challenges. During this period, safeguard your physical well-being, especially concerning your hips, legs, and liver. Moderation in alcohol intake is advisable, given the potential sensitivity of your liver.

Fast forward to April 1–26, Mercury enters his first pronounced retrograde of the year. This retrograde is accentuated by a potent eclipse on April 8, making the period particularly tumultuous. However, with Mercury's retrograde unfolding in Aries, you might weather these cosmic storms with slightly more resilience than some, being that Aries is a fellow fire sign. Though you might encounter moments of confusion, unexpected mishaps, and fleeting forgetfulness, it's also a time rich in synchronicities and meaningful coincidences. Be prepared for some disruptions, especially if you're involved in travel, education, publishing, or media. Relationships with individuals from different cultural or international backgrounds as well as in-laws or educators, might require extra attention. Yet, in the wisdom of the cosmos, patience remains your most valuable ally during such times.

August unfolds with another Mercury retrograde, this time in the meticulous sign of Virgo from August 4 to 14. This phase nudges you to pay attention to dietary choices and digestive health. Also, be mindful of your professional sphere, interactions with colleagues, and the structure of your daily routines. Financial matters might come to the fore, prompting reflections on self-worth and personal values. From August 15 to 29, Mercury shapeshifts into Leo. This transit can lead to moments of impulsive expression, so it's essential to be discerning in how you present yourself to the world. Yet, in every challenge, there's a hidden opportunity. This might be your cosmic cue to pivot, reinvent, and embrace a fresh perspective on your brand, relationship with your body, style, and image.

Summary of Mercury Retrograde Dates

- January 1–January 2: Sagittarius.
- April 1–26: Aries (Red Alert around April 8 due to a total solar eclipse).
- August 4–14: Retrograde in Virgo.
- August 14–29 Retrograde in Leo.
- November 25–December 16 Sagittarius (Red Alert from December 6–16 since Mars is retrograde).

RED ALERT! SHIELDS UP

Mars often gets a bad rap. As the co-ruler of Scorpio—represented by the "Death" Tarot card—and the unequivocal ruler of Aries, the sign symbolizing war, Mars has long been linked with destruction and chaos. His Tarot representation, "The Tower," illustrates people tumbling from a burning building, which hardly seems promising. However, fewer realize that Mars was also revered as the ancient god of vegetation, seeds, and planting. So, Mars does have his benevolent side too.

As 2024 draws to a close, Mars will begin his retrograde in Leo starting December 6, 2024, and will only go direct (in Cancer) on February 24, 2025. As such, it's advisable to complete your significant tasks for the year before December 6, and calling it a year, go have fun and relax. If Mars is the god of planting, then during his retrograde, it's an ideal time to weed out and discard what's no longer necessary in your life.

With Mars retrograding in your sign, anticipate potential tensions in all aspects of your life but especially in your romantic relationships, as well as conflicts with your children or what you might think of as the "children of your mind": projects or ventures that you passionately care about. Exercise caution during physical training or, in general, to avoid injuries and be particularly wary around sharp objects.

The retrograde Mars in your kingdom can cause health concerns, facing increased risks of accidents or injuries, and experiencing unexpected changes in your direction in life. Emotionally, matters of the heart might prove more complex. Your mood may swing unpredictably, you might also feel tired and lazy. Yet, this period is an ideal moment to return to and rejuvenate the creative endeavors that may have been sidelined in the past.

Since Mars' shadow begins on October 5, it would be prudent to be more vigilant from this point forward. It's as if you're navigating treacherous straits or passing through an asteroid belt. Stay alert and keep your shield up.

Below you will find Mars' Table Coordinates that highlight areas in your life where you can channel your passion, energy, and leadership. However, remember that wherever Mars is positioned, he can also introduce conflict and strife in those aspects of life. When Mars occupies your sign (November 4, 2024–January 5, 2025), you might feel invigorated and passionate, but also more impulsive, aggressive, impatient, and susceptible to conflicts and accidents.

- **November 24, 2023, Mars adventures in Sagittarius**: A surge of passion invigorates your romantic relationships, creative pursuits, and interactions with children. This period favors physical activities and hobbies. However, it's vital to avoid unnecessary risks and conflicts, especially with the younger generation. Prioritize honesty in all dealings.
- **January 4, 2024, Mars scales Capricorn**: Mars exalted and while he boosts your energy, potential conflicts with career superiors, elder individuals, and both personal and professional partners might arise. It's an opportune moment for health check-ups.
- **February 13, 2024, Mars glides in Aquarius**: Your energy gravitates towards friends, communities, and organizations. However, beware of disagreements with work and life partners, and stay vigilant against potential adversaries. A time to engage in partnership activities.

- **March 22, 2024, Mars surfs in Pisces**: This phase favors collaborative ventures, especially those involving shared finances and talents. Embrace your passion and sexuality and in addition, release lingering resentments. Activities in and near water are favored.
- **April 30, 2024, Mars comes home to Aries**: Mars truly thrives. It's a period of enhanced connection to one's body, leadership, and initiation. Stand up for your beliefs and seek knowledge through travel and education. Be careful of conflict with in-laws.
- **June 9, 2024, Mars strides in Taurus**: The pace of energy slows but remains steadfast. Effort is the key during this period, especially in the professional realm. Be cautious, though, as conflicts with authority figures might emerge. A time for a promotion or taking initiative in career.
- **July 20, 2024, Mars takes flight in Gemini**: Direct your focus towards conveying your message, business dealings, and contractual matters. This is the time to articulate your needs assertively. Watch out for disputes with friends and potential issues with machines or electronics.
- **September 4, 2024, Mars swims in Cancer**: This isn't Mars' preferred position. While you might be prone to defensiveness or passive aggression, family disputes can arise. On the positive side, it's an excellent period to purge excesses and offer assistance to those in need.
- **November 4, 2024, Mars parties with Leo**: Your vitality receives a significant boost. Stay aware of how you present yourself, as your energy might be overwhelming to some. Reconnect with your playful side and experiment with new physical activities. Embrace leadership and initiation wholeheartedly.

LOVE INTEREST AND ALLIES

Venus loves you, she does—it's in her nature. However, she has her moments of whimsiness and can act out. She's not your mama who adores you no matter what, she has her list of conditions, like a spiritual prenuptial agreement.

Below is the list of where Venus journeys this year, offering insights into potential areas of assistance in financial support, creative boosts, enhanced self-worth, and perhaps even a romantic connection. We're fortunate this year, as Venus remains direct, avoiding her retrograde phase. When she graces your sign (July 11–August 4), you'll likely notice a heightened sense of beauty, feel and look better, experience a stronger connection to your talent, and perhaps an improved financial situation. Essentially, you're channeling the goddess of beauty and sensuality. However, this might also make you more susceptible to spending money or a tad more self-absorbed than usual. Jupiter and Venus come together on these love-filled days: May 22–23. A great time for art, dating, meeting the love of your life, or just feeling good.

Below you'll find her celestial coordinates and the areas of your life she'll likely influence, ushering in some good fortune and support from allies and loved ones.

- **December 29, 2023, Venus travels in Sagittarius:** Venus graces you with enhanced love and creativity. Opportunities for financial gain through risky pursuits. Relationships with children and romantic love are enhanced. Your inner child thrives.
- **January 23, 2024, Venus climbs Capricorn:** Venus enhances bonds with elders or those you've known for a long time. You might experience workplace accolades or greater artistic expression. Harmonious connections with coworkers blossom.
- **February 16, 2024, Venus befriends Aquarius:** This period favors connecting with life or work partners and possibly attracting a new relationship. This is the best time of the year for dating and finding your better half. Focus on design, art, beauty, justice, and deeper friendships.
- **March 11, 2024, Venus flows into Pisces:** Exalted Venus assists particularly in connections with passionate partners, intimacy, and sensuality. Joint artistic and financial pursuits prosper, making it an opportune time for investments.
- **April 5, 2024, Venus charges Aries:** Though not Venus' preferred environment, especially during eclipses and retrogrades, and yet she can help expose your leadership talents. Bonds with educators, students, judges, and foreigners improve.

- **April 29, 2024, Venus returns home to Taurus**: Your professional life shines. A raise or promotion beckons. Enrich your workspace with fun, art, and beauty. Improved relationships with bosses and superiors.
- **May 23, 2024, Venus takes flight in Gemini**: Connect with friends and new organizations as well as technology. You'll encounter individuals and groups fostering fruitful future connections. Art in community is encouraged.
- **June 17, 2024, Venus swims in Cancer**: Venus strengthens familial bonds and reveals talents from past lives. This period is excellent for couples' therapy. Dive into your imagination.
- **July 11, 2024, Venus charms Leo**: Love flourishes, along with creativity, sports, and entertainment. Embrace your inner child, and you might find financial rewards. Radiate harmony and beauty, attracting abundant opportunities.
- **August 5, 2024, Venus works with Virgo**: Not the easiest place for Venus but she can still strengthen your workplace relationships and fine-tune your health and diet. Discover new talents and boost your self-worth. Great for raises and increasing your income. Delve into creative pursuits.
- **August 29, 2024, Venus balances Libra**: With Venus in her domicile, justice prevails. Heal relationships, particularly with close relatives and friends. Combine art with communication, enhancing sales endeavors.
- **September 23, 2024, Venus deep dives into Scorpio**: Venus beckons you to explore intimacy, sensuality, and self-reflection. Focus on home and family, considering renovations or office redesigns. A good time for relocation.
- **October 17, 2024, Venus journeys Sagittarius**: As Venus completes her cycle, she helps heal relationships with children, romantic partners, and creative associates. Consider learning something new, preferably in connection to art.
- **November 11, 2024, Venus mounts Capricorn**: Connect with older people or professional leads. Venus smoothens coworker relations and adds beauty to your workspace and career.

- **December 7, 2024, Venus wings into Aquarius**: Prioritize friendships and collaborations involving shared finances and talents. This period is ripe for romance and relationship healing.

ALIEN ENCOUNTER PROTOCOL

As a cosmic navigator, you are bound to encounter what some might call aliens. But to be intergalactically correct, let's refer to them as "extra-terrestrial sentient beings." These beings are represented by Uranus, the Awakener.

Since 2018, Uranus has been journeying through Taurus, bringing along unexpected shifts, particularly in your career and community standing. Uranus through Taurus poses challenges for you, inducing friction and urging you to act outside your comfort zone. However, this influence on your professional life isn't solely disruptive. Uranus can usher in youthful, innovative individuals to your work environment and catalyze a powerful drive to modernize and enhance your professional pursuits. Think upgrade and update. Additionally, you might experience an intensified desire for creative freedom and moments of brilliant inspiration. It's time to intro-duce innovation and technology into your career. Don't be afraid to make a leap of faith.

Moreover, Uranus nudges you to perceive through your five senses in novel ways: indulge in diverse music genres, savor unfamiliar cuisines, explore fresh income avenues, and refine the manner in which you present yourself to the world. Embracing the unique, venturing into uncharted territories, and exploring new horizons will allow you to reap the most benefits from this once-in-an-84-year transit.

CONCLUSION:

In 2024, you're undergoing a profound transformation, reminiscent of a journey from death to resurrection. This year beckons you to delve into the Underworld, seeking the latent talents and gifts that lie hidden in your shadow. The Dragon challenges you to assume the role of an adventurer and explorer. You are embarking on voyages to faraway places, as well as educational and intellectual journeys in pursuit of obtaining and sharing wisdom. The key lies in your authenticity—be genuine, forthright, and unflinchingly honest. If you heed these calls, Jupiter promises to shower you with blessings in your professional realm during the year's first half, and luck and fortune with your friends and community as the year wanes. Carrying Pluto into your opposing sign intensifies your year, pushing you to scrutinize your significant relationships.

TAROT: STRENGTH

The card reveals the anima gracefully pacifying the fierce lionlike animus. This imagery invites you to journey into the Underworld, guided by the snake that embodies the mysteries of the unknown. The infinity symbol, floating gracefully above, illuminates 2024 numerological value and meaning.

HEBREW LETTER: TET

Meaning: coiled serpent, as well as Tov, Hebrew for goodness.

VIRGO AND
VIRGO RISING—I SERVE
Becoming a Wizard and a Sage

MISSION (NOT) IMPOSSIBLE—YOUR
ASSIGNMENT CARD

Virgo—the cosmic purificator, watchmaker, universe's engineer, and Hand of God, your mission for 2024 is to guide Pluto, the nuclear reactor of the zodiac, from Capricorn star system into the Aquarius nebula. This journey is fraught with challenges, most notably from Saturn, Lord of the (Three) Rings and Master of Karma, who currently resides in the sector of chart intertwined with your significant others, primary partners, contractual relationships, and, most importantly, your adversaries. But more on that later, when we cover your antagonists. For now, let's stick to the most important service you need to provide the Zodiac Federation.

The mission, while straightforward, is perilous. You must usher Pluto, the embodiment of death and rebirth, into Aquarius, the sign of friends, community, and technological advancement. This task may be daunting, especially when you're transporting Pluto directly to the galactic sector that your sign cherishes: service, work, diet, health, and routine. Essentially, you're bringing Pluto, the Lord of the Underworld, to your doorstep, and asked to host him for a span of two decades!

But I have confidence in your clan. After all, in Kabbalah, Yod is the letter associated with your sign, and in Hebrew Yod means "hand," therefore you are the Hand of God. Pluto is also the ruler of sexuality, and according with Kabbalah, Yod in addition to being the hand of God is also the divine seed or DNA. Who better to guard the sperm of God and egg of Goddess than the chaste Virgo?

Your Assignment Card: Safely guide Pluto from Capricorn (representing the past) into Aquarius (symbolizing the future). Since 2008, Pluto has been reshaping your interactions with children, romantic liaisons, creative ventures, physical pursuits, hobbies, happiness, and entertainment. Being a sign that typically operates behind the curtains, this spotlight was both a boon and a challenge. But in 2024, change is coming, summoning you to integrate Pluto into a realm you resonate deeply with: service. This calls for a reformation in your work, dietary habits, and time management. The next two decades promise to bring about significant professional shifts, potentially amplifying your career, especially from late May for the ensuing year. Pluto's influence on health and diet means the forthcoming two decades demand caution and proactive healing efforts.

From 2024 to 2044, Pluto seeks to metamorphose your workplace dynamics, interactions with colleagues, employees, and potentially, your professional direction itself. Remember, Pluto's path is seldom easy. His meticulous nature obliterates impediments, urging an in-depth exploration of the way you serve humanity. Yet, his greatest gift to your vocation is unbridled passion and a transformative zeal. Serendipitously, the celestial Dragon this year soars in the realms of death and transformation—domains Pluto reigns supreme over. This alignment will significantly aid in supporting your professional commitments with personal passions. This year is rife with cosmic magic and alignments, beckoning you to embrace the mystical and the ethereal, setting you on a path to become both a wizard and a sage. Embrace the wondrous and let the supernatural infuse your life.

Pluto's Pickup Location

From June 11, 2023–January 21, 2024, and September 2–November 19, Pluto is in Capricorn, located at the sector of your chart that relates to happiness, love, creativity, sports, children, entertainment, hobbies, speculation, and even gambling.

From January 22–August 31 and then November 20–January 2044 (final-destination), Pluto needs to be dropped in Aquarius, the sector in your chart that relates to work, health, diet, routine, employees, coworkers, detox, acts of kindness and service, as well as pets.

OPERATING LIMITATIONS: ENCOUNTERS WITH YOUR ANTAGONIST

As previously highlighted, from March 2023 to February 2026, Saturn, the embodiment of Lord Karma, voyages through Pisces, your opposite sign. This journey presents its challenges. Why? Because as you forge ahead, Saturn obstructs your view and halting your progress, like an ever-present shadow. He casts doubt upon your aspirations, questions your aptitudes and expertise, reminiscent of an overbearing boss micromanaging your every action.

Being in your opposite sign, Saturn prompts you to re-evaluate all your relationships, that includes life and work partners and everyone pivotal in your life. Many Virgos might find themselves at crossroads in their relationships—some facing separations, others entering unions, and a few experiencing both. Saturn reinforces existing relationship dynamics, intensifying the good and exacerbating the challenges. This time may also necessitate confronting adversaries, pushing you to stand firm against those that hinder or harm. Astrologically speaking, there's little distinction between soulmates and nemeses; both serve as mirrors reflecting your true self.

Given the anticipated confrontations, it's prudent to have sound legal counsel on standby. Potential legal entanglements might surface. Yet, it's essential to understand Saturn's intentions. While he might seem like your foe, he's actually steering you away from unauthentic alliances, highlighting those who, under the guise of friendship, might undermine you.

To gain insights into potential challenges or pinpoint your antagonist, revisit the hurdles you faced in 1995 and 1996. Issues from that era may reemerge or manifest in similar ways. Recall the analogy presented in the introduction, likening Saturn's transits to both waves and particles. A story started in those years might be repeating or evolving.

On the brighter side, managing Saturn in Pisces is easier if you can have peaceful sleep and rest more often. Einstein, a Pisces himself, frequently lauded the rejuvenating qualities of brief siestas. Recent studies have corroborated this, demonstrating the brain's potential to expand during a short midday nap. Keeping a dream journal could prove enlightening, with profound wisdom emerging from your nocturnal flights. Seeking communities that emphasize yoga, dance, movement, mysticism, or meditation can also provide comfort. Immerse yourself in water, when possible, use creative visualization, and maintain faith—in yourself and the universe—the rest will naturally follow.

MENTORS AND TUTORS: ENCOUNTER WITH YOUR MASTER

In "*Rock 'n' Roll Suicide*," Bowie, with the fervor of a musical prophet, declares, "Oh no love, you are not alone, no matter what or who you've been, no matter when or where you've seen, all the knives seem to lacerate your brain, I've had my share, I'll help you with the pain. You're not alone!" He might as well have channeled Jupiter!

Jupiter, the grand luminary of our Solar System, nods in agreement. This benevolent giant has your back. For the initial five months of the year, he journeys through Taurus, a fellow earth sign. This is a boon doubled for you. Under Jupiter's tutelage, doors to study, learn, and teach will swing wide open. Anticipate spirited adventures, enlightening travels, and meaningful engagements with mentors and guides, particularly those from distant lands. Stand true to your essence and values, be authentic, walk the talk, and Jupiter will reward you with moments of serendipity and fortune. In addition, your rapport with in-laws may see a significant upswing.

Come May 26, Jupiter embarks on his voyage through Gemini. Given Gemini's airy nature, this phase could pose some challenges for you. Moreover, both you and Gemini lay claim to Mercury's guardianship, sometimes leading to a sibling rivalry for his benevolence. However, Jupiter, ever the magnanimous guide, rises above such skirmishes. His grace remains undeterred, showering you with bounties and fortunate opportunities in your professional sphere. Be it a raise, promotion, or enhanced camaraderie with superiors, the winds of favor are blowing your way. If the idea of launching a business or veering onto a new career path has been playing on your mind, now might be the opportune time to act. Jupiter's illuminating presence will guide your steps. Until June 9, 2025, his wish is to see you flourish in your chosen vocation, heightening your esteem within your community and workplace. The constellations are aligned for your triumph!

BATTLEGROUNDS PROCEDURES—ECLIPSE AND CREATURES OF THE NIGHT

Buckle up; this is of paramount significance. From December 2021 to July 13, 2023, the North Node, often termed the Dragon's Head, beckoned you to embrace your authentic self, embodying and vocalizing your true convictions. You crossed paths with insightful mentors, learning how to inspire others and share your sagacity. However, between July 2023 and January 2025, the Dragon soars in the sector of your chart intertwined with transformation, mortality, wizardry, joint assets, insurance, taxes, intimacy, the occult, and sexuality. You've pinpointed it accurately; these realms are ruled by Pluto, currently accompanying you closely. Hence, this year, your quest holds immeasurable importance.

The Dragon signifies the lessons your soul desires you to master. This annum, your enlightenment revolves around shedding inhibitions, those barriers keeping you from realizing your true potential, while simultaneously recognizing, nurturing, and disseminating your divine spark. In 2024, you possess a magnetism that draws the tools and experiences you need to ascend in every facet of your life. Call upon the Dragon daily, envisioning him as your guardian deity, like Ganesha, leveraging his might to remove obstacles from your path. Seek daily transformative moments, embracing the secrets of the universe. This year, you're on the path to mastering the mystical arts, emerging as a sorceress or a sage.

Reflect on 2005–2006 and 1986–1987; the North Node graced this identical position in your chart during those times. To unlock its potential now, channel the spirit of Aries embodied by the key phrase "I Am," mastering leadership, initiation, championing your beliefs, conquest, and refining your persona.

During the eclipses, the pace of events intensifies. These cosmic occurrences can make the journey tumultuous and unpredictable. Gear up for celestial confrontations, resplendent with energy rays and astral showers. Here are the pivotal celestial coordinates marking intensity:

- **Lunar Eclipse in Libra, March 24–25**: The Sun illuminates your passion, intimacy, sexuality, granting you access to collective resources and magic. The Moon acts as a conduit, linking you to your innate talents, skills, and financial prowess. Balance your personal financial ambitions with those of significant others. This period resonates with the profound liberation celebrated during Moses' Passover and Jesus' Last Supper. Note: 2024's Passover celebrations witness a delay due to lunar calendar intricacies.
- **Total Solar Eclipse in Aries, April 8**: This New Moon, amidst a Mercury retrograde, proves challenging. With its presence in Aries, both the Moon (mama) and Sun (daddy) urge you to dive deep into your power, healing ability, and transformative skills.
- **Partial Lunar Eclipse, September 17–18**: The Pisces Moon juxtaposes the Sun in Virgo during the Harvest Full Moon. This is your celestial dance! An omen of the wonders 2025 and 2026 will unfurl. The spotlight, however, will likely be on your significant relationships, urging a kinder, more pliable demeanor. This is your power Moon, being a Virgo. You are harvesting your well-earned gifts.
- **Annular Solar Eclipse, October 2**: Under the Libra New Moon, it's a golden period for peace initiatives, diplomacy, or budding relationships

and romances. New beginnings in the financial realms or new talents bud. An enhancement in self-esteem, potentially even a financial upswing, may be on the horizon.

ORANGE ALERT! SHAPESHIFTERS AND TRICKSTERS

When Mercury retrogrades, he takes on his trickster and shapeshifter role. It's a cosmic cue to pause and recalibrate. Make sure to bring your spacecraft to a halt and start flying in reverse. I know, it can be hard on the neck having to look back or relying on your reverse camera mode. Anticipate delays, energetic and emotional traffic jams. It's the worst time to sign documents or start a new project. But you know all this if you carefully read the first part of your pilot manual.

However, as a Virgo who is ruled by Mercury, these periods are full of potential since everyone is asked to do what you do best: edit, pay attention to small details, and recommit to a healthier diet.

As the year begins, particularly on its first two days, you might feel some resistance powering up your spacecraft. This is due to Mercury being stationary in Sagittarius, a sign that doesn't particularly resonate with you. The dawn of 2024 might feel somewhat demanding, especially when dealing with family and domestic matters. Mercury will once again retrograde in Sagittarius later in the year, from November 25 to December 16. During this span, exercise added patience with family, your home, its appliances, and matters related to your origins or real estate. You might find yourself navigating deeper emotions and addressing early childhood insecurities.

The primary Mercury retrograde of 2024 spans from April 1 to 26. Compounded by a potent eclipse peaking on April 8, this period may present its challenges. With the eclipse in Aries, you're beckoned to journey into the Underworld, potentially facing setbacks in your partner's finances or with investments, productions, collaborative artistic and financial endeavors, and intimate partnerships.

Come August 4–14, Mercury retrogrades in Virgo. Given that this is your sign, proceed with extra care. Keep a close eye on your dietary choices, digestive health, internal organs, professional relationships, and daily routine.

This phase can be particularly tricky, potentially impacting your health, personal image, and branding. Nonetheless, it provides a ripe moment for self-reinvention. From August 15–29, the mercurial shapeshifter transitions, retrograding into Leo. As this position in your chart aligns with past lives, the subconscious, imagination, confinement, solitude, and healing spaces, so please tread gently. Yet, with Mercury as your guiding planet, this time can usher in the reclamation of long-lost talents and perhaps even reconnections with souls from past lifetimes.

Summary of Mercury Retrograde Dates
- January 1–January 2: Sagittarius.
- April 1–26: Aries (Red Alert around April 8 due to a total solar eclipse).
- August 4–14: Retrograde in Virgo.
- August 14–29 Retrograde in Leo.
- November 25–December 16 Sagittarius (Red Alert from December 6–16 since Mars is retrograde).

RED ALERT! SHIELDS UP
Mars often gets a bad rap. As the co-ruler of Scorpio—represented by the "Death" Tarot card—and the unequivocal ruler of Aries, the sign symbolizing war, Mars has long been linked with destruction and chaos. His Tarot representation, "The Tower," illustrates people tumbling from a burning building, which hardly seems promising. However, fewer realize that Mars was also revered as the ancient god of vegetation, seeds, and planting. So, Mars does have his benevolent side too.

As 2024 draws to a close, Mars will begin his retrograde in Leo starting December 6, 2024, and will only go direct (in Cancer) on February 24, 2025. As such, it's advisable to complete your significant tasks for the year before December 6, and calling it a year, go have fun and relax. If Mars is the god of planting, then during his retrograde, it's an ideal time to weed out and discard what's no longer necessary in your life.

With Mars retrograding in Leo, anticipate potential tensions and hurdles in your romantic relationships, as well as conflicts with your children or what you might think of as the "children of your mind": projects or ventures that you passionately care about. Exercise caution during physical training or, in general, to avoid injuries and be particularly wary around sharp objects. Mars retrogrades in the lion's den may stir up challenges, particularly in areas of your life connected to hospitals, unexpected events, and emotional or physical distress. Thus, navigate these times with caution, being present in each moment. Echoes of conflicts from past lives might emerge, as well as potential reunions with kindred spirits from those eras. You may find yourself feeling more fatigued, drawn to moments of solitude and reflection.

Since Mars' shadow begins on October 5, it would be prudent to be more vigilant from this point forward. It's as if you're navigating treacherous straits or passing through an asteroid belt. Stay alert and keep your shield up.

Below you will find Mars' Table Coordinates that highlight areas in your life where you can channel your passion, energy, and leadership. However, remember that wherever Mars is positioned, he can also introduce conflict and strife in those aspects of life.

- **November 24, 2023, Mars strides into Sagittarius**: You'll find an abundance of energy swirling around your home and family. This is an opportune moment for renovations and home repairs. You might also consider investing in a vacation property abroad. Be aware, though, of potential disagreements with family members.
- **January 4, 2024, Mars exaltedly enters Capricorn**: Mars is showcasing his most influential stance. While he bestows energy, be mindful of potential conflicts with superiors, older individuals, and in your professional sphere. On the romantic front, passion abounds, offering a chance at new partnerships or a surge in creative endeavors.
- **February 13, 2024, Mars makes his way into Aquarius**: Mars infuses you with extra energy with your circles of friends, community, and organizations. But tread carefully: disagreements might flare up with coworkers or employees. Exercise caution around sharp objects and strenuous training. Still, this period is ripe for seizing initiative at work.

- **March 22, 2024, Mars delves into Pisces**: Brace for possible tensions and disagreements in primary relationships, particularly with a marital partner. Stay alert, as adversaries may lurk nearby. Mars can help deal with enemies.
- **Apr 30, 2024, Mars charges into Aries**: This is a time to harness your inner leadership, connect deeply with your body, and embrace your passions, sexuality, and inherent power. Great for investment and shared resources.
- **June 9, 2024, Mars grounds himself in Taurus**: Though energy may flow slower, it's unwavering and persistent. Expect to work diligently for desired outcomes, but rest assured, accomplishments on the material plane are within reach. Direct this energy towards education and travel but stay cautious of potential disputes with in-laws.
- **July 20, 2024, Mars flies into Gemini**: urging you to hone in on your communication, business dealings, and contracts. Raise your voice, assert your needs, and place your career center stage. It's an ideal phase to pioneer new ventures (though be wary of Mercury's retrograde phase). Still, anticipate potential clashes with authoritative figures.
- **September 4, 2024, Mars surfs in Cancer**: Not his most cherished abode. This placement might tempt you into over-defensiveness or passive-aggressive behaviors, possibly leading to familial disputes. Nevertheless, Mars can pave the way for bonds with younger men or cultivating new friendships. Find your siblings in arms.
- **November 4, 2024, Mars reveling in Leo**: Mars strives to amplify your vitality and enthusiasm. Monitor your interactions and ensure you assert yourself appropriately. Consider setting aside personal time for introspection and reconnection. It's a period rife with opportunities for spiritual and mystical pursuits.

LOVE INTEREST AND ALLIES

Venus loves you, she does—it's in her nature. However, she has her moments of whimsiness and can act out. She's not your mama who adores you no matter what, she has her list of conditions, like a spiritual prenuptial agreement.

Below is the list of where Venus journeys this year, offering insights into potential areas of assistance in financial support, creative boosts, enhanced self-worth, and perhaps even a romantic connection. We're fortunate this year, as Venus remains direct, avoiding her retrograde phase. When she graces your sign (August 5–August 28), you'll likely notice a heightened sense of beauty, feel and look better, experience a stronger connection to your talent, and perhaps an improved financial situation. Essentially, you're channeling the goddess of beauty and sensuality. However, this might also make you more susceptible to spending money or a tad more self-absorbed than usual. Jupiter and Venus come together on these love-filled days: May 22–23. A great time for art, dating, meeting the love of your life, or just feeling good.

Below you'll find her celestial coordinates and the areas of your life she'll likely influence, ushering in some good fortune and support from allies and loved ones.

- **December 29, 2023, Venus graces Sagittarius**: It's an ideal time to nurture bonds with teachers, in-laws, students, and foreigners. The goddess of love bestows her blessings upon family ties, making it a delightful period to infuse some exotic flair into your home. Great for real-estate.
- **January 23, 2024, Venus climbs to Capricorn**: The goddess of love ushers in a romantic interest or enhances your bond with children. A wave of creativity, particularly for long-haul projects, ensues. Also, Venus nurtures harmony with those senior to you, be they more experienced individuals or superiors.
- **February 16, 2024, Venus bonds with Aquarius**: A season of camaraderie, laughter, spontaneity, and innovation. Group artistic ventures are favored, and Venus lends her charm to your workspace, enhancing coworker relationships. Favors functional and useful artistic projects.
- **March 11, 2024, Venus exalts in Pisces**: Venus is in her element. This phase shines in financial and artistic spheres. It's arguably the year's best Venusian influence for mending ties, drawing in romantic partners, and solidifying unions.

- **April 5, 2024, Venus ventures into Aries**: not her preferred haven, especially amidst eclipses and retrogrades. Embrace assertiveness, leadership, and passion. She still aids in pooling resources and collaborating on art ventures. Investments look promising.
- **April 29, 2024, Venus returns home to Taurus**: With her in her domain, your gifts and expertise radiate. It's a prime window to encounter enlightening mentors and connecting to foreigners. Maintain transparency in partnerships. Truth is of the essence. Also, an opportune time for justice and legal victories.
- **May 23, 2024, Venus dances with Gemini**: Venus links you to realms of marketing, writing, and public relations. Enhance ties with relatives and anticipate career advancements. It's a propitious moment for that pay bump or promotion you deserve.
- **June 17, 2024, Venus immerses in Cancer**: fortifying connections with loved ones and friends. This time stands out as the year's prime for befriending new souls or embarking on group art projects.
- **July 11, 2024**: Venus parties with Leo: Venus amplifies love and joy. Dive into creative pursuits and sports, preferably paired. It's a phase of reuniting with familiar souls and reigniting skills from past lifetimes.
- **August 5, 2024, Venus refining Virgo**: Venus adorns you with charm and poise. All aspects of your life could be blessed. Life in all its hues seems to flourish under her touch, with your inner artist thriving. A good time for rebranding.
- **August 29, 2024, Venus balances Libra**: Echoing themes of justice and relational healing. She favors your finances and may reveal latent talents or novel income avenues. This is an exemplary phase for design, music, culinary arts, fashion, and artistic ventures.
- **September 23, 2024, Venus delves into Scorpio**: Venus might restrain her lavishness. Yet, she beckons you to deepen intimacy, explore sensuality, and contemplate your attractions. Connect with relatives, resolve disputes with co-dwellers or neighbors, and anticipate contractual opportunities. Concentrate on marketing and sales.

- **October 17, 2024, Venus journeys into Sagittarius**: A prime time to mend family rifts and revamp your living space. Opportunities may come from abroad.
- **November 11, 2024, Venus climbs Capricorn**: Venus establishes ties with people older than you. Whether refining existing romantic ties or kindling new flames, Venus assists. Creative hobbies prosper.
- **December 7, 2024, Venus allies with Aquarius**: Focus on friendship and elevate your organizational stature. The work atmosphere and coworker relations are set to improve. Sprinkle artistic nuances into your professional endeavors.

ALIEN ENCOUNTER PROTOCOL

As a cosmic navigator, you are bound to encounter what some might call aliens. But to be intergalactically correct, let's refer to them as "extraterrestrial sentient beings." These beings are represented by Uranus, the Awakener.

Since 2018, Uranus has journeyed through Taurus, a fellow earth sign, bringing with him unexpected twists, particularly concerning education, in-laws, travel, publishing, and your interactions with the truth and mass media. You might've noticed shifts in your values, philosophy, and overall outlook on life. Perhaps there were some unforeseen legal challenges. In addition, Uranus encourages you to delve into innovation and science, be it through fresh academic pursuits or by immersing yourself in diverse cultures and traditions. Now is a splendid moment to pick up a new language or venture to a locale you never thought would pique your curiosity. Do your utmost to refresh and enhance your understanding, especially regarding technology and innovation. Remain alert, as unforeseen matters with in-laws, judges, educators, or students may still arise.

Moreover, Uranus nudges you to perceive through your five senses in novel ways: indulge in diverse music genres, savor unfamiliar cuisines, explore fresh income avenues, and refine the manner in which you present yourself to the world. Embracing the unique, venturing into uncharted territories, and exploring new horizons will allow you to reap the most benefits from this once-in-an-84-year transit.

CONCLUSION

In 2024, you're beckoned to journey into the depths of your deepest fears. This year isn't just about facing and overcoming these insecurities, but also about drawing strength from the process of mastering them. Relationships, both in your professional realm and personal life—be it marital or romantic—will present challenges. These bonds call for your earnest attention, urging you to either deepen the connection or release them. As Pluto transitions the most important sector of your chart, the one that corresponds with your archetype, you may experience a jolt in your professional life and health. Yet, Pluto also offers a silver lining: the chance to transform your vocation and rediscover a renewed way of serving humanity. Amidst these shifts, your career stands to gain, potentially bringing you the respect and an acknowledgment you've long sought.

TAROT: THE HERMIT

This card illuminates your path, transforming you into a lighthouse for those aiming to ascend the sacred mountain—a journey you've already undertaken. With a pronounced focus on your relationships, work, and service, this card encourages you to serve others selflessly. It speaks to the profound "Service" language of love, calling upon you to guide and uplift.

HEBREW LETTER: YOD

Meaning: Representing the Hand of God, Yod symbolizes both the divine sperm and egg, denoting creation and the genesis of life.

LIBRA AND
LIBRA RISING—I BALANCE

I Versus Thou

MISSION (NOT) IMPOSSIBLE—YOUR ASSIGNMENT CARD

Libra—Balancer of Universal Justice, God's advocated, the beautifier, diplomat, and peacemaker, in 2024, your mission is grand: transport Pluto, the nuclear reactor of the zodiac, from the Capricorn star system to the Aquarius nebula. Yet, this voyage won't be a smooth sail. Saturn, Lord of the (Three) Rings and the Master of Karma, casts his watchful eye from his position in the sector of your chart governing work, health, diet, routine, and service. As you escort Pluto, the Lord of Death and Rebirth, you're bound to halt at every planet where souls grapple with ailment or despair, offering healing. The universe beckons you to embody the roles of a healer, a doctor, a sanctuary for the ailing. However, amid this, you must prioritize your own well-being, reevaluate your methods of service, and recalibrate your workplace and professional life.

2024's directive, though straightforward, is rife with peril. Pluto, the Guardian of Mysteries, seeks passage to Aquarius, the sign of camaraderie, humanity, society, and innovation. To your credit, among your zodiacal kin, your task appears a shade lighter. Pluto's residence in your chart since 2008, encompassing the Great Recession, unleashed profound alterations concerning your home, familial bonds, real estate, and inner emotional landscape. The demands were immense; Pluto's gravity at your chart's nadir stirred tumultuous shifts, prompting introspection into long-buried familial wounds and insecurities. Yet, let's steer our gaze towards the horizon. For the next two decades, Pluto will illuminate and transform realms of your life tied to happiness, creativity, children, hobbies, romance, sports, and all other sources of genuine elation. While Pluto's presence isn't a ceaseless jubilee, he compels you to introspect: to discern genuine joy and, true to your Libran nature, project that joy onto people around you. Relationships with offspring or cherished creative endeavors may evolve under Pluto's gaze until 2044.

Your Assignment Card: Beam Pluto aboard your cosmic vessel, steering him from Capricorn (representing the past) to Aquarius (symbolizing the future). Considering Pluto's past emphasis on home and familial bonds since 2008, your challenge is to channel those rich lessons about emotional tapestries, ancestral legacies, and even genetic heritage and direct this wisdom towards nurturing your children, romantic partners, creative projects, and unbridled joy. You're summoned to exude authentic cheerfulness, to captivate and uplift. Given Pluto's profound nature, your jubilation must resonate deeply. Perhaps it's a season to immerse yourself in studying positive psychology.

2024 tasks you with bringing forth life—be it through offspring or projects—and employing artistry to guide humanity towards the dawn of the Aquarius era. Still, proceed with caution. Avoid taking too many risks, whether in finance, emotions, or ventures.

Pluto's Pickup Location

From June 11, 2023–January 21, 2024, and September 2–November 19, Pluto is located in Capricorn in the sector of your chart that relates to family, emotionality, real estate, security, genetics, ancestral karma, and the past. A time for relocation, renovation, selling and buying a house, pregnancy, healing relationships with family members.

From January 22–August 31 and November 20–January 2044 (final-destination), Pluto needs to be dropped in Aquarius, the sector in your chart that relates to happiness, children, sports, hobbies, recreation, entertainment, risky endeavors, stocks trade, gambling, romantic love, and creativity.

OPERATING LIMITATIONS: ENCOUNTERS WITH YOUR ANTAGONIST

As highlighted earlier, from March 2023 to February 2026, Saturn, known as Lord Karma, sails through Pisces. In this role, the Lord of the (Three) Rings acts much like a vigilant guardian, reminiscent of a governess ensuring Alice doesn't venture too deep into her Wonderland.

So, where does this challenge manifest for you? Within your professional realm, your health, daily dietary habits, established routines, and how you serve people. Remember the adage, "The devil is in the details"? This holds especially true for you in the coming two years. It's a period beckoning you to zero in on specifics, to take an analytical approach without sliding into perfectionism. Choose the precision of a microscope over the broad sweep of a telescope and realign how you contribute to others' well-being (in your profession), how you nourish your body (through diet), and how others support you (think colleagues or subordinates). Saturn may introduce scenarios that question the effectiveness and efficiency of your routine, prompting adjustments if they aren't beneficial. Moreover, prioritize your health, especially aspects like immunity, bones, teeth, joints, skin, allergies, and any lingering chronic ailments. Ensure you undergo comprehensive medical evaluations and embrace preventive health measures.

Since Saturn's modus operandi involves revealing deep-rooted challenges, changes might occur in your workplace setting—not necessarily a career shift but rather alterations in how you advance your profession daily. You could also encounter occasional hiccups with colleagues or subordinates. On a brighter note, you may feel compelled to adopt a pet, and if you already have one, be prepared to address any issues they might face.

To gain insights into potential challenges or pinpoint your antagonist, revisit the hurdles you faced in 1995 and 1996. Issues from that era may reemerge or manifest in similar ways. Recall the analogy presented in the introduction, likening Saturn's transits to both waves and particles. A story started in those years might be repeating or evolving.

On the brighter side, managing Saturn in Pisces is easier if you can have peaceful sleep and rest more often. Einstein, a Pisces himself, frequently lauded the rejuvenating qualities of brief siestas. Recent studies have corroborated this, demonstrating the brain's potential to expand during a short midday nap. Keeping a dream journal could prove enlightening, with profound wisdom emerging from your nocturnal flights. Seeking communities that emphasize yoga, dance, movement, mysticism, or meditation can also provide comfort. Immerse yourself in water, when possible, use creative visualization, and maintain faith—in yourself and the universe—the rest will naturally follow.

MENTORS AND TUTORS: ENCOUNTER WITH YOUR MASTER

In "*Rock 'n' Roll Suicide*," Bowie, with the fervor of a musical prophet, declares, "Oh no love, you are not alone, no matter what or who you've been, no matter when or where you've seen, all the knives seem to lacerate your brain, I've had my share, I'll help you with the pain. You're not alone!" He might as well have channeled Jupiter!

Jupiter, the largest planet in the Solar System, concurs. He would never leave you alone and this year he travels for the first five months in Taurus, amplifying your passion, sexual drive, mojo, as well as your magic, therapeutic and healing abilities, nurturing your inner wizard and enchantress. Jupiter's timing is fortuitous since Pluto, your passenger, governs these very aspects of life: death, rebirth, sensuality, mysticism, the occult, the afterlife, as well as investigative and research pursuits. Thus, until May 25, you're bestowed with a penetrative intellect, adeptness in exploration, and a flair for transformative research. In other words, you are full of enchantment and magic. This is a potent period for personal metamorphosis and for bolstering the self-worth, talents, and financial prospects of your partners.

From May 26, Jupiter begins his dance through Gemini, a fellow air sign, ensuring the celestial favors cascade seamlessly upon you. For the ensuing year, guidance may manifest in the form of a new teacher, mentor, or perhaps someone from a divergent cultural or traditional backdrop. This is a great time for publishing as well. This is attributed to Jupiter's benevolent influence on the sector of your chart linked with travel, education, truth, justice, and optimism. As long as you remain genuine, anchoring firmly to your beliefs, an abundance of luck, opportunities, and success will gravitate towards you. An unfamiliar country or culture might intrigue you, possibly leading to travel related to your profession or chances to educate and guide others.

Jupiter's kiss can also foster harmony with in-laws or introduce a new familial connection, perhaps through a budding relationship of a relative. Until June 9, 2025, Jupiter's ambition is to magnify your faith in life, in your-self, and in others. Let his support in as he diligently works to elevate you.

BATTLEGROUNDS PROCEDURES—ECLIPSE AND CREATURES OF THE NIGHT

This is paramount, so buckle up. From December 2021 to July 13, 2023, the North Node, known as the Dragon's Head, beckoned you to master the teachings of the Underworld, particularly those of Pluto, the Sovereign of Death and Resurrection. The call was for a profound reflection on your passions, your sexuality, and your perspectives on the inevitabilities of life and death. However, from July 2023 to January 2025, the Dragon takes flight towards the sector of your chart dedicated to relationships, partnerships, and significant bonds. The Dragon's head will be in Aries, your opposite sign, suggesting that the Dragon's Tail now aligns with your sign. Being saddled with the Dragon's rear end doesn't sound that nice, I agree. What it means is that for the next 18 months you must sidestep the classic Libran collective, "we," and embrace the individualistic Aries stance, "I." Paradoxically, the North Node's aim is to impart the wisdom of partnerships and collaboration, steering you back to an "us" mindset and away from the singular "me." It might seem like a conundrum straight out of Wonderland, but the essence of this alignment is decipherable. With Pluto anchoring himself in the romantic sphere of your life and the Dragon emphasizing partnership, 2024 emerges as a pivotal year for understanding equilibrium between personal desires and those of others. It's about firmly recognizing and asserting your individuality (Aries = I AM) while simultaneously nurturing partnerships (Libra = I Balance). The quintessential question: within the confines of work or personal relationships, can you truly be yourself? And further, do you appreciate the version of yourself that such associations shape you into? If the bonds, be it in professional arenas or personal realms like marriage and romance, resonate with your core and elevate you, then dive in with full conviction. If not, harness Jupiter's teachings from the year's initial five months to sever ties with relationships that drain or diminish you.

For context, the North Node previously occupied this same celestial space during 2005–2006 and 1986–1987. Reflect what were the relational lessons back in those times.

During eclipses you'll experience events quickening dramatically. Here are the coordinates and key dates to monitor as you navigate the year:

- **Lunar Eclipse in Libra, March 24–25**: The Sun casts a spotlight on your collaborative endeavors and partnerships, while the Moon graces your sign. The dynamic between the self ("I") and the other ("thou") takes center stage. This celestial event harkens back to significant religious moments: Moses' Passover and Jesus' Last Supper, both symbolic of emancipation and the conclusion of captivity. It's worth noting that in 2024, the commemoration of Passover experiences a delay due to complications with the Lunar calendar.
- **Total Solar Eclipse in Aries, April 8**: Navigating this New Moon may prove challenging, especially with Mercury in retrograde. However, its positioning in Aries brings a particular emphasis. Both celestial luminaries, the nurturing Moon (mama) and the radiant Sun (daddy), steer your attention towards partnerships and binding commitments.

The stage is set for the potential birth of new relationships but be wary; adversaries might come to the forefront, gaining visibility and momentum.

- **Partial Lunar Eclipse, September 17–18**: With the Piscean Moon in opposition to the Sun in Virgo, this Harvest Full Moon prompts introspection. It encourages you to recognize and counter any tendencies to withdraw or self-isolate. Dive deep into your work and let your dedication shine brightly. This period is fertile ground for reaping the rewards of seeds sown earlier in the year, particularly around March and April.
- **Annular Solar Eclipse, October 2**: The New Moon in Libra signifies a time of balance and connection. It's an opportune moment for fostering peace, engaging in diplomacy, or kindling the flames of new romantic endeavors. As this eclipse aligns so closely with your sign, it beckons you to embrace its energies fully. Indulge in self-enhancement, discover fresh avenues of tranquility, or embark on exhilarating ventures, be they projects or personal relationships.

ORANGE ALERT! SHAPESHIFTERS AND TRICKSTERS

When Mercury retrogrades, he takes on his trickster and shapeshifter role. It's a cosmic cue to pause and recalibrate. Make sure to bring your spacecraft to a halt and start flying in reverse. I know, it can be hard on the neck having to look back or relying on your reverse camera mode. Anticipate delays, energetic and emotional traffic jams. It's the worst time to sign documents or start a new project. But you know all this if you carefully read the first part of your pilot manual.

As you set forth on your 2024 journey, the first two days might feel akin to trying to ignite your spacecraft with dampened fuel. Mercury, stationary in Sagittarius, isn't giving you the spark you need. Though Sagittarius, the fiery archer, usually complements your energy, he governs your departments of communication, sales, marketing, and contracts. These are precisely the sectors Mercury tends to throw into disarray during his retrogrades. So, brace yourself: the dawn of 2024 may challenge your business dealings, communications, and even relations with relatives, neighbors, or roommates. Mercury revisits his retrograde in Sagittarius again at the end of the year from November 25 to December 16. Be judicious with your words, whether spoken, texted, posted, or liked. Sales, marketing, and negotiations may also hit some snags.

The inaugural Mercury retrograde of 2024 unfurls from April 1 to 26. Coinciding with a potent eclipse on April 8, this retrograde could prove particularly testing. The combination of the eclipse and Mercury's backspin occurring in your opposite sign, Aries, might stir up turbulence with partners and close associates. It's crucial not to ignite conflicts or, worse, forge adversaries. Breathe deep, dear cosmic voyager, and practice patience.

The retrograde from August 4–14 settles in Virgo, often dubbed the zodiac's conscientious caretaker. Proceed with caution, for this phase alights upon the sectors of your life linked to hospitals, distress, release, addictions, and befuddlement. Perhaps it's wise to seek solitude during this time—consider a retreat, meditation sessions, or tranquil saunters amidst nature's bosoms. This period may also bring about familiar faces or long-forgotten skills from past lives. It's an opportune window for therapeutic ventures and dreamwork. Mercury, the ever shapeshifter changes into Leo garments and continues his retrograde August 15–29, potentially ushering in a wave of dramatic episodes within friendships or group settings. Navigate with care when engaging with colleagues, pals, or members of your community or organization. A peculiar "Pauli Effect" might even manifest, causing technology around you to behave erratically.

Summary of Mercury Retrograde Dates
- January 1–January 2: Sagittarius.
- April 1–26: Aries (Red Alert around April 8 due to a total solar eclipse).
- August 4–14: Retrograde in Virgo.
- August 14–29 Retrograde in Leo.
- November 25–December 16 Sagittarius (Red Alert from December 6–16 since Mars is retrograde).

RED ALERT! SHIELDS UP

Mars often gets a bad rap. As the co-ruler of Scorpio—represented by the "Death" Tarot card—and the unequivocal ruler of Aries, the sign symbolizing war, Mars has long been linked with destruction and chaos. His Tarot representation, "The Tower," illustrates people tumbling from a burning building, which hardly seems promising. However, fewer realize that Mars was also revered as the ancient god of vegetation, seeds, and planting. So, Mars does have his benevolent side too.

As 2024 draws to a close, Mars will begin his retrograde in Leo starting December 6, 2024, and will only go direct (in Cancer) on February 24, 2025. As such, it's advisable to complete your significant tasks for the year before December 6, and calling it a year, go have fun and relax. If Mars is the god of planting, then during his retrograde, it's an ideal time to weed out and discard what's no longer necessary in your life.

With Mars retrograding in Leo, anticipate potential tensions and hurdles in your romantic relationships, as well as conflicts with your children or what you might think of as the "children of your mind": projects or ventures that you passionately care about. Exercise caution during physical training or, in general, to avoid injuries and be particularly wary around sharp objects. Furthermore, this retrograde may also amplify complications when dealing with governmental entities. Be particularly vigilant with issues related to taxes, permits, and other bureaucratic matters. Given Mars' influence, it's prudent to meticulously review all documentation, exercise patience when handling administrative tasks, and, if feasible, seek advice from experts in these fields to sidestep any potential pitfalls. In addition, be extra patient with your friends.

Since the shadow of Mars begins October 5, you should start being cautious from the onset of October. It is as if you are navigating an asteroid belt. Take heed and bring your protective shields up.

Below you will find Mars' Table Coordinates that highlight areas in your life where you can channel your passion, energy, and leadership. However, remember that wherever Mars is positioned, he can also introduce conflict and strife in those aspects of life. This year Mars will not visit your sign.

- **November 24, 2023, Mars strides into Sagittarius**: A surge of energy surrounds business, communication, marketing, and writing. Approach teachers, students, and relatives with care and tact.
- **January 4, 2024, Mars ascends into Capricorn**: Mars' most potent position. He offers strength to revamp your living space or delve into real estate ventures. However, tread lightly with family, particularly the elders, as tensions might arise.
- **February 13, 2024, Mars befriends Aquarius**: Mars is channeling additional vigor towards friendships, community activities, and organizational engagements. While he energizes sports, hobbies, and creativity, be wary of potential disagreements with children, co-creators, or romantic partners.
- **March 22, 2024, Mars dives into Pisces**: The waters may get a bit turbulent at your workplace, with possible disputes among colleagues. Exercise caution against injuries, accidents, and safeguard your health, especially your immune system.
- **April 30, 2024, Mars ignites Aries**: A powerful manifestation that promotes body connectivity, leadership, and the kickstart of new projects. Relationships might run hot with both passion and contention. Stay vigilant against potential adversaries.
- **June 9, 2024, Mars treks through Taurus**: The energy might feel slow, but its resolve is unwavering. Effort may be required in all pursuits, but this is a prime period to revisit your passions and sexuality. It's conducive for investments and collaborative artistic or financial ventures.
- **July 20, 2024, Mars takes the helm in Gemini**: Emphasizing the significance of messages, businesses, and contracts. It's an opportune phase to be firm in communications and vocalize your needs. While travel and education prospects are favorable, be watchful of disagreements with in-laws, mentors, or teachers.
- **September 4, 2024, Mars anchors in Cancer**: This isn't Mars' preferred territory. This might spark defensiveness or passive-aggressive tendencies. While familial discord is possible, Mars can bolster your

professional standing, letting you assert your role and climb the career ladder. Mind your superiors, though, and anticipate some professional rivalry.

- **November 4, 2024:** Mars celebrates in Leo: Mars is revitalizing your spirit. The ambiance among friends is electric, perhaps some youthful, assertive newcomers inspire you. However, be mindful of potential clashes within your company or friend circles.

LOVE INTEREST AND ALLIES

Venus loves you, she does—it's in her nature, besides, you Libra folks are ruled and blessed by the goddess of love and beauty. However, she has her moments of whimsiness and can act out. She's not your mama who adores you no matter what, she has her list of conditions, like a spiritual prenuptial agreement.

Below is the list of where Venus journeys this year, offering insights into potential areas of assistance in financial support, creative boosts, enhanced self-worth, and perhaps even a romantic connection. We're fortunate this year, as Venus remains direct, avoiding her retrograde phase. When she graces your sign (August 29–Sep 22), you'll likely notice a heightened sense of beauty, feel and look better, experience a stronger connection to your talent, and perhaps an improved financial situation. Essentially, you're channeling the goddess of beauty and sensuality. However, this might also make you more susceptible to spending money or a tad more self-absorbed than usual. Jupiter and Venus come together on these love-filled days: May 22–23. A great time for art, dating, meeting the love of your life, or just feeling good.

Below you'll find her celestial coordinates and the areas of your life she'll likely influence, ushering in some good fortune and support from allies and loved ones.

- **December 29, 2023, Venus graces Sagittarius:** This period fortifies relationships with teachers, in-laws, students, and foreigners. Venus, the goddess of love, enhances your bonds with relatives and roommates while paving the way for rewarding contracts and associations. Combine art and communication.

- **January 23, 2024, Venus enters Capricorn**: Venus' presence here can improve relationships with people older than you. Relationships with family members stand to benefit, making it a prime time for home renovations or redecorations.
- **February 16, 2024, Venus dances with Aquarius**: Embrace a season of new friendships, spontaneous laughter, and innovative endeavors. Dabble in art and technology. The goddess of love blesses your bonds with children, creative projects, and romantic partners. It's an auspicious period for dating.
- **March 11, 2024, Venus exalted in Pisces**: Finances and artistic endeavors flourish. This is an optimum position for Venus to enhance workplace relationships and infuse your service with an artistic touch.
- **April 5, 2024, Venus ventures into Aries**: Though not her favored realm, especially during eclipses and retrogrades, Venus encourages you to be assertive and take on the helm. This period is conducive to strengthening marital bonds, romantic relationships, and business partnerships.
- **April 29, 2024, Venus settles in Taurus**: Here, your innate talents and self-worth are accentuated. It's a time ripe for passionate expression, sexuality, and collaborative ventures involving mutual assets and talents. Venus descends into the underworld.
- **May 23, 2024, Venus soars through Gemini**: Venus enhances endeavors in marketing, writing, and public relations. Your bonds with educators, students, and in-laws are strengthened. A favorable time for artistic learning and travel.
- **June 17, 2024, Venus nestles in Cancer**: Experience improved relations with those you deem family. Your professional life could see advancements, and artistic endeavors in your career may bear fruit.
- **July 11, 2024, Venus radiates in Leo**: Love and camaraderie pervade, with heightened enjoyment in creative pursuits and sports, especially with a partner. Artistic collaborations might form, and new friendships could blossom.

- **August 5, 2024, Venus transitions to Virgo**: In this sign, Venus is more reserved, resembling a discerning nun. Yet, she assists in detoxing and distancing yourself from unsavory influences. There is a strong connection to your imagination. Skills and familiar souls from past lifetimes might re-emerge.

- **August 29, 2024, Venus rejuvenates in Libra**: Venus flourishes in her home sign, emphasizing justice and healing in relationships. Her influence benefits all facets of your life. You're likely to feel invigorated, making it an opportune moment for personal reinvention.

- **September 23, 2024, Venus delves into Scorpio**: Though not entirely at ease, Venus still assists you in harnessing your talents and perhaps discovering new income avenues. Elevated self-worth and awards abound.

- **October 17, 2024, Venus revisits Sagittarius**: This is a potent period for mending ties with relatives and colleagues. Infuse artistry into your business and communications.

- **November 11, 2024, Venus climbs Capricorn**: Engage with those wiser and older people. Venus fosters improved family dynamics and is conducive for design projects at home and work.

- **December 7, 2024, Venus mingles with Aquarius**: Direct your attention to friendships and elevate your stature within groups or organizations. Love, creativity, and enhanced relationships with children and romantic partners are in the offing. It's an auspicious period for partner-centric sports.

ALIEN ENCOUNTER PROTOCOL

As a cosmic navigator, you are bound to encounter what some might call aliens. But to be intergalactically correct, let's refer to them as "extra-terrestrial sentient beings." These beings are represented by Uranus, the Awakener.

Since 2018, Uranus has journeyed through Taurus, generating unanticipated shifts, particularly in areas of your chart linked to death, transformation, release, intimacy, and your interactions with others' finances and talents. Uranus is determined to shake things up in these realms until

2026. His aim? To ignite your passion and help you harness your fervor and healing capacities.

Make a concerted effort to refresh and elevate your mindset, particularly in how you perceive and engage with technology and innovation. Moreover, Uranus nudges you to perceive through your five senses in novel ways: indulge in diverse music genres, savor unfamiliar cuisines, explore fresh income avenues, and refine the manner in which you present yourself to the world. Embracing the unique, venturing into uncharted territories, and exploring new horizons will allow you to reap the most benefits from this once-in-an-84-year transit.

CONCLUSION

In 2024, you are called upon to revamp your daily routines, dietary habits, and professional endeavors, all with the noble aim of nurturing your well-being and contributing positively to the world. Transformation is the keyword for the year, touching every facet of your existence. Embrace these changes and equip yourself with the skills to adapt seamlessly.

The year beckons you to refine, harmonize, and forge relationships that resonate with your authentic self and amplify your inherent strength. Yet, amidst these shifts and evolutions, the heart of 2024 is a journey towards joy. It's an invitation to rediscover love, to seek out and nurture the playful spirit within, and to unshackle the boundless enthusiasm of your inner child. This year, let your inner light guide you.

TAROT: JUSTICE

The card represents the need for balance and equilibrium. With the South Node in your sign, you can benefit from uprooting whatever prevented you in the last 18/19 years from gaining harmony and balance.

HEBREW LETTER: LAMED

Meaning: The letter means both "learn" and "teach, it is also the acronym of lev, Hebrew for "heart." Its shape derives from the shepherd's crook, designed to teach the flock where to go. Your letter learns as it teaches the rest of the signs.

SCORPIO AND
SCORPIO RISING—I TRANSFORM
Finding, Cultivating, and Sharing Joy

MISSION (NOT) IMPOSSIBLE—YOUR ASSIGNMENT CARD

Scorpio—The transformer, witch and warlock, investigator supreme, financier, spymaster, and Keeper of the Secret Keys, your mission in 2024 is to transport Pluto, your ruler, also known as the nuclear reactor of the zodiac, from the Capricorn star system into the Aquarius nebula. Though your bond with Pluto runs deep, this journey promises to be fraught with challenges, especially under the watchful gaze of Saturn, the Lord of the (Three) Rings, and the Master of Karma. This year, Saturn anchors himself in the realms of your chart tied to children, joy, creativity, love, sports, hobbies, and entertainment. While other signs might rejoice, you, who prefer to work from behind the scenes, might balk from being pushed into centerstage. Yet, Saturn has set his intent, at least till February 2026, to make you bring the entertaining, childlike, and creative aspects of your personality, into the light. We'll delve deeper into your challenges and their origins in the year ahead soon. But for now, let's focus on the pivotal service you must render to the Zodiac Federation.

Your 2024 mission is to safely transport Pluto, the Lord of the Underworld, into the domain of Aquarius, which symbolizes community, friendship, and the modern marvels of technology. Fortunately, among your zodiac brethren, you hold an edge. Pluto and you share a soul connection. From 2008 until 2024, Pluto has been influencing areas of your life that involve communication, contracts, kinship, and the realms of writing, marketing, and sales. Since the times of the Great Recession in 2008, Pluto has steered the course of your business and implored you to reassess all your contracts, be they spiritual, financial, emotional, or intellectual. Remember, you, Scorpio, possess the unique gift of transformation—the ability to reincarnate without dying, akin to the phoenix.

Now, 2024 beckons you to welcome Pluto, the harbinger of endings and new beginnings, into the sector of your chart associated with home and family, security, and emotions, for the next two decades. During this period, Pluto will bring to light all that's been hidden, challenging you to confront your deepest fears and secrets. This transformative phase will profoundly impact your personal and professional domains. You'll find yourself navigating significant shifts, especially in dealings with family, property matters, security concerns, and planning for the latter stages of life. It's an intense period, even for someone as profound as you. Pluto will urge you to delve into childhood traumas, ancestral karma, and even inter-generational impositions. Relocation, whether prompted by a career move or a career change because of relocation, may be on the cards. Embrace all emotional currents. Familial transitions or the necessity to part ways with someone dear might surface. However, with your intrinsic understanding of these realms and the amplified power of Jupiter enhancing your intuitive and transformative faculties in the latter half of the year, you're well-equipped to deal with everything.

Your Assignment Card: Safeguard Pluto, your ruler, as you journey from Capricorn (representing the past) into the promise of Aquarius (symbolizing the future). Recall the last 16 years, where Pluto honed your intimate powers and magical energies in communication and business. Now, the universe beckons you to channel this acquired wisdom into nurturing your home, family, and professional spheres. Maybe finding a new home for your business, a new abode to your information. Accept this new role, for you are to uplift others with the knowledge you've amassed over the years.

Pluto's Pickup Location

From June 11, 2023–January 21, 2024, and September 2–November 19, Pluto is located in Capricorn, in the sector of your chart that relates to business and communication, and yes, there is still some information and data you need to collect, process, investigate, and research.

From January 22–August 31 and then November 20–January 2044 (final-destination), Pluto needs to be dropped in Aquarius, the sector in your chart that relates to family, emotionality, real estate, security, genetics, ancestral karma, and the past. A time for relocation, renovation, selling and buying a house, pregnancy, healing relationships with family members.

OPERATING LIMITATIONS: ENCOUNTERS WITH YOUR ANTAGONIST

From March 2023 to February 2026, Saturn, the enigmatic Lord of Karma, drifts through the mystical realm of Pisces. In this journey, the austere Lord of the Three-Rings behaves somewhat like the cosmic party pooper, casting his stern gaze over the vibrant sectors of your life associated with love, joy, recreation, sports, entertainment, and occasional indulgences. You, inherently reticent toward these lighter shades of life, might be tempted to disregard this transit. However, when Saturn hints at creating rifts with your beloved or perhaps unsettling your connection to children or grandchildren, it's an entirely different game. Suddenly, the stakes rise.

Having Saturn in the realm of your chart that oversees progeny—be it flesh and blood or creations of the mind—signifies a period of keen attention and potential challenges. This might manifest in hurdles faced by your children, or perhaps, key projects you consider your "babies". Contemplating parenthood or embracing the title of a grandparent might come into focus now. But remember, Saturn isn't just a taskmaster; he also brings with him the wisdom of discipline, commitment, and strategy.

Kabbalistic teachings suggest that Saturn unveils the processes of mending "Tikkun," in our lives. Reflecting on 1995–1996 might offer insights, shedding light on past challenges that connect with what's unfolding in 2024 and 2025.

Saturn wants you to become a Leo for the next two years. Don't shun the stage or limelight, welcome the attention and the opportunity to shine. Find ways to increase your joy, what was once fun is no longer, there is a need to reevaluate what ticks you. Delve into the realm of positive psychology, discover what sparks joy, and embody it. While your depth and intensity are commendable, infusing them with laughter and light will be a refreshing change. Saturn, resonating with the watery cadence of Pisces, might just ease his lessons for you. Heed your intuition and be attuned to the universe's subtle signals.

On the brighter side, managing Saturn in Pisces is easier if you can have peaceful sleep and rest more often. Einstein, a Pisces himself, frequently lauded the rejuvenating qualities of brief siestas. Recent studies have corroborated this, demonstrating the brain's potential to expand during a short midday nap. Keeping a dream journal could prove enlightening, with profound wisdom emerging from your nocturnal flights. Seeking communities that emphasize yoga, dance, movement, mysticism, or meditation can also provide comfort. Immerse yourself in water, when possible, use creative visualization, and maintain faith—in yourself and the universe—the rest will naturally follow.

MENTORS AND TUTORS: ENCOUNTER WITH YOUR MASTER

In "*Rock 'n' Roll Suicide*," Bowie, with the fervor of a musical prophet, declares, "Oh no love, you are not alone, no matter what or who you've been, no matter when or where you've seen, all the knives seem to lacerate your brain, I've had my share, I'll help you with the pain. You're not alone!" He might as well have channeled Jupiter!

Jupiter, the grand luminary of our Solar System, concurs. He's a steadfast ally, ensuring you're never left alone. For the first five months this year,

Jupiter sojourns through Taurus, your opposite sign. In doing so, he acts as a counterbalance to Saturn's love limitations, potentially summoning a significant partner, be it in life or profession. If you're already bound to a partner, Jupiter's benevolence works to resolve conflicts, weaving a tapestry of understanding, compromise, and serenity. Consequently, up until May 25, you bask under a protective aura, warding off adversaries and naysayers. This period also fortifies your bonds to artistry and design and paves the way for favorable outcomes in any legal entanglements that might surface.

As May 26 dawns, Jupiter, for the span of a year, ventures into the vibrant realm of Gemini. In this transit, he brings you into the territory that resonates with your very essence, the domain overseen by Pluto, your guiding luminary: the spheres of transformation, in-depth exploration, intimacy, sensuality, and the profound ability to nurture others in amplifying their skills and wealth. For an entire revolution around the sun, Jupiter aligns you with your inner mage and mystic. The ambiance is charged with enchantment, conjuring marvels from the void. It's an opportune phase for judicious investments, discerning your true calling, and syncing with the forces that truly stir your soul. Welcome this enticing dance of passion and intimacy!

BATTLEGROUNDS PROCEDURES—ECLIPSE AND CREATURES OF THE NIGHT

This is super important, so buckle up. From December 2021 through July 13, 2023, the North Node, revered as the Dragon's Head, beckoned you to prioritize relationships, even at the expense of self. With the South Node settled in Scorpio, it was a challenging transit, to say the least. But as the winds shifted in July 2023, and they will persist until January 2025, the Dragon has chosen to wing his way into the sector of your chart associated with work, service, health, routine, coworkers, employees, and selfless acts. Now is the moment to champion the greater good, rise in your professional realm, enhance rapport with coworkers, and elevate your health and nutrition regimen. Such is the bounty the Dragon pledges.

Meanwhile, the South Node, often visualized as the Dragon's Tail, beseeches you to disengage from feelings of solitude, and break away from entrenched habits, or any escapist tendencies. You're encouraged to side-step aspirations of heightened mysticism or spirituality, instead, focus on channeling the likes of Mother Teresa, Mary Poppins, or the supernanny. In your pursuit to serve others, the Dragon reminds you not to neglect your own self-care.

With the North Node nestled in Aries, it's a golden opportunity to draw inspiration from the sign that is ruled by Mars, your co-ruler. Embrace the mantra "I Am," while still sidestepping egocentric tendencies. It's paramount to assert your identity and leadership, especially within your work sphere. Seize the initiative, advocate for that raise, or undertake more responsibilities.

For context, the North Node previously occupied this same celestial space during 2005–2006 and 1986–1987. What did you experience back then with work, health, and service?

During eclipses you'll experience events quickening dramatically. Here are the coordinates and key dates to monitor as you navigate the year:

- **Lunar Eclipse in Libra, March 24–25**: The Moon lights up your imagination and gives you a rare window into your subconscious, past lifetime memories and skills and plots of hidden enemies. At the same time the Sun shines on your work and service, allowing you to push forward and bring to completion projects at work. This is the original Full Moon of Moses (Passover) and Jesus (Last Supper), a time of liberation and ending bondage. As mentioned before, Passover in 2024 is delayed due to issues with the Lunar calendar.
- **Total Solar Eclipse in Aries, April 8**: This is a tough New Moon since it takes place during Mercury retrograde. Both the Moon (mama) and Sun (daddy) are focusing on service, work, health, and diet. A good time to reboot a project in work you failed to complete in the past.
- **Partial Lunar Eclipse, September 17–18**: Pisces Moon opposite Sun in Virgo (Harvest Full Moon). This eclipse is much easier for you to

handle. You might feel a push and pull between the need to focus on your children (priority) versus your company or friends. You might be harvesting whatever you planted in March/April.

- **Annular Solar Eclipse, October 2**: Libra New Moon. A great time for peacemaking, diplomacy, or to start a new relationship or romantic love. The energies provide a rare window into your past lives, offering both protection against hidden enemies and those who harbor ill intentions towards you. There could be a meeting with a soulmate from a past lifetime.

ORANGE ALERT! SHAPESHIFTERS AND TRICKSTERS

When Mercury retrogrades, he takes on his trickster and shapeshifter role. It's a cosmic cue to pause and recalibrate. Make sure to bring your spacecraft to a halt and start flying in reverse. I know, it can be hard on the neck having to look back or relying on your reverse camera mode. Anticipate delays, energetic and emotional traffic jams. It's the worst time to sign documents or start a new project. But you know all this if you carefully read the first part of your pilot manual.

The year's initial two days may find you struggling to ignite your spacecraft due to Mercury's stationary stance in Sagittarius. This positioning may bring about financial tensions and challenges to your sense of self-worth. If someone questions your values or abilities, you might find yourself becoming particularly assertive or even unyielding. So, brace yourself; the commencement of 2024 might test your financial stability and confidence. Mercury will retrograde again in Sagittarius from November 25 to December 16, therefore, remain vigilant about your financial dealings at that period again, especially if traveling abroad. During this period, potential misunderstandings with in-laws, mentors, or students might also arise.

2024's first significant Mercury retrograde spans from April 1 to 26, coinciding with a potent eclipse that reaches its peak on April 8. With both the eclipse and retrograde occurring in Aries, a sign overseen by your esteemed leader, Mars, expect heightened miscommunications or misunderstandings, particularly in your professional sphere or with team members. Prioritize your health, with a focus on your nervous system, vital organs, and diet. This phase offers a prime opportunity to revisit, refine, and perhaps even reinitiate past work endeavors that hadn't reached fruition earlier.

Between August 4 and 14, Mercury's retrograde in Virgo, the zodiac's vigilant caretaker. As you navigate this period, hone in on your health, dietary choices, and professional responsibilities. Additionally, this retrograde may influence your interactions with acquaintances, friends, governmental personnel, organizational associates, and even your digital companions like computers and phones. From August 15–29, Mercury, the ever shapeshifter, retrogrades in Leo. Anticipate potential theatrics and drama in your professional life. Leo's energies may not always gel well with yours, leading to potential ego tussles with colleagues or those in positions of authority. Tread with caution and tact, especially when engaging with higher-ups.

Summary of Mercury Retrograde Dates

- January 1–January 2: Sagittarius.
- April 1–26: Aries (Red Alert around April 8 due to a total solar eclipse).
- August 4–14: Retrograde in Virgo.
- August 14–29 Retrograde in Leo.
- November 25–December 16 Sagittarius (Red Alert from December 6–16 since Mars is retrograde).

RED ALERT! SHIELDS UP

Mars often gets a bad rap. As the co-ruler of Scorpio—represented by the "Death" Tarot card—and the unequivocal ruler of Aries, the sign symbolizing war, Mars, your ruler, has long been linked with destruction and chaos. His Tarot representation, "The Tower," illustrates people tumbling from a burning building, which hardly seems promising. However, fewer realize that Mars was also revered as the ancient god of vegetation, seeds, and planting. So, Mars does have his benevolent side too.

As 2024 draws to a close, Mars will begin his retrograde in Leo starting December 6, 2024, and will only go direct (in Cancer) on February 24, 2025.

As such, it's advisable to complete your significant tasks for the year before December 6, and calling it a year, go have fun and relax. If Mars is the god of planting, then during his retrograde, it's an ideal time to weed out and discard what's no longer necessary in your life.

As Mars goes into retrograde in Leo, it may stir up tensions and disagreements in your professional life, particularly with those in leadership roles or positions of authority. Ego conflicts may become a recurring theme during this period. Leverage your inherent qualities of discretion and privacy. Instead of discussing your future plans or intentions, it might be wiser to share only your accomplished deeds. Mars' retrograde can sometimes cloud others' perceptions, leading them to misconstrue your actions and intentions. Navigate this phase with caution and discernment. Since Mars' shadow begins on October 5, it would be prudent to be more vigilant from this point forward. It's as if you're navigating treacherous straits or passing through an asteroid belt. Stay alert and keep your shield up.

Below you will find Mars' Table Coordinates that highlight areas in your life where you can channel your passion, energy, and leadership. However, remember that wherever Mars is positioned, he can also introduce conflict and strife in those aspects of life.

- **November 24, 2023, Mars adventures into Sagittarius**: Embrace a surge of energy surrounding your finances and talents. This is a prime moment to shine and gain accolades for your expertise. However, tread lightly with teachers, students, foreigners, and in-laws.
- **January 4, 2024, Mars climbs Capricorn**: Mars exalted and ready to inject your ventures with unmatched vigor. This is your cue to propel your business forward, amplify sales, or launch that marketing initiative. Nurture the bonds with relatives, roommates, and neighbors. Revisit contracts if they seem amiss. Be careful of conflict with superiors.
- **February 13, 2024, Mars rendezvous with Aquarius**: Feel an added zest around friends, community, and organizations. Mars offers you the stamina to rejuvenate your dwelling or workspace. However, sidestep unnecessary family skirmishes.

- **March 22, 2024, Mars drifts to Pisces**: Watch for possible tiffs with your children or romantic liaisons. It's an ideal phase for sports and vigorous activities near or around water. Yet, curb any overzealous impulses or risks.
- **April 30, 2024, Mars homecoming in Aries**: Mars in his elemental essence, propelling you to reconnect with your physique, leadership, and spark new ventures. Your zeal for work escalates, matched with an earnest drive to serve. Yet, be wary of potential injuries, mishaps, or altercations, especially on the work front.
- **June 9, 2024, Mars marches to Taurus**: While the energy pace moderates, your resolve stands unyielding. Persistence is key now, bearing fruit in the material domain. Anticipate possible discord with partners, be it in business or personal spheres. Opponents might turn up their intensity.
- **July 20, 2024, Mars' flight in Gemini**: Channel your energies on your messages, enterprises, and agreements. This is an apt phase to assertively communicate and express your needs. Mars kindles heightened passion, echoing the core attributes of your sign: intimacy, sexuality, research, shared resources, healing, and mystic realms.
- **September 4, 2024, Mars swims through Cancer**: Though Mars feels a tad uneasy here, be watchful of being overly guarded or indirectly confrontational. Family ties, especially with in-laws, might waver. Nevertheless, this Mars phase favors scholarly pursuits, travel, and standing up for your convictions.
- **November 4, 2024, Mars parties in Leo**: Allow Mars to rejuvenate your spirit, heightening your vitality. The professional realm brims with potential, making it prime to seek advancements or pioneer initiatives. Yet, handle relations with higher-ups delicately. Stay alert, for envy or subversion might lurk close.

LOVE INTEREST AND ALLIES

Venus loves you, she does—it's in her nature. However, she has her moments of whimsiness and can act out. She's not your mama who adores you no matter what, she has her list of conditions, like a spiritual prenuptial agreement.

Below is the list of where Venus journeys this year, offering insights into potential areas of assistance in financial support, creative boosts, enhanced self-worth, and perhaps even a romantic connection. We're fortunate this year, as Venus remains direct, avoiding her retrograde phase. When she graces your sign (September 23–October 16), you'll likely notice a heightened sense of beauty, feel and look better, experience a stronger connection to your talent, and perhaps an improved financial situation. Essentially, you're channeling the goddess of beauty and sensuality. However, this might also make you more susceptible to spending money or a tad more self-absorbed than usual. Jupiter and Venus come together on these love-filled days: May 22–23. A great time for art, dating, meeting the love of your life, or just feeling good.

Below you'll find her celestial coordinates and the areas of your life she'll likely influence, ushering in some good fortune and support from allies and loved ones.

- **December 29, 2023 Venus journeys into Sagittarius**: Harness the energy to enhance bonds with educators, in-laws, learners, and those from afar. Venus, the divine goddess of love and prosperity, extends an invitation to bolster your finances, reconnect with your innate talents, and fortify your self-worth.
- **January 23, 2024, Venus ascends to Capricorn**: Under the watchful gaze of Venus, the goddess of love, anticipate the blossoming of fresh business endeavors, especially those involving wiser or older collaborators. Paint your marketing and sales with an artistic brushstroke, and let creativity flow, drawing closer ties with kinsfolk, roommates, and neighbors.
- **February 16, 2024, Venus aligns with Aquarius**: A period to cultivate friendships, embrace joy, champion spontaneity, and harvest the fruits of innovation. Venus showers blessings on your home and kin, setting a conducive mood for revamping your living and workspaces.
- **March 11, 2024, Venus exalts in Pisces**: There are illuminated pathways in finance and arts. Allow Venus' guidance to birth creations,

discover romance, rekindle childhood wonders, and deepen connections with the young.

- **April 5, 2024, Venus ignites Aries**: While Aries might not be Venus' cherished companion, especially during cosmic disturbances, she beckons you to unleash your leadership skills. Fortify work relations and ornament your workspace with an artistic touch.

- **April 29, 2024, Venus returns home to Taurus**: Bask in the glow of Venus in her domicile. Let your abilities radiate, alongside your self-value. A harmonious phase unfolds, beckoning new allies and resolving disputes. A great time for dating, winning disputes, and making compromises.

- **May 23, 2024, Venus flirts with Gemini**: Venus crafts conduits in marketing, writing, sales, and public outreach. Immerse yourself in collaborative ventures, both artistic and fiscal, and explore the depths of connection. Consider it a propitious phase for couples' therapy.

- **June 17, 2024, Venus sojourns in Cancer**: Within Cancer, Venus nurtures bonds, especially familial ones. Reap her blessings in academia, and relationships with mentors, foreigners, and in-laws. Great for travel.

- **July 11, 2024, Venus lusters in Leo**: Romantic vibes prevail. Engross yourself in artistic ventures and athletic pursuits, preferably paired. Under Venus' sparkle, careers flourish; let artistry guide you to prosper. Elevate ties with superiors and ponder a salary appraisal.

- **August 5, 2024, Venus fine-tunes Virgo**: Though Virgo's austerity may slightly dim Venus' sense of style, she still nurtures camaraderie and refines your professional image. Collaboration in art, especially in digital realms, can flourish—a prime era for social media creativity.

- **August 29, 2024, Venus equilibriums Libra**: Rejoice as Venus graces her home sign, symbolizing justice. Revive and heal partnerships, tap into forgotten skills, and encounter souls from previous lives.

- **September 23, 2024, Venus deep dives into Scorpio**: Though Venus treads cautiously in Scorpio, she generously aids in your personal transformation. Revel in her gifts to reinvent, rebrand, and embellish your surroundings and self. You are shining bright, let everyone see you.

- **October 17, 2024, Venus returns to Sagittarius**: Harness Venus energy to mend ties with scholars, educators, foreigners, and in-laws. Travel and arts education beckon, with prosperity linked to creativity.
- **November 11, 2024, Venus climbs Capricorn**: Engage with older people or figures of authority. With Venus as your guide, you can heal relationships with relatives, neighbors, and roommates. Inject artistry into your business and writing.
- **December 7, 2024, Venus befriends Aquarius**: Prioritize companionship and elevate your stature in your company or organization. It's a golden period to infuse aesthetics into your personal and professional domains, enhancing familial bonds in the process. Great for remodeling.

ALIEN ENCOUNTER PROTOCOL

As a cosmic navigator, you are bound to encounter what some might call aliens. But to be intergalactically correct, let's refer to them as "extraterrestrial sentient beings." These beings are represented by Uranus, the Awakener. Since 2018, Uranus has journeyed through Taurus, your opposite sign, weaving a tapestry of unexpected twists, particularly in your primary relationships, which encompasses both business and personal partnerships. Perhaps you've yearned for liberation, desiring more personal space, or the tables turned, and it was your partner seeking freedom from the ties that bind. Regardless, this dance of highs and lows with all your contractual bonds remains a theme for the coming two years.

Uranus mission is to rejuvenate your relationships, to add some spark. If you are single, he might introduce a significant someone to accompany. Thankfully, Jupiter extends a hand, assisting you in navigating Uranus's revelations during the year's initial five months. However, with Uranus traversing Taurus, your mirror sign, you might find yourself more attuned to his invigorating energy. He encourages you to sprinkle your relationships with laughter and spontaneity. Moreover, he offers guidance in freeing yourself from antiquated familial patterns tied to love and partnership.

Uranus nudges you to perceive through your five senses in novel ways: indulge in diverse music genres, savor unfamiliar cuisines, explore fresh income avenues, and refine the manner in which you present yourself to the world. Embracing the unique, venturing into uncharted territories, and exploring new horizons will allow you to reap the most benefits from this once-in-an-84-year transit.

CONCLUSION

In 2024, you stand at the cusp of a transformative journey centered around relationships and love. Saturn, ever the wise mentor, strives to illuminate the path to genuine happiness and creativity, a reconnection with your inner child. This year, your children or grandchildren might command more of your attention, heralding a reminder to invite unbridled creativity and joy into your existence. The Dragon promises serendipitous moments in your work and health. In the year's second half, let Jupiter mend, balance, and magnetize beneficial partnerships, be it in love or profession. In addition, there could be major changes with family members as well as relocation due to Pluto's transition into your abode.

TAROT: DEATH

This card represents the transformational aspects of Scorpio and the importance of allowing death and resurrection into your life. This year the old ideals of happiness are dying and a new way to connect to joy arises instead.

HEBREW LETTER: NUN

Meaning: The "snake." Scorpio is the only sign with three glyphs representing its essence: the scorpion, snake, and eagle. The snake sheds its skin and symbolizes transformation, healing, and magic.

SAGITTARIUS AND SAGITTARIUS RISING

The Journey Homeward

MISSION (NOT) IMPOSSIBLE—YOUR ASSIGNMENT CARD

Sagittarius—The prophet, explorer, social reformer, the zodiac's Indiana Jones, lover of wisdom, Guardian of Truth, your mission in 2024 is to transport Pluto, also known as the nuclear reactor of the zodiac, from the Capricorn star system into the Aquarius nebula. While you're a beacon of optimism, embodying the "Yes I Can" spirit, this year presents you with a considerable challenge. You must confront Saturn, the Lord of the (Three) Rings and Master of Karma, who is currently residing in the realm of your chart dedicated to home and family. Indeed, you are a born explorer, always seeking the next great adventure. However, since March of 2023, Saturn has impelled you to anchor down at home, urging you to address deep-seated emotional challenges, and battle childhood insecurities. Much like Agamemnon, held back from sailing to Troy, you too find yourself tethered, compelled to address issues of security, property, ancestral karma, and family ties. Imagine Indiana Jones, forever the adventurer, now tasked with parenting triplets. We'll delve deeper into the challenges posed by other planetary placements later. For now, let's focus on your primary mission for the Zodiac Federation.

Your mission for 2024, amidst the cacophony of wailing triplets, is unequivocal yet perilous: You must transport Pluto, the Lord of the Underworld, into the realm of Aquarius, the sign of friendship, community, and innovation. From 2008 to 2024, Pluto resided in the sector of your chart concerned with finances, self-worth, talents, and skills. This phase was challenging, especially for someone as affirmative as you. You were nudged to adopt frugality, re-evaluate your earning methodologies, and possibly invest in honing your skills. You might have even had your ego bruised and felt lower self-esteem. There were significant transformations, both endings and beginnings, in your financial stature, innate talents, and values. So, in retrospect, ushering Pluto away from Capricorn might be a welcome change.

Come 2024, your task is to safely transport Pluto, the deity of death and rebirth, into the domain of your chart linked with communication, writing, marketing, and business. In essence, Pluto's influence will compel you to introspect over the next two decades: What is the essence of your message? What narrative do you wish to broadcast to the world? As a mutable fire sign and the overseer of mass media and publishing, what stories do you wish to share? In what manner do you intend to communicate, promote, and resonate with the masses? Representing the embodiment of truth in its purest form, you bear a profound responsibility over information and how it's disseminated.

Your Assignment Card: Safely transport Pluto from Capricorn (representing the past) into Aquarius (symbolizing the future). While it might seem a daunting task, remember that since 2008, Pluto has been instrumental in reshaping your values and skills. Now, harness this transformative energy to craft your message for humanity, your magnum opus. Accept your role as the philosopher, prophet, and teacher; it's time to pen your manifesto.

Pluto's Pickup Location

From June 11, 2023, to January 21, 2024, and between September 2 to November 19, Pluto is located in Capricorn in the sector of your chart that relates to money, talents, values, self-worth, skills and gifts. There is still time to transform and change the way you make your living, so that it's congruent with your creed and truth.

From January 22–August 31 and November 20–January 2044 (final-destination), Pluto needs to be dropped in Aquarius, the sector in your chart that relates to business, communication, information, data, words, network, relatives (especially siblings and their offspring), roommates and neighbors. Pay extra attention to the contracts you sign and businesses you create.

OPERATING LIMITATIONS: ENCOUNTERS WITH YOUR ANTAGONIST

As highlighted previously, from March 2023 until February 2026, Saturn, the Lord Karma, voyages through Pisces. In this role, the Lord of the (Three) Rings navigates a water sign that squares off with your fiery tendencies. Consequently, you may frequently find yourself pushed into taking actions that you don't necessarily align with. Moreover, Saturn is currently traversing the Nadir of your chart—the foundation of your edifice, akin to the basement where you've stored your insecurities and where the boogeyman lurks. Confronting these deep-rooted emotional issues will demand every ounce of your celebrated courage, tenacity, and creativity. It's as if you're being beckoned to journey back to the formative years of your childhood and reprogram yourself.

However, amidst these challenges lies a glimmer of hope. By bravely addressing these innermost emotional specters and coming to terms with your ancestral karma, you stand to unearth profound treasures including genetic gifts bestowed by your ancestors. This introspective work paves the way for unparalleled growth, notably in your professional sphere (during the initial five months of the year) and in personal relationships (in the latter half of 2024). And it's essential to note that Saturn's influence in this sector isn't solely about confronting past shadows. His presence could also signify joyous milestones such as expanding your family, creating a homestead, purchasing a home, relocating, or even resolving long-standing familial issues. Consider this period as an emotional detox, and you, undoubtedly, are primed for this transformative journey.

To gain further insight into Saturn's influence, reflect upon the years 1995-1996. Recognize what Saturn nudged you towards then and consider the major challenges you confronted during that period. They might hold clues to the core issues emerging in 2024 and 2025.The good news is that the transit of Saturn in Pisces can be dealt with much easier if you can allocate time to sleep or rest longer. Einstein, who was a Pisces, spoke frequently about the restorative powers of short siestas. Recent studies confirmed that indeed the brain can expand during a short midday nap. Also, try to keep a dream journal, you will find much wisdom channeled through these nightly flights. You can also find solace in groups that practice yoga, dance, movement, mysticism or meditation. Spend time near and in water as much as you can. Imagine where you want to be and have faith, the rest would follow.

MENTORS AND TUTORS: ENCOUNTER WITH YOUR MASTER

In "*Rock 'n' Roll Suicide*," Bowie, with the fervor of a musical prophet, declares, "Oh no love, you are not alone, no matter what or who you've been, no matter when or where you've seen, all the knives seem to lacerate your brain, I've had my share, I'll help you with the pain. You're not alone!" He might as well have channeled Jupiter!

Jupiter, your ruler, concurs. He stands steadfast by your side, and this year, for the initial five months, he journeys through Taurus. This sign holds relevance to your work, service, health, dietary choices, relationship with pets, and daily routines. While Jupiter functions as your personal mentor, harnessing his wisdom, his sojourn in Taurus requires proactive engagement on your part. His blessings are not simply handed out; they must be earned. So, even as you glimpse expansive opportunities in work as well as in a healing journey, you'll be summoned to align with a greater purpose—something transcending your individual needs and desires. However, amidst these calls to a higher mission, anticipate positive and practical developments like salary hikes, job promotions, and an overall chance to improve your health. To fully enjoy these rewards, be sure to cultivate a balanced lifestyle and heed the earlier mentioned teachings of Saturn.

Come May 26, for the succeeding year, Jupiter embarks on his expedition into Gemini, your complementary and opposite sign. This shift heralds promising tidings for your partnerships, be it in business or personal life. If you've been single, there could be a change, ushering in romance, especially with the Dragon traveling the area of your chart associated with love and happiness. For those already tethered in relationships, anticipate delightful enhancements, or potentially a collaborative venture at work. Furthermore, Jupiter offers a protective shield, mitigating challenges from adversaries or providing relief in legal matters. His benevolence seeks to fortify all your primary connections. However, exercise caution not to overextend or dilute your energies. Jupiter is considered in exile when he transits in Gemini, and at times, you too might feel like a stranger in a strange land.

BATTLEGROUNDS PROCEDURES—ECLIPSE AND CREATURES OF THE NIGHT

Buckle up, this is important. Between December 2021 and July 13, 2023, the North Node, often referred to as the Dragon's Head, sought to impart essential lessons about your health, employment, dietary habits, and daily regimen. And certainly, for all the diligence shown during that period, Jupiter will reward you during the initial five months of this year. But the story evolves: from July 2023 until January 2025, the Dragon takes flight into the region of your chart associated with children, romantic love, joy, athletic pursuits, risky endeavors, hobbies, leisure, and artistic expression. This signals the beckoning of your inner child, a rejuvenation of spirit that promises a reconnection to happiness. With Jupiter fortifying your relationships and the Dragon infusing romance, the celestial energies are surely smiling upon you.

The Dragon's location and sign points to our soul's deepest yearnings. This year, it's a clarion call for happiness, love, and romantic endeavors. Reflect upon the desires of your inner child and strive to fulfill them. Furthermore, address your inherent talents this year, especially those that are hereditary and could be harnessed professionally. Engage in physical activities; perhaps pick up a new sport. Your primary focus should shift towards nurturing children and cultivating cheerfulness, setting aside the incessant demands of your company, friends, or circle of peers. This shift will be profoundly evident during the eclipse seasons.

The North Node occupied the position in your chart during 2005–2006 and 1986–1987. To truly tap into the North Node's potential, embody the spirit of Aries, your fellow fire sign. Embrace his mantra "I Am," and focus on developing your leadership skills and identity.

The eclipse periods will quicken these processes by ushering in a whirlwind of events, demanding a firm grip on your spacecraft's navigational stick. Expect celestial turbulence. Here are some significant dates:

- **Lunar Eclipse in Libra, March 24–25**: The Sun lights up your creativity, romantic love, and connection to children, while the Moon shines on your friendships, organization, and organizations. However, there could be some conflicts between your children or lover's need (prioritize) to those of your corporation, friends, or company, (less important). This is the original Full Moon of Moses (Passover) and Jesus (Last Supper), a time of liberation and ending bondage. As mentioned before, Passover in 2024 is delayed due to issues with the Lunar calendar.
- **Total Solar Eclipse in Aries, April 8**: Falling during Mercury's retrograde, this eclipse might render you more susceptible to irritation. However, both the Moon (mama) and Sun (daddy) are focusing you on love, children, and creativity.
- **Partial Lunar Eclipse, September 17–18**: Pisces Moon opposite Sun in Virgo (Harvest Full Moon). This eclipse is much harder since both square off with your sign. Once again, you might feel a push and pull between home and career. You might be harvesting whatever you planted in March/April.
- **Annular Solar Eclipse, October**: Libra New Moon. A great time for peacemaking, diplomacy, or a new relationship or romantic love. Perhaps a new friendship or an offer from a company is entering your life.

ORANGE ALERT! SHAPESHIFTERS AND TRICKSTERS

When Mercury retrogrades, he takes on his trickster and shapeshifter role. It's a cosmic cue to pause and recalibrate. Make sure to bring your spacecraft to a halt and start flying in reverse. I know, it can be hard on the neck having to look back or relying on your reverse camera mode. Anticipate delays, energetic and emotional traffic jams. It's the worst time to sign documents or start a new project. But you know all this if you carefully read the first part of your pilot manual.

On the first two days of the year, you may find it challenging to power up your spacecraft. This is because Mercury, the messenger, is stationary, in your sign, and in exile as well. This cosmic position might make you feel lethargic, with a reduced resistance to both emotional and physical ailments, potentially casting a shadow over various spheres of your life. This celestial configuration may also cause a disconnect in communication, leading to misunderstandings with those you aim to lead. The same Mercury retrograde induced haziness will repeat at the end of the year between November 25 to December 16, as Mercury will pace backwards in your sign once again. This period can be especially perplexing; you may grapple with indecisiveness and doubt your instincts. Disagreements or miscommunications with in-laws, mentors, students, or individuals from diverse backgrounds might also crop up. Be extra careful if you plan to travel or while making important presentations.

The foremost Mercury retrograde of 2024 spans from April 1 to 26. Taking place during a potent eclipse (April 8), this retrograde promises to be exceedingly intense. Given that both the eclipse and the retrograde transpire in Aries, a fellow fire sign, you have a familiar energy to navigate. Nevertheless, tread carefully, for disruptions might arise in your romantic endeavors, creative projects, or with your children. Additionally, there's an amplified risk of injuries during athletic activities.

The subsequent retrograde, occurring between August 4 and 14, unfolds in Virgo, the zodiac's quintessential caretaker. This phase might prove a tad more challenging, potentially propelling you into actions you'd rather not take. Your career might become a hotbed of complexities, with potential misalignments with superiors, father figures, or bosses. From August 15 to 29, Mercury continues retrograding but shifts into theatrical Leo. This phase could usher in heightened drama, particularly with educators, students, in-laws, or those from foreign lands. If travel is on your agenda during this time, exercise added caution to circumvent potential pitfalls.

Summary of Mercury Retrograde Dates

- January 1–January 2: Sagittarius.
- April 1–26: Aries (Red Alert around April 8 due to a total solar eclipse).
- August 4–14: Retrograde in Virgo.
- August 14–29 Retrograde in Leo.
- November 25–December 16 Sagittarius (Red Alert from December 6–16 since Mars is retrograde).

RED ALERT! SHIELDS UP

Mars often gets a bad rap. As the co-ruler of Scorpio—represented by the "Death" Tarot card—and the unequivocal ruler of Aries, the sign symbolizing war, Mars has long been linked with destruction and chaos. His Tarot representation, "The Tower," illustrates people tumbling from a burning building, which hardly seems promising. However, fewer realize that Mars was also revered as the ancient god of vegetation, seeds, and planting. So, Mars does have his benevolent side too.

As 2024 draws to a close, Mars will begin his retrograde in Leo starting December 6, 2024, and will only go direct (in Cancer) on February 24, 2025. As such, it's advisable to complete your significant tasks for the year before December 6, and calling it a year, go have fun and relax. If Mars is the god of planting, then during his retrograde, it's an ideal time to weed out and discard what's no longer necessary in your life.

Since Mars is retrograding in Leo, he can cause conflict and strife with in-laws, mentors, teachers, and foreigners, all aspects that your sign is associated with. You might also experience betrayal and disloyalties. Perhaps a sense that life isn't fair. When Mars retrogrades people can easily misunderstand and misinterpret your actions and intentions, so take heed.

Since Mars' shadow begins on October 5, it would be prudent to be more vigilant from this point forward. It's as if you're navigating treacherous straits or passing through an asteroid belt. Stay alert and keep your shield up.

Below you will find Mars' Table Coordinates that highlight areas in your life where you can channel your passion, energy, and leadership. However, remember that wherever Mars is positioned, he can also introduce conflict and strife in those aspects of life. When Mars occupies your sign (November 24, 2023–January 3, 2024), you might feel invigorated and passionate, but also more impulsive, aggressive, impatient, and susceptible to conflicts and accidents.

- **November 24, 2023, Mars enters Sagittarius**: There's a surge of energy permeating all aspects of your life. This period beckons you to take the lead, initiate actions, and truly embody your identity. Physical activities flourish, however, be careful of overexertion and potential injuries. Embrace a gentle pace in your movements and conversations.
- **January 4, 2024, Mars climbs Capricorn**: Mars is at his mightiest in this position, empowering you to boost your finances and fostering confidence in your abilities. This alignment can also usher in opportunities to reach your objectives.
- **February 13, 2024, Mars ventures into Aquarius**: The atmosphere buzzes with heightened energy centered around friendships, community ties, and collective endeavors. Let Mars motivate you to launch a new enterprise, promote your business, and communicate your ideas. However, stay vigilant against potential disputes with relatives, roommates, or neighbors.
- **March 22, 2024, Mars flows into Pisces**: Domestic arenas might witness tensions or disagreements. While household gadgets might act up, it's a conducive period for remodeling and enhancing your living space.
- **April 30, 2024, Mars ignites Aries**: Mars resonates powerfully here, enhancing romantic pursuits, athletic engagements, and facilitating a deep connection with your inner child. Creativity flows abundantly.

But, in his fiery essence, Mars might instigate clashes with your loved ones or offspring.

- **June 9, 2024, Mars anchors in Taurus**: The energy might be unhurried, but it's unwavering. Rewards come to those who persevere, especially in tangible endeavors. Mars lends a hand in spearheading work projects; however, balance is key to avoid unsettling coworkers or employees. Healthwise, remain alert to inflammation, fevers, and potential injuries.
- **July 20, 2024, Mars soars into Gemini**: The spotlight now is on effective communication, business pursuits, and building bridges. Relationships could face turbulence if not nurtured by quality time. Also, stay guarded against potential adversaries, as their aggressiveness might escalate.
- **September 4, 2024, Mars sails into Cancer**: This isn't Mars' most favored spot, potentially leading to heightened defensiveness or passive-aggressive tendencies. Nevertheless, it's a prime time for investments, tapping into the skills of others, and financial collaborations. It's also a period conducive for in-depth research, exploration, and passionate endeavors.
- **November 4, 2024, Mars celebrates in Leo**: Experience a rejuvenated vitality and zest for life with Mars in Leo. There's an added appetite for travel and education. However, ensure harmonious ties with teachers, in-laws, or mentees. If wanderlust beckons, steer clear of unnecessary confrontations during your journeys.

LOVE INTEREST AND ALLIES

Venus loves you, she does—it's in her nature. However, she has her moments of whimsiness and can act out. She's not your mama who adores you no matter what, she has her list of conditions, like a spiritual prenuptial agreement.

Below is the list of where Venus journeys this year, offering insights into potential areas of assistance in financial support, creative boosts, enhanced self-worth, and perhaps even a romantic connection. We're fortunate this year, as Venus remains direct, avoiding her retrograde phase. This year Venus graces your sign twice, December 29 to January 22 and

October 17–November 10. You'll likely notice a heightened sense of beauty, feel and look better, experience a stronger connection to your talent, and perhaps an improved financial situation. Essentially, you're channeling the goddess of beauty and sensuality. However, this might also make you more susceptible to spending money or a tad more self-absorbed than usual. Jupiter and Venus come together on these love-filled days: May 22–23. A great time for art, dating, meeting the love of your life, or just feeling good.

Below you'll find her celestial coordinates and the areas of your life she'll likely influence, ushering in some good fortune and support from allies and loved ones.

- **December 29, 2023, Venus graces Sagittarius**: Embrace this time to fortify relationships with educators, in-laws, students, and those from abroad. With the goddess of love and prosperity accompanying you, it's the perfect moment for personal reinvention and rebranding. You are shining!
- **January 23, 2024, Venus ascends Capricorn**: Venus bestows her charm, unveiling new business opportunities, particularly with seasoned or older individuals. Let her guide you toward a raise, promotions, and pathways to showcase your unique skills and gifts. It's an inspiring phase to hone your abilities and make money in new ways.
- **February 16, 2024, Venus aligns with Aquarius**: Revel in making fresh connections, indulging in spontaneous joys, and cherishing intellectual insights. Venus casts her blessings over your business, communication and writing, infusing creativity into your marketing and sales efforts. Bonds with relatives, roommates, and neighbors are poised to thrive. As you search for your message this year, this period may bring clarity.
- **March 11, 2024, Venus is exalted in Pisces**: The celestial muse assists in financial matters and beckons your innate artistic flair. Consider delving into home renovations and exploring family talents passed down through generations. It's a harmonious time to nurture familial ties.
- **April 5, 2024, Venus embarks on Aries**: Venus finds Aries a challenging companion, especially amidst eclipses and retrogrades. Yet,

relationships with offspring may flourish, and a surge of creativity awaits. Romance may knock on your door. Revel in the moment; Venus craves enjoyment.

- **April 29, 2024, Venus luxuriates in Taurus**: At home in Taurus, Venus amplifies your talents and instills a robust sense of self-worth. Adorn your workspace with beauty and imagination. Collaborations at work prosper, and it's a fitting moment to discuss raises or partnerships. Yet, moderation in dietary indulgences is advised.

- **May 23, 2024, Venus dallies in Gemini**: Your communicative efforts, be it in marketing, writing, or public relations, gain an artistic, Venusian touch. Harmony pervades your primary relationships and professional liaisons. It's a wonderful time for compromise and reconciliation. Venus harmonizes and attracts partnerships in your life.

- **June 17, 2024, Venus dances with Cancer**: Foster bonds with those you hold dear. Let Venus reignite passion and intimacy in your relationships. Collaborative artistic and financial projects flourish.

- **July 11, 2024, Venus revels in Leo**: Love electrifies the atmosphere. Dive into creativity, sports, and travel, preferably with companions. Relationships with mentors, teachers, and students are poised for growth. If you have a message, it's prime time to broadcast it.

- **August 5, 2024, Venus hones Virgo**: Venus may feel restrained in meticulous Virgo. Yet, she continues to enhance your professional image, strengthening your rapport with superiors and older individuals.

- **August 29, 2024, Venus graces Libra**: In her element, Venus promotes justice, diplomacy, and reconciliation. Relationships with friends and colleagues receive a healing touch. Reconcile with technology and consider digital upgrades.

- **September 23, 2024, Venus probes Scorpio**: While Scorpio's depths can overwhelm Venus, this period amplifies your imagination and recalls gifts and skills from past incarnations. You might reunite with souls or talents from past lifetimes. Release toxic relationships.

- **October 17, 2024, Venus circles back to Sagittarius**: Relationships with educators, students, and diverse cultures thrive. Embrace her guidance to refine your persona, update your digital presence, and enhance your wardrobe.

- **November 11, 2024, Venus scales Capricorn**: Build connections with the wise and experienced. Venus promises prosperity and an avenue to broadcast your unique gifts. Seek a new skill to invest in. There could be a boost in your income.
- **December 7, 2024, Venus allies with Aquarius**: Prioritize friendships and fortify your position within your community. It's a prosperous phase for creative endeavors, marketing, and networking.

ALIEN ENCOUNTER PROTOCOL

As a cosmic navigator, you are bound to encounter what some might call aliens. But to be intergalactically correct, let's refer to them as "extra-terrestrial sentient beings." These beings are represented by Uranus, the Awakener. Since 2018, Uranus has journeyed through Taurus, ushering in unforeseen shifts, particularly in areas of your work, pets, health, diet, routine, and your interactions with service—both given and received. Uranus seeks to rejuvenate your professional realm, jolting you from stagnation, all in anticipation of 2026 when he will venture into your opposite sign, Gemini, and that would be far more intense.

Uranus's sojourn in Taurus will persistently nudge you over the next two years to revolutionize your work. This isn't merely about staying current; it's about leaping forward. Given your sign's prophetic nature, ponder upon where your industry or profession might stand a decade from now and initiate that vision in the present. ChatGPT 14? Rest assured, that's not just a quirky typo.

As Uranus reconfigures your work dimensions, he also beckons you to reassess your diet and health, prompting a shift towards more contemporary, science-backed nutrition. It's a call to invigorate your health so you can get into peak form. Nevertheless, Uranus's essence is one of disruption, which can usher chaos, particularly if he discerns that the order and routine in your life lack genuine structure. Brace for some winds of change. Fortunately, with Jupiter lending a hand in refining your work for the initial five months of the year, navigating the reformation of your work and health from January to May might just be a smoother sail.

Moreover, Uranus nudges you to perceive through your five senses in novel ways: indulge in diverse music genres, savor unfamiliar cuisines, explore fresh income avenues, and refine the manner in which you present yourself to the world. Embracing the unique, venturing into uncharted territories, and exploring new horizons will allow you to reap the most benefits from this once-in-an-84-year transit.

CONCLUSION

In 2024, the cosmic currents anchor you, urging you to center on foundations—home, family, and the mending of ancestral legacies. Yet, you're not journeying this path in solitude. Jupiter, your guiding planet, introduces a potential partner in work or life during the year's latter half, even as the Dragon bestows his grace on your romantic pursuits and bonds with children. This year calls you to harness joy from your core, less wandering, more rootedness. Your pivotal task? Unearth the word—*logos*—the message, which Pluto urges you to disseminate over the forthcoming two decades. As Uranus reshapes your professional landscape and daily rhythms, it's to align with this very purpose. Now's the moment to reconnect with the whims and wonders of your inner child!

TAROT: TEMPERANCE

In 2024 you have one foot in Aquarius (future) and the other in Capricorn (past). You are tasked with finding temperance between the young and old. The card shows your angelic potential if you manage to navigate extremes.

HEBREW LETTER: SAMECH

Meaning: "Trust" and "support," as well as "nearby." The letter's shape resembles a chair's backrest. Sagittarius draws its optimism from the knowledge that life supports them. That support is granted whenever one comes "nearby" Oneness.

CAPRICORN AND
CAPRICORN RISING—I USE

First was the Word and the Word was God

MISSION (NOT) IMPOSSIBLE—YOUR
ASSIGNMENT CARD

Capricorn, master builder, the cosmic mason and Keeper of Tradition, the coming year beckons you to play the vital role of interstellar transporter. Your objective? To safely carry Pluto, the nuclear reactor of the zodiac, from your Capricorn constellation into the Aquarius nebula.

Having played host to Pluto, the Lord of Death and Rebirth since 2008, hasn't been a light task. Few, if any, could withstand such intensity. But in your grand cosmic design, you have been molded with unparalleled resilience. However, the challenge isn't over. This year Pluto will be on and off in your sign.

The world often misunderstands you, Capricorn. They link you with the stark Tarot image of "The Devil" and point fingers at Saturn, your ruler, whom many view as the Grand Malevolent. You're labeled calculated, frugal, and rigid. Yet, this perception stems from ignorance. Your zodiac position lies in winter's heart, when survival rests on foresight and prudence. The Devil? A manifestation of our primal fears and survival instincts. It's a profound cosmic misunderstanding you've had to bear.

Saturn's position in 2024 and 2025, calls for you to hone your self-representation, business, marketing and discovering your "logos," your word—message. It's an opportunity to reshape your narrative, especially now, when the daunting presence of Pluto is about to leave your realm.

From 2008 to 2024, Pluto's sojourn in Capricorn, an event spanning once in 250 years, upturned structures and definitions of success. Your foundations shook as Pluto relentlessly probed every facet of your existence, a sentiment especially felt between 2019 and 2021, when you had to also host Saturn in your realm. Memories of 2020, when both celestial bodies conjoined in your space, still linger. But now, as 2024 emerges, it's Aquarius' turn to host Pluto. It's okay to quietly say "good riddance."

This year, you're entrusted with the mighty task of transferring Pluto to a new domain in your chart, where finance, self-worth, and talent converge. As Pluto signifies transformation, anticipate a metamorphosis in the way you deal with finances, your talents and self-worth. However, this isn't just about dissolution; it's a deep excavation of passions, values, and latent skills. After Pluto's long haul in your sign, your identity has morphed, possibly demanding a fresh set of skills and avenues to generate wealth.

An intriguing consideration: with Pluto being synonymous with power, some Capricorns might resist relinquishing this influential planet. You'll observe this tug-of-war in global politics and personal spaces. Ensure you're not clinging to outdated power edifices, particularly in your professional realm. Embracing transformation, especially in monetary matters, is the need of the hour.

Your Assignment Card for 2024: Embark on the celestial voyage, transporting Pluto from Capricorn (representing the past) to Aquarius (symbolizing the future). Utilize the wisdom accrued since 2008 especially concerning your identity and self-awareness and materialize it, by exploring new talents and ways of making money. Courageously evolve and redefine your core values and the principles you champion.

Pluto's Pickup Location

From June 11, 2023, to January 21, 2024, and between September 2 to November 19, Pluto is located in Capricorn in the sector of your chart that relates to your body, personality, image, health, vitality, identity, leadership, self-awareness, and initiation.

From January 22–August 31 and then November 20–January 2044 (final-destination), Pluto needs to be dropped in Aquarius, the sector in your chart that relates to money, talents, skills, values, self-worth, and gifts.

OPERATING LIMITATIONS: ENCOUNTERS WITH YOUR ANTAGONIST

As previously noted, from March 2023 to February 2026, Saturn, the Lord of Karma and your often austere ruler, journeys through Pisces. During this time, the Three-Ringed Master finds himself meandering through the whimsical territory reminiscent of *Alice in Wonderland*, calling for you to temperate practicality with mysticism. The year 2024 stands out for you. As you release Pluto from your grasp, Saturn navigates Pisces, a sign that might puzzle your grounded nature. While you embrace the concrete, Pisces, with its dreamy landscapes, might seem nebulous and distant to you. Yet, Saturn's sojourn in Pisces offers a precious opportunity: to anchor your practicality in the seas of imagination and empathy. Over these two years, consider delving deeper into meditation and becoming receptive to insights from dreams and visions. You are embracing the healer in you.

Saturn's directive over this period is clear: discern your message, the authentic voice that you wish to broadcast to the world. It should resonate with your passions, talents, and unique offerings. Remember, Pluto, in his relentless scrutiny, will shed anything disingenuous. This pivotal year beckons you to pen your thoughts, embark on ventures that mirror your new sense of self, and determine the knowledge you wish to share. As the sign symbolized by the Sacred Mountain, you possess a vantage point from which the horizons are clear. Guide us, share what you discern, and illuminate the authentic path ahead.

However, Saturn's influence might ripple tensions with siblings, relatives, roommates, neighbors, or business associates. Be vigilant about these relationships. Their challenges might be a call for your support or intervention. Additionally, ensure the solidity of contracts—having proficient legal advice might prove invaluable.

Reflecting on 1995–1996 could provide insights, as the themes Saturn introduced during that period might echo in the challenges and focuses of 2024 and 2025.

On the brighter side, managing Saturn in Pisces is easier if you can have peaceful sleep and rest more often. Einstein, a Pisces himself, frequently lauded the rejuvenating qualities of brief siestas. Recent studies have corroborated this, demonstrating the brain's potential to expand during a short midday nap. Keeping a dream journal could prove enlightening, with profound wisdom emerging from your nocturnal flights. Seeking communities that emphasize yoga, dance, movement, mysticism, or meditation can also provide comfort. Immerse yourself in water, when possible, use creative visualization, and maintain faith—in yourself and the universe—the rest will naturally follow.

MENTORS AND TUTORS: ENCOUNTER WITH YOUR MASTER

In "*Rock 'n' Roll Suicide,*" Bowie, with the fervor of a musical prophet, declares, "Oh no love, you are not alone, no matter what or who you've been, no matter when or where you've seen, all the knives seem to lacerate your brain, I've had my share, I'll help you with the pain. You're not alone!" He might as well have channeled Jupiter!

Jupiter, the grand luminary of our Solar System, concurs. This benevolent giant won't abandon you. For the initial five months of 2024, his journey through a fellow earth sign, Taurus, ushers in abundant blessings. This translates to the potential of happiness, deepening romantic connections, improved relationship with children (whether it's the joy of conception or fostering deeper bonds), and a surge in leisurely pursuits like sports, hobbies, and entertainment. Indeed, delightful moments await.

Starting May 26, and for the subsequent year, Jupiter graces Gemini. This shift heralds significant enhancements in your professional sphere, health, dietary choices, and relations with colleagues. This phase is opportune not only to crystallize and articulate your message but also to rejuvenate your nervous system. Embark on a nutritious diet that bolsters your health, ascend the professional ladder with promotions or salary hikes, and discover innovative avenues to contribute to the greater good of humanity. Moreover, it is a great time to get a pet.

BATTLEGROUNDS PROCEDURES—ECLIPSE AND CREATURES OF THE NIGHT

This is super important, so buckle up. From December 2021 until July 13, 2023, the North Node—often referred to as the Dragon's Head—beckoned your attention to your creativity, joy, and affection. And as you've just read, Jupiter will gracefully continue this theme in the first half of 2024. Yet, from July 2023 to January 2025, the Dragon takes to the skies, guiding you towards the facets of your chart linked to home, ancestral karma, security, real estate, and the healing of familial ties. The Dragon's flight in Aries presents challenges; he nudges you into realms you might be hesitant to tread—like contemplating relocation, addressing deeply-rooted childhood insecurities, or confronting intergenerational traumas. The wisest approach with the Dragon being in Aries is to staunchly preserve your individuality, after all, Arie's key phrase is "I Am," especially in matters relating to home and family. Your task is to become the beacon of warmth and light for your clan, akin to the Sun—steadfast and central. Embrace the leadership mantle, initiate family endeavors, and steer your loved ones towards brighter horizons.

With the South Node gracing Libra, a sign that governs your career, you might sense a taut tension between familial commitments and career responsibilities. This equilibrium is particularly tricky around the eclipses (specified below). However, this year, the scales ought to tilt towards home, despite the inherent Capricornian drive towards professional achievement.

2024 is ripe for embracing parenthood, investing in real estate, relocating, refurbishing your residence, and indulging in your emotional landscape.

Eclipses typically turbocharge events. The pace of unfolding can feel dizzying—requiring a firm grip on your navigational controls, as the journey becomes turbulent and filled with unforeseen challenges. Steel yourself for some space battles, complete with laser showdowns. Here are the pivotal cosmic waypoints:

- **Lunar Eclipse in Libra, March 24–25**: The Sun illuminates facets like your abode, lineage, emotional tapestry, and security. Meanwhile, the Moon casts her glow on your career sphere. If caught at crossroad, home and family take precedence. This eclipse is the Full Moon of Moses (Passover) and Jesus (Last Supper), moments symbolizing liberation and transcendence. Note that Passover in 2024 witnesses a temporal shift due to lunar calendar nuances.
- **Total Solar Eclipse in Aries, April 8**: This New Moon bears challenges, intensified by the Mercury retrograde and its placement in the square of Aries. Both celestial luminaries—the Moon (the maternal) and Sun (the paternal)—urge you to emphasize familial bonds, property matters, and healing ancestral karma.
- **Partial Lunar Eclipse, September 17–18**: With the Moon in Pisces and the Sun in Virgo (the Harvest Full Moon), this celestial event aligns more harmoniously with your energies. The eclipse favors writing, focus on business, as well as travel and education. Reflect on the seeds sown in March/April this year, now might be the time they bear fruit.
- **Annular Solar Eclipse, October 2**: The Libra New Moon heralds a period ripe for reconciliation, diplomacy, and potentially blossoming new romantic liaisons. It signifies a fresh chapter in your professional trajectory, ideal for fostering strategic alliances.

ORANGE ALERT! SHAPESHIFTERS AND TRICKSTERS

When Mercury retrogrades, he takes on his trickster and shapeshifter role. It's a cosmic cue to pause and recalibrate. Make sure to bring your spacecraft to a halt and start flying in reverse. I know, it can be hard on the neck having to look back or relying on your reverse camera mode.

Anticipate delays, energetic and emotional traffic jams. It's the worst time to sign documents or start a new project. But you know all this if you carefully read the first part of your pilot manual.

As the new year dawns, right at the outset of your cosmic voyage, propelling your spacecraft might prove challenging with Mercury stationary Sagittarius January 1 and 2. This pause might summon feelings of letting go, coupled with a fog of fatigue, try to rest more than act. Mercury will take another retrograde in Sagittarius between November 25 to December 16. This won't be an easy so please navigate with heightened awareness, as Mercury retraces its path through realms of your chart linked with surrender, anguish, hospitals, letting go, hidden enemies and isolation. On the brighter side, this retrograde might direct you deeper into the realms of introspection, meditation, mysticism, and imagination.

The foremost palpable Mercury retrograde in 2024 unfolds between April 1 to 26. Its intensity is magnified as it coincides with a potent eclipse (climaxing on April 8). With both the eclipse and retrograde ensconced in Aries, the ambiance might feel unsettling. This particular retrograde phase could see a flurry of misinterpretations and disconnects, especially with family members, home, and domestic appliances.

Come August 4–14, Mercury retrogrades in Virgo, the cosmic custodian. While this phase might be slightly more congenial, tread carefully if you're embarking on travels or diving into realms of education. Misunderstandings might arise with in-laws, educators, students, or those from foreign lands. Be extra careful if you travel abroad. From August 15 to 29, Mercury continues retrograding but shapeshifts into Leo. This could introduce a flair of theatricality, especially in close relationships, as well as nuances related to financial aspects like taxes, insurances, and investments. Your friends might feel egocentric and self-centered.

Summary of Mercury Retrograde Dates
- January 1–January 2: Sagittarius.
- April 1–26: Aries (Red Alert around April 8 due to a total solar eclipse).
- August 4–14: Retrograde in Virgo.

- August 14–29 Retrograde in Leo.
- November 25–December 16 Sagittarius (Red Alert from December 6–16 since Mars is retrograde).

RED ALERT! SHIELDS UP

Mars often gets a bad rap. As the co-ruler of Scorpio—represented by the "Death" Tarot card—and the unequivocal ruler of Aries, the sign symbolizing war, Mars has long been linked with destruction and chaos. His Tarot representation, "The Tower," illustrates people tumbling from a burning building, which hardly seems promising. However, fewer realize that Mars was also revered as the ancient god of vegetation, seeds, and planting. So, Mars does have his benevolent side too.

As 2024 draws to a close, Mars will begin his retrograde in Leo starting December 6, 2024, and will only go direct (in Cancer) on February 24, 2025. As such, it's advisable to complete your significant tasks for the year before December 6, and calling it a year, go have fun and relax. If Mars is the god of planting, then during his retrograde, it's an ideal time to weed out and discard what's no longer necessary in your life.

With Mars retrograding in Leo, anticipate potential tensions and hurdles in your romantic relationships, as well as conflicts with your children or what you might think of as the "children of your mind": projects or ventures that you passionately care about. Exercise caution during physical training or, in general, to avoid injuries and be particularly wary around sharp objects.

For you, Capricorn, the retrograde Mars may stir turbulence, especially in the realms of intimate partnerships and shared artistic or financial endeavors, Issues around death, and intimacy might rise, perhaps feeling less sexual or wanting to explore different intimate directions. Be particularly vigilant with monetary matters such as taxes, insurance, investments, and inheritances. But within this challenging tapestry lies a silver lining. This phase is a golden window for introspection. Reflect upon the passions that drive you, where you channel your vitality, what seeds you're sowing in your life's garden, and your approach towards death and endings as well as rebirth and new beginnings.

Since Mars' shadow begins on October 5, it would be prudent to be more vigilant from this point forward. It's as if you're navigating treacherous straits or passing through an asteroid belt. Stay alert and keep your shield up.

Below you will find Mars' Table Coordinates that highlight areas in your life where you can channel your passion, energy, and leadership. However, remember that wherever Mars is positioned, he can also introduce conflict and strife in those aspects of life. Mars occupies your sign between January 4–February 12 and since he is exalted in Capricorn, you might feel invigorated and passionate, but also more impulsive and aggressive.

- **November 24, 2023, Mars sojourns into Sagittarius**: This period boosts your imagination and creativity while urging you to relinquish what doesn't serve you. Mars encourages you to cut ties with toxic people and behaviors and could even unlock skills or memories—perhaps even physical aptitudes—from past lives.
- **January 4, 2024, Mars ascends into Capricorn**: Mars finds his zenith of power here, exalted in your sign. His influence fortifies you in all spheres of life, imbuing you with strength and magnetic allure. This is a stellar time to exercise leadership and to connect with your body for healing.
- **February 13, 2024, Mars cruises into Aquarius**: Mars invigorates your social circles, communal endeavors, and organizational activities. His fiery energy can help you boldly request a pay hike or better employ your managerial skills. Use this phase to act assertively in financial matters.
- **March 22, 2024, Mars dives into Pisces**: Mars stokes your entrepreneurial spirit, especially in areas like marketing and sales. He also offers the zest needed to articulate and share your ideas. Exercise caution, though, as he could also fuel conflicts with relatives, roommates, and neighbors.
- **April 30, 2024, Mars ignites Aries**: This transit showers you with creative vitality but can also spark domestic tensions or bring erratic behavior from household appliances. Nonetheless, it's an opportune period for home renovations and improvements.

- **June 9, 2024, Mars plods into Taurus**: Mars moves deliberately but firmly, asking you to labor for your rewards. This is a time when you can manifest material gains through persistent efforts. Mars aids you in the realms of romantic love, sports, recreation, and connecting with the youthful spirit within you and in children.
- **July 20, 2024, Mars zips into Gemini**: Now's the moment to concentrate on your message, business ventures, and communication skills. Mars grants you the momentum to initiate and steer projects at your workplace, but exercise restraint to avoid burnout. Note that coworkers may be easily rattled during this phase. Stay vigilant for possible inflammations, fevers, infections, and injuries.
- **September 4, 2024, Mars navigates Cancer**: Mars is somewhat ill-at-ease in this emotional sea, potentially making you over-defensive or passive-aggressive. It's an ideal time to zero in on relationships but be mindful; neglecting quality time can lead to strains. Be cautious, as competitors and foes could become more antagonistic.
- **November 4, 2024, Mars revels in Leo**: Mars invigorates your life force and magnetism, making this an excellent period for investments and for collaborating on financial or talent-based ventures. This is a favorable time for research, investigation, as well as rekindling sexuality and passion.

LOVE INTEREST AND ALLIES

Venus loves you, she does—it's in her nature. However, she has her moments of whimsiness and can act out. She's not your mama who adores you no matter what, she has her list of conditions, like a spiritual prenuptial agreement.

Below is the list of where Venus journeys this year, offering insights into potential areas of assistance in financial support, creative boosts, enhanced self-worth, and perhaps even a romantic connection. We're fortunate this year, as Venus remains direct, avoiding her retrograde phase. In 2024, Venus graces your sign twice: January 23 to February 15 and November 11 to December 6. In these periods you'll likely notice a heightened sense of beauty, feel and look better, experience a stronger connection to your talent, and perhaps an improved financial situation. Essentially, you're channeling the goddess of beauty and sensuality. However, this might also make you more susceptible to spending money or a tad more self-absorbed than usual. Jupiter and Venus come together on these love-filled days: May 22–23. A great time for art, dating, meeting the love of your life, or just feeling good.

Below you'll find her celestial coordinates and the areas of your life she'll likely influence, ushering in some good fortune and support from allies and loved ones.

- **December 29, 2023, Venus explores Sagittarius**: Strengthen bonds with teachers, in-laws, students, and those from foreign lands. Venus connects you to individuals, locations, and talents from previous lifetimes. This is an opportune time for couples' therapy, dance, art, and diving into your dreams.

- **January 23, 2024, Venus climbs Capricorn**: Venus bestows blessings on every facet of your existence. You're a beacon of beauty and attraction. A perfect window to reinvent your image. Fill yourself with the love goddess's aura, welcoming bountiful opportunities, particularly with those seasoned by age or experience. It's your time to shine.

- **February 16, 2024, Venus aligns with Aquarius**: Celebrate friendships, embrace spontaneity, and harness innovation. Try to connect technology and artistic abilities. There may be a raise or promotion, as well as fresh ways of translating talents into money.

- **March 11, 2024, Venus exalted in Pisces**: Venus showers financial wisdom and amplifies your artistic endeavors. As she graces your businesses, consider infusing artistry in all you undertake. Fortify ties with relatives, roommates, and neighbors. Anticipate favorable contracts or new acquaintances.

- **April 5, 2024, Venus rushes into Aries**: Venus finds Aries challenging, more so during the Mercury retrograde and Solar eclipse. Yet, it's ideal for remodeling, tapping into talents that are coded in your DNA. A good time to mend familial ties.

- **April 29, 2024, Venus strolls into Taurus**: Venus, radiant in her domain, brings your talents to the fore, enhancing self-worth. Foster relationships with children and bask in creativity. Great for romance.
- **May 23, 2024, Venus saunters into Gemini**: Elevate your work and workplace with Venus's touch in marketing, writing, sales, and PR. Beautify your workspace, and expect harmonious coworker relations. Negotiate that salary bump or find a collaborative counterpart. However, moderation is key in your dietary choices.
- **June 17, 2024, Venus coasts through Cancer**: Deepen bonds with significant others. Great time for dating and healing relationships. Venus spreads her charm on work and personal relationships. Perfect for healing issues in relationships and attracting new partners. Embrace design, art, music, and fashion.
- **July 11, 2024, Venus sparkles in Leo**: Let love reign. Indulge in joyful creations and paired athletic endeavors. Sexuality, passion, and collaborations on artistic and financial ventures are coming centerstage. Prosper in investments and inheritance.
- **August 5, 2024, Venus crafts in Virgo**: Venus feels restrained, like a diva forced into a convent. Ideal for overseas journeys and mingling with diverse traditions. Strengthen connections with mentors, in-laws, and students. Try to work aboard.
- **August 29, 2024, Venus graces Libra**: At home in Libra, Venus embodies diplomacy and harmony. She aids in elevating your career stature and workplace reputation. Infuse art into your professional journey.
- **September 23, 2024, Venus plunges into Scorpio**: While the depths of Scorpio can be overwhelming for Venus, it's a time to reconcile with friends and peers. Seek harmony, connect to technology, and cultivate your connection to technology.
- **October 17, 2024, Venus revisits Sagittarius**: Heal ties with educators, learners, and diverse souls. Recognize kindred spirits from previous lives. Detach from harmful connections and let imagination soar.
- **November 11, 2024, Venus rediscovers Capricorn**: Engage with people who are older than you. Venus stands ready to refine every aspect of your life. A good time for a rebrand and stylize yourself anew.

- **December 7, 2024, Venus mingles with Aquarius**: Focus on camaraderie and bolster your standing amongst peers. Venus aids in financial growth and unearthing latent talents. Seek a new skill to nurture and develop.

ALIEN ENCOUNTER PROTOCOL

As a cosmic navigator, you are bound to encounter what some might call aliens. But to be intergalactically correct, let's refer to them as "extraterrestrial sentient beings." These beings are represented by Uranus, the Awakener. Since 2018, Uranus has journeyed through Taurus, a fellow earth sign, weaving unpredictable narratives particularly within your romantic endeavors, relationships with children, creative pursuits, and happiness. Uranus wants you to smile, be happy, let go of your natal seriousness. Unless you tenaciously cling to gravity and overburden yourself, Uranus should make you laugh and connect you to your inner child. Learn from comedic geniuses like Andy Kaufman and Jim Carrey, both Capricorns, to harness this energy.

In the upcoming two years, Uranus in Taurus urges you to be lively, think outside the box, and infuse life with playful abandon. Embrace moments of whimsy, lightness, and sheer joy. Bind your rising creativity and apply it to pragmatic ventures, especially if they intertwine with technology and modernization. This period is ripe for diving into ecommerce and refining your digital footprint. As the year commences, Jupiter aligns with Uranus, both uniting with a singular aim: your happiness. This synergy also marks an auspicious phase for delving into hobbies and new sports. However, your children might go through a rebellious phase or act unpredictably.

Moreover, Uranus nudges you to perceive through your five senses in novel ways: indulge in diverse music genres, savor unfamiliar cuisines, explore fresh income avenues, and refine the manner in which you present yourself to the world. Embracing the unique, venturing into uncharted territories, and exploring new horizons will allow you to reap the most benefits from this once-in-an-84-year transit.

CONCLUSION

In 2024, you are tasked with finding your voice, as well as the message you need to impart to the world. The eclipses will create tension between your career and home life, urging you to anchor your heart and priorities in the realms of home, family, children, and creative aspirations.

This year Pluto makes the last adjustments in your identity and begins to transform your financial standing, linking you to your true talents, and deepen your sense of self-worth.

Capricorns, this year is your clarion call. You're beckoned to embrace unwavering faith in yourself and those around you, recognizing and asserting your well-deserved place under the Sun, in the realms of joy and enlightenment.

TAROT: THE DEVIL

The card symbolizes our dread of oblivion, as well as fear of failure and success. You are the "John Constantine" of the Zodiac, ever ready to confront the devil and exorcise his malevolent spirits. In the card, Adam and Eve, shackled by their insatiable desires, could easily take off the chains but are ignorant. In the same vein, in 2024 you can break free of any barriers that seem insurmountable.

HEBREW LETTER: AIN

Meaning: "eye." Capricorn represents practicality and can tend to be skeptical, only believing what they can see. This year have faith in the power of your word.

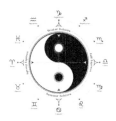

AQUARIUS AND AQUARIUS RISING—I KNOW (THAT I DON'T KNOW)

Power to the People

MISSION (NOT) IMPOSSIBLE—YOUR ASSIGNMENT CARD

Aquarius—The electromagnetic bearer, visionary, inventor, revolutionary, Guardian of the Yet to Come, your mission in 2024 is to shepherd Pluto, the zodiac's nuclear reactor, from the realm of Capricorn into your own domain—the Aquarius nebula. Among King Sun's twelve champions, it is you who is chosen to safeguard the Holy Grail of the Zodiac: Pluto, the Sovereign of Death and Rebirth, from 2024 until 2044. The last time this responsibility fell upon your shoulders, humanity basked in the Age of Reason, giving birth to pivotal events like the Industrial and French Revolutions and the inception of the American Constitution.

From 2008, Pluto thrust upon you the weighty themes of dealing with letting go, anguish, confinement, sickness, and seclusion. You've journeyed your spacecraft through the murkiest reaches of your astrological chart, reconciling with karmic debts from past lifetimes. Your odyssey entailed a general detox—body, mind, and soul—all to prime you for the upcoming task: aiding Pluto in humanity's metamorphosis and its alignment with emerging tech frontiers like A.I. and Quantum Computing. As the sign of progress, humanitarianism, extraterrestrial realms, and technological evolution, you're tasked with amalgamating these concepts. In this Pluto phase, humanity's Aquarian essence confronts death and renewal. You are to ensure we retain our core amidst the tumult.

For 16 years, you've shed whatever was blocking your ultimate potential. However, Saturn, your erstwhile ruler and occasional adversary, casts a shadow of doubt, sometimes eroding your self-worth, creating moments of skepticism, self-distrust, escapism, and cynicism. As the embodiment of the Tarot's "The Star," you're our beacon in these stormy ages. Shine valiantly, our stellar luminary.

Your 2024 directive, though arduous, is simple: Transport Pluto, the Lord of Shadows, from Capricorn (representing the past) into your sign, synonymous with the future. As mentioned, from 2008 to 2024, Pluto's voyage through the sector of your chart associated with past lifetimes, the subconscious realm, hospitals, jails, and unseen adversaries. In Aquarian context, this translates to humanity navigating hardships (the Great Recession), adversities (surge of populism and misinformation), and isolation (pandemic, global lockdowns). This became especially pronounced from March 2020 to March 2023, with Saturn's presence in your sign.

From 2024 to 2044, Pluto promises a rebirth in every facet of your existence: from your physical body to your worldview. This epoch urges a metamorphosis—a fresh identity, dwelling, and purpose. Channel your inner Captain Picard, boldly going where no Aquarius has gone before. Propel us into novel horizons, vanquish our collective phobias, and embrace the potency that Pluto brings to your sign. Like the Water Bearer you are, prepare to harness this monumental force. Since Pluto is power and Aquarius represents the people—your job is to bring power back to the people.

Your Assignment Card: Usher Pluto into your spacecraft, transitioning him from Capricorn (what you accumulated in the last 16 years), into your sign. Employ the wisdom garnered since 2008 across various life sectors: finances (under Saturn's gaze), writing and commerce (the Dragon's domain), and family and offspring (Jupiter's territory), into a new identity—the Super Aquarius.

Pluto's Picup Location:

From June 11, 2023, to January 21, 2024, and between September 2 to November 19, Pluto is located in Capricorn in the sector of your chart that relates to letting go, past lives, imagination, healing, and isolation. A great time for meditation, hiking in nature, and working with your dreams. Sleep is essential.

From January 22–August 31 and then November 20–January 2044 (final-destination), Pluto changes all aspects of your life since he is traveling in your sign.

OPERATING LIMITATIONS: ENCOUNTERS WITH YOUR ANTAGONIST

From March 2023 to February 2026, as previously touched upon, Saturn, Lord of Karma, and your traditional ruler (until Uranus took the mantle in 1781), voyages through Pisces. In this role, the Lord of the (Three) Ringed confronts you about self-worth, financial prowess, innate talents, and core values. This phase doesn't necessarily signal losing money or grim financial forecasts. Instead, Saturn nudges you with probing inquiries: Are you capitalizing on your true talents for income? Does your earnings source resonate with your values? Could your worth be undervalued? Have any talents remained dormant or unexplored? What pillars support your values?

While you needn't address every query immediately, delving deep into these concerns is essential in the next two years. A word of caution: if you sidestep these issues, Saturn might present you with scenarios you'd rather avoid. Given Pluto's transit in your sign, Pluto would also force you to look into your passion, sexuality, and relationship to your power.

The silver lining? The Dragon's influence activates the spheres of your life linked to writing, marketing, and sales. By honing in on the right talents and principles, you can leverage the North Node in Aries—a sign in harmony with yours—to broadcast and market your gifts and expertise in 2024. Time is on your side, but resist the urge to dawdle, lest you stifle your own growth.

Aligning with Saturn's essence requires embodying focus, strategy, discipline, tenacity, and pragmatism. Upon recognizing a talent that holds practical value, craft a two-year blueprint outlining its translation into a viable income source. And while realism is key, don't tether yourself too tightly. For instance, if guitar mastery is your chosen path but recording an album within two years feels daunting, that's okay. Perhaps the discipline acquired from consistent practice sparks an epiphany, catalyzing a previously dormant skill. This newfound prowess might bolster your self-esteem, paving the way for professional advancements. The key is unwavering faith, complemented by meticulous attention to your finances, talents, and confidence.

Reflect upon 1995–1996—what lessons did Saturn impart then? Were there significant challenges that might have sown the seeds for the issues emerging in 2024 and 2025?

Fortunately, Saturn's passage through Pisces can be navigated more smoothly by dedicating time for rejuvenating slumbers. Dreams might offer practical insights. Einstein, a Piscean himself, extolled the virtues of siestas. Modern studies support the brain's expansive capabilities during short naps. Maintaining a dream journal can further elucidate wisdom from nocturnal journeys. For balance, immerse yourself in communities that resonate with yoga, dance, mysticism, or meditation. Regularly seek solace in water's embrace. Creative visualization bolstered by unwavering faith—and the universe will pave the way.

MENTORS AND TUTORS: ENCOUNTER WITH YOUR MASTER

In "*Rock 'n' Roll Suicide*," Bowie, with the fervor of a musical prophet, declares, "Oh no love, you are not alone, no matter what or who you've been, no matter when or where you've seen, all the knives seem to lacerate your brain, I've had my share, I'll help you with the pain. You're not alone!" He might as well have channeled Jupiter!

Jupiter, the grandest planet in our Solar System, concurs. In the first five months, he sojourns through Taurus, a fixed sign akin to yours, which may challenge your synergy. This transit suggests you might feel compelled to make decisions impulsively, which you could later regret. Hence, practice measured thought before action, particularly when tempers flare. On the brighter side, Jupiter's presence in Taurus can fortify your home, familial ties, welcoming a child or expanding your family, relocation, property acquisition, home or office renovations, or healing past emotional scars. Taurus's influence can also help unfold artistic talents embedded in your genetic code. Consider delving into your ancestry; there may be artisans whose legacy flows in your veins. Harnessing these inherited gifts becomes more attainable, especially with Saturn stoking the flames of your innate talents.

Starting May 26 and spanning an entire year, Jupiter makes his graceful transition into Gemini, where his benevolent energies will align more harmoniously with yours. This phase promises blessings, potentially in the form of a new child or perhaps a grandchild. Existing relationships with offspring may deepen, and doors to romantic love, creativity, and an overarching aura of joy might open. This jovial energy is a much-needed counterbalance, especially with the intense undertow of Pluto's presence in your sign. Jupiter's essence urges you to embrace happiness, indulge in merry-making, and perhaps kickstart a new sport or hobby. Indeed, this year has a recurring theme of rediscovering and honing your talents and gifts. Reconnect with the desires of your inner child and fulfill them.

BATTLEGROUNDS PROCEDURES—ECLIPSE AND CREATURES OF THE NIGHT

Buckle up, for this is crucial. From December 2021 until July 13, 2023, the North Node, often termed as the Dragon's Head, focused your attention on your home and kin. The Dragon, representing what your soul desires you to learn, guided you into parenthood, relationships with family, real estate, and issues of security. But, as the tides shift from July 2023 to January 2025, the Dragon majestically takes flight into the sector of your chart dedicated to communication, writing, business, networking, marketing, sales, contracts, and even associations with relatives, neighbors, and roommates. Embrace these domains with mindfulness and the lessons they unfold this year could be your greatest blessings. To simplify, this period could be a golden era for your entrepreneurial and communicative endeavors, but only if you distill the essence of your message. What do you wish to convey? Seek that singular word or phrase that encapsulates your life's purpose. The Dragon's position in Aries, a sign symbolizing identity, will help you be true to your authentic self. And with Pluto aligned with your sign, introspection regarding your core identity becomes pivotal for the forthcoming decades. In 2024, ascertain your narrative, be it through writing, marketing, sales, posts, or promotions, aiming at the betterment of human society. While not everyone can be a Gandhi or Mandela, as an Aquarian, you possess an innate humanitarian spirit.

With the South Node in Libra, another airy sign, you might experience a tension between self-interest and altruism. The coming year nudges you to trust your own intuition, sidelining mentors and guides, unless they're introducing you to a novel talent or expertise.

2024 heralds opportunities for you to disseminate your insights and wisdom, striking a harmonious balance between expression and reception, talking and listening, writing and reading. Familial ties might flourish, perhaps you'll embrace a new role as an uncle or aunt or deepen bonds with siblings and neighbors.

During eclipse seasons, these thematic undertones intensify. The pace of unfolding events accelerates, urging you to hold steady amidst turbulent times. The key eclipses coordinates:

- **Lunar Eclipse in Libra, March 24–25**: The Sun illuminates your intellect with innovative concepts and words, fostering growth in business and communication. The Moon amplifies your educational pursuits, philosophies, and could instigate travel, especially business-related. This eclipse corresponds Moses' Passover and Jesus' Last Supper—periods symbolic of emancipation and breaking free. Notably, 2024's Passover encounters a monthlong delay due to lunar calendar intricacies.

- **Total Solar Eclipse in Aries, April 8**: Although this New Moon is challenging due to its concurrence with Mercury in retrograde, its alignment in Aries is advantageous for you. The celestial duo of the Moon (mama) and Sun (dad) urge you to formulate and reassess your message for humanity. This period becomes pivotal for your business undertakings, the specifics of which rest in your hands.
- **Partial Lunar Eclipse, September 17–18**: With the Pisces Moon opposing the Sun in Virgo, this eclipse might test your resilience, attempting to anchor your usually buoyant spirit. There's an evident tension between personal talents and finance, vis-a-vis those of a partner. Prioritize self-worth and personal skills over appeasing others. You might be harvesting projects and processes that you started March/April.
- **Annular Solar Eclipse, October 2**: Coinciding with the Libra New Moon, this is an opportune moment for reconciliation, diplomacy, and possibly, the commencement of romantic ventures. It marks a fresh start in your education, teaching, publishing, counseling, and a wonderful time to travel.

ORANGE ALERT! SHAPESHIFTERS AND TRICKSTERS

When Mercury retrogrades, he takes on his trickster and shapeshifter role. It's a cosmic cue to pause and recalibrate. Make sure to bring your spacecraft to a halt and start flying in reverse. I know, it can be hard on the neck having to look back or relying on your reverse camera mode. Anticipate delays, energetic and emotional traffic jams. It's the worst time to sign documents or start a new project. But you know all this if you carefully read the first part of your pilot manual.

As you set out on your journey at the dawn of the year, the initial two days (January 1–2) might prove challenging in jumpstarting your spacecraft. This is attributed to Mercury being stationary in Sagittarius. It would be especially challenging in your interactions with friends, colleagues, and government officials. Tread carefully within bureaucratic environments and maintain harmony with your coworkers. Mercury will once again retrograde to Sagittarius at the end of the year from November 25 to

December 16. This retrograde could cause issues within your company, in your interactions with friends and colleagues, as well as with machines, gadgets, electronics and your digital pals. Given your intrinsic connection with community and people, these Mercury retrogrades may pose added challenges with interpersonal relations and organizations. Additionally, anticipate potential complications with in-laws, educators, students, and those from diverse backgrounds.

The inaugural Mercury retrograde of 2024 spans from April 1 to 26. Its concurrence with a potent eclipse, peaking on April 8, can amplify its intensity. However, take solace in the fact that both the eclipse and retrograde are in Aries, a sign you harmoniously resonate with. Hence, you might navigate this tumultuous phase with greater ease than most. Yet, be wary of possible miscommunications or misunderstandings involving your children, romantic partners, or creative ventures. Exercise prudence with speculative activities like stock trading or gambling and please stay vigilant during physical exertions.

The retrograde stretching from August 4 to 14 finds its home in Virgo, often referred to as the zodiac's meticulous caretaker. This phase could be particularly burdensome, testing the resilience of your intimate bonds, sexual partners, as well as influencing decisions with investors, while casting shadows over joint financial and artistic ventures. From August 15 to 29, Mercury shapeshifts, dresses like a lion, and retrogrades in Leo. Expect heightened drama in your primary relationships, encompassing both personal and professional partners. Not a good time to start a new relationship or sign partnership agreements.

Summary of Mercury Retrograde Dates
- January 1–January 2: Sagittarius.
- April 1–26: Aries (Red Alert around April 8 due to a total solar eclipse).
- August 4–14: Retrograde in Virgo.
- August 14–29 Retrograde in Leo.
- November 25–December 16 Sagittarius (Red Alert from December 6–16 since Mars is retrograde).

RED ALERT! SHIELDS UP

Mars often gets a bad rap. As the co-ruler of Scorpio—represented by the "Death" Tarot card—and the unequivocal ruler of Aries, the sign symbolizing war, Mars has long been linked with destruction and chaos. His Tarot representation, "The Tower," illustrates people tumbling from a burning building, which hardly seems promising. However, fewer realize that Mars was also revered as the ancient god of vegetation, seeds, and planting. So, Mars does have his benevolent side too.

As 2024 draws to a close, Mars will begin his retrograde in Leo starting December 6, 2024, and will only go direct (in Cancer) on February 24, 2025. As such, it's advisable to complete your significant tasks for the year before December 6, and calling it a year, go have fun and relax. If Mars is the god of planting, then during his retrograde, it's an ideal time to weed out and discard what's no longer necessary in your life.

During Mars retrograde in Leo, expect a surge of tensions and obstacles in your romantic affairs. Additionally, clashes with your children or with the "offspring of your mind"—those projects or endeavors you hold dear—are likely. When engaging in physical activities, tread with care to sidestep potential injuries, especially around sharp instruments. It's a period that calls for heightened awareness and patience in all your significant relationships and partnerships. The retrograde can also embolden your enemies and competitors, so take heed. There also could be some legal issues, and close people misinterpreting your action.

Since Mars' shadow begins on October 5, it would be prudent to be more vigilant from this point forward. It's as if you're navigating treacherous straits or passing through an asteroid belt. Stay alert and keep your shield up.

Below you will find Mars' Table Coordinates that highlight areas in your life where you can channel your passion, energy, and leadership. However, remember that wherever Mars is positioned, he can also introduce conflict and strife in those aspects of life. When Mars occupies your sign (February 13–March 21), you might feel invigorated and passionate, but also more impulsive, aggressive, impatient, and susceptible to conflicts and accidents.

- **November 24, 2023, Mars ventures into Sagittarius**: Your thirst for adventures intensifies, but tread carefully to avoid needless risks. Energy surges when engaging with groups, friends, and within your organization. Consider traveling or taking on an intellectual journey.
- **January 4, 2024, Mars climbs into Capricorn**: Mars exalted offers you the vigor to break free from barriers to your growth. Your imaginative and creative capacities are amplified, and you may rediscover talents and memories, especially physical ones, from past lives. There may be meetings with siblings in arms.
- **February 13, 2024, Mars allies with Aquarius**: You'll emanate strength and charisma, making it an opportune time to showcase your leadership skills. This period beckons you to connect deeply with your body and initiate healing. Energy surrounding friends, community, and organizations is also heightened.
- **March 22, 2024, Mars drifts into Pisces**: Mars ensures you have the drive, vitality, and confidence to pursue financial advancements. It's a prime period to assertively manage your finances.
- **April 30, 2024, Mars steps boldly into Aries**: Mars energizes you to venture into new businesses, promote yourself or your products, dominate debates, boost sales, and ardently communicate your concepts. However, stay alert to potential disagreements with relatives, cohabitants, and neighbors.
- **June 9, 2024, Mars takes a determined path into Taurus**: Energy here may feel unhurried but unwavering. Efforts need to be consistent and diligent, but the tangible outcomes can be rewarding. Anticipate potential discord within the home or with family members. Household appliances might act up, but it's an opportune phase for home renovations.
- **July 20, 2024, Mars focuses on Gemini**: It's the season to concentrate on your message, enterprise, and communication. Mars assists in deepening romantic connections, engaging in sports and leisure, and bonding with the young at heart or actual children. Passion and creativity are in the limelight.

- **September 4, 2024, Mars gently sails into Cancer:** Not his favored abode, leading you to possibly display heightened defensiveness or subtle aggression. Mars does, however, bolster your ability to kickstart and generate initiatives at work. Tread carefully; coworkers may be more sensitive around you. Stay vigilant against potential ailments, inflammations, and injuries. Suppressed emotions could lead to digestive discomforts.

- **November 4, 2024, Mars strides confidently into Leo:** Mars here rejuvenates you with zest and enthusiasm. It's a period conducive for nurturing relationships, but remain mindful of potential strains with partners, especially if you neglect quality interactions. Rivalries might become more confrontational, so stay prepared.

LOVE INTEREST AND ALLIES

Venus loves you, she does—it's in her nature. However, she has her moments of whimsiness and can act out. She's not your mama who adores you no matter what, she has her list of conditions, like a spiritual prenuptial agreement.

Below is the list of where Venus journeys this year, offering insights into potential areas of assistance in financial support, creative boosts, enhanced self-worth, and perhaps even a romantic connection. We're fortunate this year, as Venus remains direct, avoiding her retrograde phase. This year, Venus graces you twice as she walks in your sign between February 16–March 10 and December 7, 2024–January 2, 2025. At those times you'll likely notice a heightened sense of beauty, feel, and look better, experience a stronger connection to your talent, and perhaps an improved financial situation. Essentially, you're channeling the goddess of beauty and sensuality. However, this might also make you more susceptible to spending money or a tad more self-absorbed than usual.

Jupiter and Venus come together on these love-filled days: May 22–23. A great time for art, dating, meeting the love of your life, or just feeling good.

Below you'll find her celestial coordinates and the areas of your life she'll likely influence, ushering in some good fortune and support from allies and loved ones.

- **December 29, 2023, Venus voyages to Sagittarius**: This is an excellent period for enhancing relationships with teachers, in-laws, students, and people from other cultures. Invite your life or work partner on an exhilarating adventure. It's also a promising time to connect with like-minded individuals for collective creativity.
- **January 23, 2024, Venus ascends to Capricorn**: Venus generously blesses your interactions with older individuals and superiors at work. This is a prime opportunity to add an artistic touch to your professional life. Venus also links you to people, places, and talents that you may have known in a previous life. It's a potent period for healing relationships and exploring your imagination and dreams.
- **February 16, 2024, Venus meets Aquarius**: Now is the time to form new friendships, revel in spontaneity, and enjoy the benefits of innovation. Venus showers blessings upon every aspect of your life, assisting you in a style makeover. You'll find yourself acting as a channel for the goddess of love, inviting numerous opportunities into your life.
- **March 11, 2024, Venus exalted in Pisces**: Venus offers her aid in financial matters and helps you tap into your artistic talents. It's an ideal period to invest your energy, funds, and dive into skills that could later turn into new revenue streams.
- **April 5, 2024, Venus confronts Aries**: Though Aries isn't Venus's preferred companion—especially during eclipses and retrogrades—she still extends her blessings to your enterprises. Your marketing and sales efforts could particularly benefit if you incorporate artistic elements. Relationships with relatives, roommates, and neighbors are likely to improve. Be on the lookout for new contracts or valuable contacts.
- **April 29, 2024, Venus returns to Taurus**: Venus feels at home here, allowing your skills and self-worth to shine brilliantly. It's a wonderful time for a home or office makeover and for exploring talents that may have been passed down through your family. Relations with family members are set to improve.
- **May 23, 2024, Venus dallies with Gemini**: Venus lends her charm to your marketing, writing, and public relations efforts, making your

workplace communications more artistic and agreeable. Relations with your children could also improve, and you might discover a more creative and entertaining side to yourself. Romance may be in the cards; Venus suggests you plan a date!

- **June 17, 2024, Venus nurtures Cancer**: Venus enhances your bonds with those you consider family. This is an opportune period to infuse your professional life with creativity and beauty. Relationships with employees, clients, and coworkers are poised for improvement. Be cautious with your dietary choices; you could be prone to overindulgence and emotional eating.

- **July 11, 2024, Venus revels in Leo**: Love and happiness abound, especially in the realms of creativity and sports, and even more so if shared with a partner. Venus bestows her blessings upon your primary relationships as well as work associates. It's a favorable period for making compromises and reaching peaceful agreements, as well as for taking your existing relationships to the next level. The arts—be it design, music, or fashion—are highly favored.

- **August 5, 2024, Venus matures in Virgo**: Though she may feel restrained, Venus still manages to reconnect you with your passions and deepen your intimacy. It's an advantageous time for joint artistic and financial endeavors, as well as for making sound investments and dealing with inheritance issues.

- **August 29, 2024, Venus balances in Libra**: Venus is back in her home sign, strengthening her ties to justice, diplomacy, and peace-making. It's an excellent period for travel and connections with people from diverse backgrounds. Relations with in-laws, mentors, teachers, and students are likely to improve, making it an opportune time for publishing and spreading your message.

- **September 23, 2024, Venus plumbs the depths of Scorpio**: While not completely at ease in Scorpio, Venus still offers her aid in your career and community standing, smoothing relations with bosses and superiors. Consider adding an artistic layer to your professional endeavors.

- **October 17, 2024, Venus returns to Sagittarius**: It's a wonderful opportunity for healing relations with educators, students, and individuals from diverse cultural backgrounds. Be prepared for technological updates and new friendships, perhaps even a job offer.
- **November 11, 2024, Venus elevates in Capricorn**: This is a favorable time for connecting with older or more experienced individuals. You might also encounter souls you've journeyed with in past lives. It's a period ripe for releasing toxic relationships and for enhancing your dreams and imagination.
- **December 7, 2024, Venus alights in Aquarius**: Focus on friendships and improving your standing within your organization or social circle. With Venus revisiting your sign, she helps refine all aspects of your life, including a personal rebranding and a general makeover.

ALIEN ENCOUNTER PROTOCOL

As a cosmic navigator, you are bound to encounter what some might call aliens. But to be intergalactically correct, let's refer to them as "extraterrestrial sentient beings." These beings are represented by Uranus, the Awakener, who is also your co-ruler ruler. Uranus was discovered in 1781, right when Pluto was last time in your sign. Since 2018, Uranus has been journeying through Taurus, a sign that challenges your equilibrium, ushering in unforeseen changes particularly in areas concerning your home, family, real estate, and emotional landscape. Uranus might inspire you to unexpectedly purchase property, move to a new location, enhance your living space, or even welcome surprise visitors. Currently positioned at the nadir of your chart, Uranus is nudging all the matters you've tucked away in the basement. This aligns with the already potent influence of Pluto residing in your sign. In essence, Uranus encourages you to truly feel, connect with your deeper emotions, and navigate life with more emotionality.

Uranu's sojourn in Taurus will persist in stirring your emotions until 2026, at which point he will transition to Gemini, an affable air sign that resonates more harmoniously with your nature. In the initial half of 2024, Jupiter aligns with Uranus, and their combined energies have the potential to manifest numerous positive transformations in your domestic sphere and familial relationships. Moreover, Uranus nudges you to perceive through your five senses in novel ways: indulge in diverse music genres, savor unfamiliar cuisines, explore fresh income avenues, and refine the manner in which you present yourself to the world. Embracing the unique, venturing into uncharted territories, and exploring new horizons will allow you to reap the most benefits from this once-in-an-84-year transit.

CONCLUSION

2024 is a potent year, where you are truly called upon to embrace Pluto's entry into your sign with open arms. Representing unbridled power, Pluto's arrival signals not just strength, but also the accompanying responsibility. Think of the next two decades as a rigorous superhero training regimen. While this influx of energy is bound to amplify your innate power, it's pivotal to comprehend that when a deliberate planet like Pluto settles into your sign, it requires a gestation period to align seamlessly. Hence, start paying more attention to your well-being, body, and diet.

Simultaneously, the cosmos nudges you towards channeling steadfast discipline, meticulous attention, and unwavering determination. This is your chance to harness your unique abilities, talents, and expertise, aiming to reinvent your financial trajectory and pioneer innovative income streams. You might grapple with moments that challenge your self-worth, but remember, every cloud has a silver lining—and yours is graced by Jupiter's magnanimity. In the initial months of 2024, Jupiter generously bestows its favor upon your home and hearth. In the second part of the year, he will magnify your happiness, deepening your connection to the playful spirit of your inner child.

TAROT: THE STAR

This card depicts a woman pouring water, symbolizing electromagnetic waves. She is naked, unashamed, and untainted by such polluting ideas as the "Original Sin." She loves humanity without judgment. In 2024 you are asked by the Lady of the Star to shine upon your talents and gifts that you must share with the rest of us.

HEBREW LETTER: TZADIK

Meaning: "Saint," or "fishhook." The letter's shape resembles a fisherman, sitting holding a rod, catching fish. The fish symbolizes intuition, and the Kabbalistic meaning of the letter is meditation. In 2024 with Saturn literally in the sign of the fish, you must try to meditate deeper and longer so you can better fish the insights you need to propel your life forward.

PISCES AND
PISCES RISING—I IMAGINE

Rebranding—From Fish to Dolphin

MISSION (NOT) IMPOSSIBLE—YOUR ASSIGNMENT CARD

Pisces—The mystic, poet, extra-dimensional voyager, dreamer (day and night), visionary, and Guardian of the Philosopher's Stone, your quest in 2024 is to guide Pluto, the zodiac's nuclear reactor, from the starry realms of Capricorn to the vast expanse of the Aquarius nebula. Of all King Sun's twelve celestial knights, it is you who has been chosen to accompany Pluto, the Lord of Rebirth and Transformation, into the Zodiac's Wonderland—your homeland. Sounds confusing? Perchance, but not to you Pisces, the sign of confusion. Allow me to elucidate...

From 2008, with Pluto residing in skeptical Capricorn, your ethereal nature, steeped in mysticism and imagination, faced challenges. This phase ushered in self-doubt, shaking not only your belief in the divine, but also in yourself. It beckoned introspection into your alliances—with friends, organizations, governments, and the many entities you engaged with. Regrettably, some friendships faltered, and allies you entrusted with your power (personified by Pluto) left you disenchanted. This period of upheaval, especially pronounced between 2018–2020 with Saturn joining Pluto, called for a profound reassessment of your relationships, often leaving you feeling solitary in a crowd.

But 2024 heralds a monumental shift. For the first time in 250 years, Pluto graces a sector of the chart that aligns with your essence—mysticism, memories of past lives, artistry, dance, introspection, dreams, empathy, and above all, boundless imagination. In essence, you are to guide Pluto through the metaphysical maze. This pivotal transition signifies welcoming Pluto's power into your sanctuary. For Pisces, the Dolphin of the Zodiac, this means undergoing a profound purification, shedding any tendencies that cloud your vision, ensuring your insights remain as pure as spring waters. This purification aids the collective transition from your era, the Age of Pisces, to the dawning of the Age of Aquarius. Pisces, you play a key role in the tapestry of our collective destiny. You are Jonah coming out of the whale, ready to deliver your prophecies.

Adding layers to this celestial journey is Saturn, the Lord of Karma, which has taken residence in your sign from March 2023 to February 2026. While hosting this stern cosmic entity can be demanding for any sign, for the dreamy and imaginative Pisces, it's particularly challenging. But it's also an invaluable opportunity to ground your ethereal nature, applying your intuitions and dreams in pragmatic ways, be it enhancing your financial status, bolstering health, or tapping into the collective unconscious, your spiritual homeland. However, believing in your innate talents becomes paramount, especially with the Dragon blessing the sector of your chart associated with self-worth and financial gains.

Your 2024 Assignment Card: Safely transport Pluto from Capricorn (representing the past) and Aquarius (symbolizing the future). Harness the wisdom you gained since 2008 and assimilate it into every aspect of your life. Guide Pluto, the underworld sovereign, into the heart of your zodiac realm, bridging past, present, and future. Your job is to combine technology with imagination, innovation with mysticism, science and poetry, intellect with faith. The juxtapositions may baffle many, but a true Pisces has the unique gift of reconciling dichotomies. Perhaps, in this cosmic dance, we might glimpse the dawn of a Geneal Artificial Intelligence, fusing power and technology.

Pluto's Pickup Location

From June 11, 2023, to January 21, 2024, and between September 2 to November 19, Pluto is located in Capricorn in the sector of your chart that relates to humanity, friends, government, technology, altruism, nonprofit organizations, manifesting wishes and hope.

From January 22–August 31, and then November 20–January 2044 (final-destination), Pluto must be dropped at the area of your chart relating to letting go, past lives, imagination, healing, and isolation. A great time for meditation, hiking in nature, and working with your dreams. Rest and sleep are essential.

OPERATING LIMITATIONS: ENCOUNTERS WITH YOUR ANTAGONIST

From March 2023 to February 2026, Saturn, the Lord of the (Three) Rings (past, present, future), graces your sign. In his majestic voyage, he questions the very essence of your Piscean spirit. There may be moments where you feel submerged, yearning for the surface, akin to the dolphin's need for air.

Yet, understand this: the initial phase of Saturn's journey through a sign often poses the most significant trials. In 2023, you were introduced to the lessons he sought to impart. As you move through 2024 and 2025, the rewards of understanding and integrating these teachings will manifest. Saturn, in his wisdom, emphasizes discipline, resilience, patience, and strategy. He yearns for tangible milestones in your journey of self-betterment. With Saturn in your realm, you're beckoned to undergo a transformative once-in-three-decades metamorphosis—a reimagining of self, a celestial makeover. Revamp your aesthetic, refresh your digital footprint, and welcome a renewed perspective on the world. Get a new hairdo, email, website. It's a call to enhance your health, invigorate your physique, and allow the emergent you to break free. Committed and disciplined transformations will be rewarded, more so with the Dragon heralding enhanced recognition (financial and emotional).

Reflect upon who you envision becoming over the next 30 years—in health, identity, and demeanor. With the Dragon in Aries, your neighboring constellation, lean into the affirmation "I Am." Define your aspirations to the Dragon, employ Pluto's powers, and harness Saturn's discipline to realize them.

To gain deeper insights of what is ahead for you this year, journey back to 1995–1996, recalling the lessons Saturn imparted when he last danced through your sign. The challenges of that era could illuminate the origins of present-day tribulations in 2024 and 2025.

However, there is a silver lining: Saturn's sojourn in your sign can be navigated with greater ease when you dedicate moments for sleeping and dreaming. Dreams can serve as practical conduits for valuable insights. Albert Einstein, a fellow Piscean, often extolled the rejuvenating virtues of brief naps. Modern research concurs, suggesting the brain's potential expansion during a short rest. Embrace the practice of maintaining a dream diary—you'll find profound wisdom through these nocturnal flights. Seek camaraderie in communities devoted to yoga, dance, movement, mysticism, or meditation. Immerse yourself in water whenever possible. Visualize your desired future, and with unwavering faith, the universe will chart the course for you.

MENTORS AND TUTORS: ENCOUNTER WITH YOUR MASTER

In "*Rock 'n' Roll Suicide*," Bowie, with the fervor of a musical prophet, declares, "Oh no love, you are not alone, no matter what or who you've been, no matter when or where you've seen, all the knives seem to lacerate your brain, I've had my share, I'll help you with the pain. You're not alone!" He might as well have channeled Jupiter!

Jupiter, the largest planet in the Solar System, who is also your co-ruler along with Neptune, agrees. He would never leave you alone and in the first five months, he travels through Taurus, Mother Nature's sign, which you vibe with very well. Taurus is like the Garden of Eden and Pisces is its four rivers. This means you can expect an expansion and fortune with contracts and contacts, improved ability to communicate and deliver your messages, flow with writing, texting, and delivering information. In addition, your businesses can thrive and your relationships with relatives, roommates, and neighbors can improve.

From May 26, for a whole year, Jupiter transits into Gemini and blesses your homestead with improved relationships with family members, maybe getting pregnant, relocate, buy a property, renovate, or heal childhood wounds. Take a close look at your family tree and see if you had writers and communicators in your ancestry, you will be able to unfold these genetic gifts, and using Saturn's discipline, make something practical with them.

BATTLEGROUNDS PROCEDURES—ECLIPSE AND CREATURES OF THE NIGHT

This is important, so buckle up. From December 2021 to July 13, 2023, the North Node, also known as the Dragon's Head, beckoned you to refine your communication and the essence of your message. What did you wish to convey? To whom, and through which means? Often, the Dragon illuminates the path, aiding you in writing, networking, marketing, and promoting yourself or your offerings. Yet, from July 2023 to January 2025, the Dragon takes flight towards the sector in your chart associated with finances, self-worth, skills, values, and talents. This is great news, and with Saturn's discipline, the Dragon can illuminate untapped talents, potentially translating to improved finances and self-esteem.

With the Dragon positioned in Aries, a sign symbolizing identity, and Saturn also advocating for your authentic self-expression, this period presents a golden opportunity to bolster your finances and explore uncharted terrains—provided you remain authentic. The South Node's presence in Libra suggests a tug-of-war between prioritizing your finances and talents versus those of a partner or associates. However, your focus should remain on yourself without veering into narcissism. For 2024, it's paramount to nurture your gifts and talents. Reflect on 2005–2006 or 1986–1987 to identify potential skills or aptitudes previously cultivated by the Dragon, now ripe for harvest. Trust in yourself, and the cosmos will reciprocate.

Eclipses tend to amplify events, making life's journey exhilarating yet unpredictable. Ready your spacecraft's joystick for some exciting turbulence. Here are the pivotal dates:

- **Lunar Eclipse in Libra, March 24–25**: The Sun amplifies your financial sphere, talents, and capabilities, allowing you to dazzle brilliantly (akin to Aries' gemstone, the diamond). The Moon, meanwhile, accentuates passions and intimacy. Opportunities may arise, but also potential conflicts between your aspirations and those of others loom large. This eclipse coincides with the Moses' Passover Full Moon, and Jesus' Last Supper—a period symbolic of freedom and transcendence. Note that Passover 2024 observance is postponed due to lunar calendar discrepancies.
- **Total Solar Eclipse in Aries, April 8**: Mercury being in retrograde makes this New Moon especially challenging. Both the Moon (mama) and Sun (dad) urge you to hone in on your talents and fiscal aspirations. Exercise caution and refrain from embarking on fresh projects unless they are previous ventures awaiting completion.
- **Partial Lunar Eclipse, September 17–18**: As the Pisces Moon opposes the Virgo Sun (Harvest Full Moon), this eclipse, occurring in your sign, intensifies the dynamics. You might experience tension between focusing on yourself or your partner. It's essential to harmonize the "I Am" with "We Are." Ensure your identity remains distinct within relationships. This period could culminate in the fruition of your endeavors from March/April.
- **Annular Solar Eclipse, October 2**: Occurring during the Libra New Moon, this is an auspicious period for forging peace, diplomacy, or even starting a new romantic chapter. It's also apt for letting go or severing ties. Favorable energies abound for intimate relationships, joint artistic endeavors, or financial collaborations.

ORANGE ALERT! SHAPESHIFTERS AND TRICKSTERS

When Mercury retrogrades, he takes on his trickster and shapeshifter role. It's a cosmic cue to pause and recalibrate. Make sure to bring your spacecraft to a halt and start flying in reverse. I know, it can be hard on the neck having to look back or relying on your reverse camera mode. Anticipate delays, energetic and emotional traffic jams. It's the worst time to sign documents or start a new project. But you know all this if you carefully read the first part of your pilot manual.

As you commence the year's journey, the initial two days might feel like trying to ignite a spacecraft with wet fuel. This is because Mercury, stationed in the fiery Sagittarius, attempts to dissipate your watery essence. There's a likelihood of being nudged into actions, particularly in the professional realm, which you'd rather avoid. To ensure a smoother take-off, perhaps consider initiating your endeavors post January 3. Mercury will again retrograde in Sagittarius between November 25 to December 16. During these times you might experience more glitches and issues in your career and with people of authority as well as in travel. Tread wisely.

The foremost significant Mercury retrograde of 2024 unravels from April 1 to 26. Amplified by a potent eclipse peaking on April 8, this period promises heightened intensity. Both the eclipse and retrograde transpire in Aries—a neighboring sign with which you often grapple over boundaries. Anticipate potential miscommunications and hitches concerning finances, self-worth, and the harnessing of your innate talents—themes underscored as pivotal this year. Refrain from making grand financial commitments during this phase.

The August 4–14 retrograde unfurls in Virgo, and your opposite sign. Brace yourself, for this retrograde could strain your core relationships and any existing partnerships. Legal matters may also come to the fore, requiring your attention. Then, from August 15-29, the ever-shapeshifting Mercury takes on a new persona, retrograding in theatrical Leo. This phase might usher in heightened drama within your workplace. Your health and dietary habits could also encounter disruptions during this time. Stay grounded and navigate with care.

Summary of Mercury Retrograde Dates
- January 1–January 2: Sagittarius.
- April 1–26: Aries (Red Alert around April 8 due to a total solar eclipse).

- August 4–14: Retrograde in Virgo.
- August 14–29 Retrograde in Leo.
- November 25–December 16 Sagittarius (Red Alert from December 6–16 since Mars is retrograde).

RED ALERT! SHIELDS UP

Mars often gets a bad rap. As the co-ruler of Scorpio—represented by the "Death" Tarot card—and the unequivocal ruler of Aries, the sign symbolizing war, Mars has long been linked with destruction and chaos. His Tarot representation, "The Tower," illustrates people tumbling from a burning building, which hardly seems promising. However, fewer realize that Mars was also revered as the ancient god of vegetation, seeds, and planting. So, Mars does have his benevolent side too.

As 2024 draws to a close, Mars will begin his retrograde in Leo starting December 6, 2024, and will only go direct (in Cancer) on February 24, 2025. As such, it's advisable to complete your significant tasks for the year before December 6, and calling it a year, go have fun and relax. If Mars is the god of planting, then during his retrograde, it's an ideal time to weed out and discard what's no longer necessary in your life.

With Mars retrograding in Leo, anticipate potential tensions and hurdles in your romantic relationships, as well as conflicts with your children or what you might think of as the "children of your mind": projects or ventures that you passionately care about. Exercise caution during physical training or, in general, to avoid injuries and be particularly wary around sharp objects. You also might have some conflict and misunderstanding around health, work, and with employees. Take extra care with your pets during the retrograde.

Since Mars' shadow begins on October 5, it would be prudent to be more vigilant from this point forward. It's as if you're navigating treacherous straits or passing through an asteroid belt. Stay alert and keep your shield up.

Below you will find Mars' Table Coordinates that highlight areas in your life where you can channel your passion, energy, and leadership. However, remember that wherever Mars is positioned, he can also introduce conflict and strife in those aspects of life. When Mars occupies your sign (March 22–April 29), you might feel invigorated and passionate, but also more impulsive, aggressive, impatient, and susceptible to conflicts and accidents.

- **November 24, 2023, Mars strides into Sagittarius**: Adventure calls, but it's wise to avoid unnecessary risks. This phase can be opportune for career pursuits, launching projects (post-January 3, 2024), and assuming leadership roles. Just watch out for potential tensions with superiors. Consider traveling or joining study groups that align with your professional aspirations.
- **January 4, 2024, Mars ascends to Capricorn**: Here, Mars is at his pinnacle of power, exalted. Energy surges in group activities, whether it's with friends or within your professional circle. It's an excellent period for team sports and collaborative endeavors.
- **February 13, 2024, Mars transitions to Aquarius**: Mars fuels your drive to liberate yourself from inhibitions, amplifying creativity and imagination. You might even tap into abilities, particularly physical ones, that feel as though they're from another lifetime.
- **March 22, 2024, Mars dives into Pisces**: Mars in your sign bestows you with strength and magnetism. Use this energy to amplify leadership and foster a connection to your body. Great for healing.
- **April 30, 2024, Mars ignites in Aries**: With Mars invigorating you, there's an enhanced vitality and confidence to negotiate better financial terms or refine managerial skills. It's an opportune time to take charge of your finances and invest in your talents.
- **June 9, 2024, Mars treads through Taurus**: The energy here is deliberate and persistent. Effort may need to be doubled, but the rewards can be equally satisfying, especially concerning finances. From starting new businesses to marketing yourself, Mars' influence is palpable. However, be on the lookout for potential disputes with relatives or some issues with contracts and how you communicate.
- **July 20, 2024, Mars soars in Gemini**: Concentrate on refining your message and business communications. Domestic squabbles or appliance

glitches might arise, but it's also a conducive period for home renovations and improvements.

- **September 4, 2024, Mars navigates Cancer**: Mars feels somewhat out of his element here, possibly leading to defensiveness or passive aggression. Nonetheless, he supports endeavors in romance, sports, and leisure, and fosters connections with your inner child or children around you. Creativity and passion are also heightened.
- **November 4, 2024, Mars dazzles in Leo**: Mars infuses you with vitality and drive, priming you for workplace initiatives. However, moderation is key. Be mindful of inadvertently ruffling colleagues' feathers. On the health front, stay alert to inflammations, infections, and potential injuries. Repressed emotions might manifest as digestive issues.

LOVE INTEREST AND ALLIES

Venus loves you, she does—it's in her nature. However, she has her moments of whimsiness and can act out. She's not your mama who adores you no matter what, she has her list of conditions, like a spiritual prenuptial agreement.

Below is the list of where Venus journeys this year, offering insights into potential areas of assistance in financial support, creative boosts, enhanced self-worth, and perhaps even a romantic connection. We're fortunate this year, as Venus remains direct, avoiding her retrograde phase. When she graces your sign, (March 11–April 4), she is exalted, and you'll likely notice a heightened sense of beauty, feel and look better, experience a stronger connection to your talent, and perhaps an improved financial situation. Essentially, you're channeling the goddess of beauty and sensuality. However, this might also make you more susceptible to spending money or a tad more self-absorbed than usual. Jupiter and Venus come together on these love-filled days: May 22–23. A great time for art, dating, meeting the love of your life, or just feeling good.

Below you'll find her celestial coordinates and the areas of your life she'll likely influence, ushering in some good fortune and support from allies and loved ones.

- **December 29, 2023, Venus graces Sagittarius**: This period is ripe for enhancing relationships with mentors, in-laws, students, and those from diverse backgrounds. Venus showers your professional path with harmony and fresh opportunities, fostering stronger bonds with authority figures. Incorporate artistry into your career for added flair.
- **January 23, 2024, Venus ventures into Capricorn**: The blessings continue, particularly in relationships with elders and those in leadership roles. This is the moment to befriend with like-minded souls and co-create. Friendship may beautifully evolve into romance. Make peace with your digital help.
- **February 16, 2024, Venus befriends Aquarius**: Embrace spontaneity, laughter, and innovative ventures. Venus bridges connections from previous lives, rejuvenating relationships and deepening your bond with your creative imagination.
- **March 11, 2024, Venus exalts in Pisces**: Venus generously aids every facet of your life. With Saturn guiding your reinvention, Venus delivers a forceful nudge. Whether it's your finances, artistic endeavors, or personal style, she's amplifying your glow, making opportunities abound.
- **April 5, 2024. Venus steps into Aries**: Though not her preferred companion, especially during celestial events like eclipses and retrogrades, Venus still enriches your financial well-being, augmenting your earnings and linking you to your innate gifts.
- **April 29, 2024, Venus returns home to Taurus**: Your inherent talents take center stage. With Venus's touch, your self-worth, business pursuits, and marketing endeavors flourish. Connections with relatives, roommates, or neighbors—deepen, and exciting new contacts or contracts may emerge.
- **May 23, 2024, Venus flirts with Gemini**: In the realms of communication—be it marketing, writing, or public relations—Venus refines and beautifies your message. A perfect moment for home or office rejuvenations, or for rediscovering inherited talents. Strengthen ties with family during this phase.

- **June 17, 2024, Venus flows into Cancer**: This period enhances your bond with those you consider family, bringing joy, creativity, and stronger ties with children. Love may come knocking; let it in and perhaps indulge Venus with a delightful date. Integrate artistry into your professional world. Sports, creative hobbies, and connecting to your inner child could be some of Venus' gifts.
- **July 11, 2024, Venus dazzles Leo**: Romance fills the air. Embrace happiness, creativity, and partner-based activities. Relationships with colleagues, clients, and employees, flourish. Consider collaborating or seeking a financial boost in your career, but mind overindulgence in your dietary choices.
- **August 5, 2024, Venus adopts Virgo**: While Venus feels restrained in Virgo, she still nurtures your primary relationships and professional associations. This is a phase ripe for compromise and peacemaking, and to elevate relationships. Creativity—be it in design, music, or fashion—is magnified. Can help with legal affairs.
- **August 29, 2024, Venus balances Libra**: Venus thrives in her native sign, enhancing your links to justice, diplomacy, and harmony. Rekindle passion and intimacy and embark on joint artistic or financial ventures. Investments and inheritances appear promising.
- **September 23, 2024, Venus plunges into Scorpio**: Though she treads cautiously in Scorpio, Venus strengthens bonds with educators, students, mentors, and extended family. Travels and diverse traditions are welcomed.
- **October 17, 2024, Venus revisits Sagittarius**: Embark on intellectual and spiritual journeys. Your professional trajectory stands to gain immensely.
- **November 11, 2024, Venus ascends to Capricorn**: Connect with wiser or older individuals. Welcome technological advancements and expand your digital circle. New affiliations and potential career opportunities loom.
- **December 7, 2024, Venus soars with Aquarius**: Prioritize friendships and elevate your position within your community or group. Reconnect

with souls from past lifetimes and shed any lingering toxic relationships. Your imaginative world deepens, opening doors to dreams and creativity.

ALIEN ENCOUNTER PROTOCOL

As a cosmic navigator, you are bound to encounter what some might call aliens. But to be intergalactically correct, let's refer to them as "extraterrestrial sentient beings." These beings are represented by Uranus, the Awakener. Since 2018, Uranus has been weaving a tapestry of unforeseen changes, particularly affecting your business, writing, communication styles, networking, and relationships with siblings, neighbors, and roommates.

With his transit through Taurus, Uranus sprinkles chaos and unpredictability around how you handle, process, and convey information. As he casts his influence over all modes of communication, it's crucial to tread carefully with contracts, negotiations, and what messages you spread. Business may be punctuated with moments of disruption, but also with the potential for serendipitous breakthroughs. The key is not to perceive this time as purely disruptive, but rather as dynamically unpredictable. By infusing humor, innovation, and modern tech into your professional and communicative endeavors, you can harness the power of this transit to your advantage.

Furthermore, Uranus encourages you to engage your senses in fresh ways. Delight in an eclectic range of music, indulge in tastes from across the globe, seek out novel financial opportunities, and consider updating how you present yourself. Embrace the unusual, delve into the unknown, and expand your horizons. This approach will empower you to maximize the blessings of this rare, once-in-an-84-year cosmic cycle.

CONCLUSION

2024 is a monumental year for you, dear dolphin. With Saturn gracing your sign, he is guiding you in the ways of the Jedi, molding you into a superhero. While this mentorship demands discipline and meticulous planning—qualities you might not naturally gravitate towards—the rewards are unparalleled. It's a golden opportunity to elevate yourself, to metamorphose. Think of it as a once-in-three-decades window to manifest the highest vision you've held for yourself.

Moreover, Pluto conspires to reconnect you to the wisdom and talents you gained in past lifetimes, invigorating your innate creativity and fueling your imagination. And as if the universe hasn't favored you enough, the Dragon and Jupiter join forces to bolster your finances and entrepreneurial endeavors.

TAROT: THE MOON

The card represents the mysteries of the night as well as the Piscean activities to connect us to Oneness: meditations, dreaming, imagination, intuition, and peace of mind.

HEBREW LETTER: KUF

Meaning: "Back of the head," or "eye of the needle." The letter's shape resembles a head and spinal cord in profile. Pisces is the sign of imagination, which flows from the parietal to the occipital centers, both located in the back of the head.

Printed in Great Britain
by Amazon

37063698R00165